PRAISE FOR *DANCING FOR THE DEVIL*

"Grace is what kept us connected to our daughter and allowed us never to give up hope for Anny while she was in the darkest places of the sex industry. Grace is what kept our daughter alive, and grace is what pulled her out of the sex-for-sale culture. Although it was excruciatingly painful to witness our child in the sex industry, it has led her to her purposes in this life of teaching, advocating, and sharing the same grace that restored her with women across the globe. Her courage to tell her story in this book and the grace she imparts to others continue to inspire us."

—Retired NCAA head basketball coach Bob Donewald and his wife, Kathy

"*Dancing For The Devil* is not just a pole-to-the-pulpit memoir, but a call to action about how the billion-dollar sex-for-sale industry is impacting our culture. Anny Donewald and her coauthor Carrie Gerlach Cecil grippingly and beautifully illustrate how one woman went from a life of privilege to surviving the underbelly of the sex industry and ultimately advocating God's grace in places others don't dare to venture."

—Brian "Head" Welch, guitarist with Love and Death, formerly of Korn, and *New York Times* bestselling author of *Save Me from Myself*

T0335362

"*Dancing for the Devil* is a heartbreaking yet powerful memoir about Anny Donewald's incredible journey that takes her from a seemingly perfect life to the darkest realms of the sex industry. *Dancing For the Devil* brilliantly recounts how Anny came from brokenness and darkness into a life of beauty and freedom through the redemptive power of Jesus. You won't be able to put this book down."

—Henry and Alex Seeley, founders of The Belonging Co.

DANCING FOR THE DEVIL

THE DEVIL

ONE WOMAN'S DRAMATIC RESCUE FROM
THE SEX INDUSTRY

A MEMOIR

Anny Donewald
with Carrie Gerlach
Cecil

MONARCH
BOOKS
Oxford, UK, and Grand Rapids, Michigan, USA

Published by Monarch Books
an imprint of
Lion Hudson plc
Wilkinson House, Jordan Hill Road,
Oxford OX2 8DR, England
Email: monarch@lionhudson.com
www.lionhudson.com/monarch

ISBN 978 0 85721 650 2
e-ISBN 978 0 85721 651 9

First published by Howard Books, a division of Simon & Schuster,
Inc., 1230 Avenue of the Americas, New York, NY 10020.

Acknowledgments
Scripture quotations are taken from The Holy Bible, New
International Version NIV®. Copyright © 1973, 1978, 1984, 2011
by Biblica, Inc. Used by Permission of Biblica, Inc. All rights reserved
worldwide.

A catalogue record for this book is available from the British Library

Printed and bound in the UK, April 2015, LH26

This book is dedicated to Jesus Christ, who decided to befriend an atheist just to show her He loved her.

And to my mother. Thank you for your consistent love and support and your familiar words, "It's all good." I strive to be half the woman and mother you are, not only to my own children but also to the thousands of women God sends my way from the pits of darkness. You showed me what God meant when He said love never gives up.

(1 Corinthians 13, paraphrased)

Through God and my mother I learned that love is the answer. His love can and does change the darkest of hearts.

I want to tell my story with gut-wrenching honesty, so that other women and men may find encouragement and hope in these pages and recognize that no one is too far gone to be healed by God's love. What I learned on my journey from the sex industry to the pulpit was that I was never meant to dance for the devil—whether that was in sexual, political, or religious cultures. This is what I know to be true: Jesus Christ does not want us to sugarcoat his best stories of redemption to pacify man.

Tell your stories, and tell them openly.

Anny Donewald, daughter of an NCAA basketball head coach, sex industry survivor, founder of Eve's Angels

contents

The names and identifying characteristics of everyone with the exception of family and known celebrities in this book have been changed to protect the guilty and the innocent. Changes were made for legal and safety concerns surrounding the people in the book, my family, and myself. While all the described actions and incidents are true, there are particular events that have been combined and condensed to maintain continuity in the story. The situations described remain accurate and true to the actual events that took place, to the very best of my memory.

Graphic descriptions of what goes on in the sex industry, as well as the explicit language of that world, have been omitted at the request of the publisher.

preface

Over the years many people had approached me about writing a book or movie about my life. The answer was always the same, "No, thank you." I had zero desire to write my memoir, as for years I was not willing to disclose elements of my childhood that had not completely healed. I was still keeping a mental file marked "Secrets."

But God had other plans, and they included a writer He had already chosen for me. Her name is Carrie Gerlach Cecil. She and I share a love of sports, God, and the Holy Spirit, and a passion to love and to restore the heartbroken. A writer and speaker, she is also my cousin.

In 2011, I began praying with Carrie as she plotted her public relations tour to promote her upcoming novel, *One Sunday*. One particular evening I prophesied over her that *One Sunday* would be an incredible gift to many when it was published, *but it would be her next book that would change lives*.

Over the next two years my relationship with my cousin blossomed as I traveled down my path, unlocking and healing my childhood. I would feverishly pray for understanding, and then one afternoon in May, I felt inspired and called Carrie and asked if she would help me write my memoir.

"All of it?" she questioned. She knew my reluctance to share my past and openly discuss my childhood and my very private family. "Are you sure?"

"All of it," I said.

What I was sure of was that God has an incredible sense of irony and timing, and there is no one that I trusted more both as writer and as confidant to help me tell my truths than I trusted Carrie. Together we would find a way to share what was important to my story: none of us need to cover up the very pitchfork that threw us into a psychological and physical mind-set of shame or pain or darkness. And no matter what walk of life you come from, evil knows no boundaries. But most important, there is no darkness that God's love cannot reach and restore to its perfect state.

"Love you, cousin," she said to me as she hung up.

"Love you back, cousin," I repeated.

Little did Carrie know that after years of encouraging me to address and tell my *whole* story, she would be the one helping me to tell it in this memoir. And interestingly, the book that I prophesied over her two years prior, *her next book that would change lives,* is this book.

It's been an amazing, therapeutic, painful, and spectacular process. And we are just getting started. Stay tuned.

Chicago, Illinois
May 2014

foreword

I never knew my cousin growing up. My mother and her father have been estranged, with only pockets of exchanges, for over thirty years. I had heard *stories* of Anny, but not the kind of stories you want repeated about you. She was an anomaly to me, as she grew up with everything that I didn't. A stay-at-home mother and a father who was a successful NCAA head basketball coach who remained faithful and present for his wife and children. She had money for private schools, designer clothes, and the college of her choice, so it was a mystery to me how such a blessed girl became one of the highest-paid strippers and prostitutes in Michigan, Chicago, and Las Vegas. More miraculous to me was how the ex-stripper had gone from the pole to the pulpit.

As cliché as it sounds, Anny and I found each other through social media, and with cautious optimism we began to slowly divulge our lives to each other. I had an incredible empathy for her, as my own youth had been riddled with shards of shame and secrets as well as joy and love. Today I consider myself to be a work-in-faith-progress, a galaxy away from being anywhere near complete. What connected Anny and me was not our shared DNA but rather our passion for Jesus Christ and a hunger to love and serve broken people.

Over the years that followed, Anny began to slowly peel back for me the captivating and constricting layers of her life, revealing how Polly-Anny had ended up a high-priced prostitute and how the prostitute had transformed into a prophetess. It was a thought- and prayer-provoking exploration, exposing this truth: no amount of privilege could have protected her. Uncovering and recounting her pain was unnerving and spellbinding at the same time for me. Some days after hearing and writing her stories, I would want to re-baptize myself in my pool after a good glass of wine. Her memories came to life on the page and kept me awake at night with my heart beating out of my chest. Even now I wonder how something so heavy could have been so elating. Anny's journey of riches, rebellion, rape, and redemption is one of the most compelling stories I have ever encountered.

At five foot nine, with a lioness mane, my outspoken and powerful cousin is striking and inspiring to be around. Our adult relationship has morphed into a full-blown, God-anointed friendship, and although our paths of pain were different, what I learned from talking, crying, hollering, praying, breaking down, and breaking through with her was that God's grace is the medicine that heals us all. Writing Anny's memoir with her has been riveting, heartbreaking, educational, and inspiring. We pray that someday our families are reconnected, if only through us and our faith in God.

From the strip clubs to the pulpit, Anny was saved from the brink of physical, emotional, and spiritual death by supernatural powers. In turn she has helped thousands of women through her nonprofit, Eve's Angels, to fight against the modern-day slavery subculture of sex for sale in America. She stands by her mantra that no matter your profession or past, God loves you where you are at. *Dancing for the Devil* is the story of one woman saved out of the pit of her shame, despair, and addictions by the simplicity of grace. My cousin, friend, and coauthor Anny Donewald is that woman, and this is her story.

Carrie Gerlach Cecil, author of *One Sunday*

prologue

On the cusp of my seventh anniversary in the sex industry, I sat on my futon counting the money I had raked in swinging upside down on a pole, center stage, wearing silver platform heels and a sequin thong and answering to the stage name Bailey. The week had been strangely profitable, as I had tucked away a few thousand for four nights of dancing and seeing clients on the side, but the price tag had left me physically and mentally exhausted, not to mention spiritually bankrupt.

With an orange soda mixed with Ketel One vodka in hand and a little bump of coke to energize me, my friend Nina and I loaded up her Lexus with our overnight bags and headed west to Los Angeles, the land of milk and honey, for the weekend. This had become my method of survival. Escape. Escape from what ailed me.

During the five-hour drive to California, I rang up a prominent music producer client who lived in the Hollywood Hills to let him know we were heading to town. He laid the groundwork with doormen and nightclub managers for us to roll into all the posh Hollywood nightspots VIP-style. Even in LA, there's no waiting in lines for girls like us. We make the patrons happy. This is how it works from coast to coast.

It was Friday night at the Wild Orchid, and the place was packed with A-list celebrities, Hollywood studio types, and wannabe starlets. In painted-on white leather pants, a black tank that hugged my breasts, and sexy lace-up boots, I was at my peak prizefighting weight. Nina and I cruised the bar to decipher who was really a player and who was just playing. It wasn't my intention to be working, but at this stage in my life, I didn't know another way.

We had cozied up next to two movie executives I'll call Mr. X and Mr. Y. The corks were popping off the two-hundred-dollar bottles of Cristal champagne like fireworks on the Fourth of July. We were snorting an occasional line of cocaine to pick us up when I felt a tug in my soul. It was that voice again, *Time for us to leave.* But our foursome kept our party going as we headed outside to the valet stand, where Mr. X's red Lamborghini pulled up.

"At least we know he has money," I whispered to Nina.

We piled in the car and headed from the Wild Orchid to an after-hours club that I vaguely remember being named something like the Hookah Lounge. My head was spinning and foggy. When Jay Z and Beyoncé's "Crazy in Love" repeated for the third time, I started to feel sick. My heart was racing faster than normal from the drugs. Something was very wrong.

I wanted to go home.

Not home to our hotel, but home home. Home to a small town in Michigan. Home to the safety of a good Christian family where I had a loving mom and basketball-coach dad. Home to my daughter. Back in time to when I wasn't such a complete disaster. I was afraid I was going to die here, and I didn't want to.

I struggled to get up as Mr. X tugged at my arm. His bloodshot, hungry eyes filleted me. He rubbed his hand down my hair and into the arch of my back and breathed his stale cigar breath on me with a growl. "How much?"

The next thing I knew I was in the heart of Beverly Hills at the L'Ermitage hotel in an oversized suite with marble floors, white linens, and sweeping views of the city. Now, let's be clear. This isn't a scene out of *Pretty Woman*, and Mr. X is no Richard Gere. He's overweight, bald, sweaty, and oily. He grinds his teeth. He's an especially lonely pervert.

Mr. Y has vanished. Nina turns to me as if to say, *What now?* I just shrug. I'm praying he'll pass out and I plan to slip a Xanax into his cocktail to make sure he does.

But Mr. X was all business. He pulled out a wad of cash and paid Nina five hundred dollars to leave and wait in another room. My heart sank. My stomach gurgled and flipped upside down for the umpteenth time. I was the one who was going to have to pay the piper, and I was going to have to do it alone.

The metallic clang of the lock on the door jolted me. Despite the gallon of alcohol I had poured into my frame, I was suddenly very alert. I eased down on the bed as he counted out a thousand dollars in hundred-dollar bills. It wasn't my first time, but this wasn't something I did easily either. Like an animal led to the slaughter, I was about to be carved up piece by piece. Every time I offered myself up for sale like this, I left a piece of me behind. Tiny morsels of my humanity, my soul, were being sliced off to satiate the devil, one scavenging meal at a time. Eventually there would be nothing left. And what then?

Take off your clothes. Be Bailey, I begged myself.

They make it look easy in the movies, but there is nothing easy about selling sex. You're naked and open for the taking. No matter how tough you are—and I was raised a champion with a winner's spirit—there is a vulnerability and fear and disgust and hatred of yourself and your client in every breath and every touch. Each minute passes like hours and each hour like days. This particular night was darker and seedier and more horrific for me than any of the others. I had imprisoned myself with my own sinister choices. The horror ended sometime before sunrise when he left.

When the morning light finally pierced through the corners of the heavy drapes, I saw my beautiful, luxurious hotel room for the dungeon that it was. A wretched smell of stale cigar smoke and body odor clung to the sheets, and a sourness filled the air. I stumbled like a zombie to the minibar and proceeded to down four small bottles of scotch. I made my way to the bathroom. I wished a shower would wash away the stain of filth on me. I inspected my body in the full-length mirror: a little bruise here, a scratch there. Where had my beauty gone? How had I gotten here? My rubbery licorice-whip legs gave way and I dropped to my knees and finally succumbed to limpness on the cool floor. I saw blood begin to trickle from my nose onto the white chenille mat. I reached out and touched the stranger with dead eyes staring back at me out of the mirror and whimpered, "Help me."

Beverly Hills, California
April 2003

chapter one
SO YOU UNDERSTAND MY LINEAGE

When kids act out, it's often the parents who get the blame. Whether the kids are getting in trouble in school or misbehaving with family, many parents worry they're doing something wrong. But that may not always be the case.

Dr. Richard Friedman, professor of psychiatry at
Weill Cornell Medical College

There were times that I couldn't forgive myself for what I put my parents through in my darkest days. It wasn't until I realized that they were the first people to show me unconditional love, and they did that through their relationship with Jesus Christ, that I was able to understand the Father's love and to forgive myself.

Anny

It is a commonly held belief that unborn children become aware of their world through the sounds they hear while in the womb. Thus, swollen and puffy soon-to-be mommas are encouraged to coo and sing nursery rhymes ad nauseam directly into their protruding tummies.

The mantras I heard while in my mother's belly were a serenade of a different sort. Instead of lullabies, I heard eighteen thousand pairs of feet stomping—*WHAM! WHAM! WHAM!*—in rhythm on metal bleachers and the pounding of bass drums in the percussion section of the Indiana Hoosiers' basketball band. Adoring fans cheered and belted out, "Indiana, our Indiana, we're all for you! Never daunted, we cannot falter, in the battle, we're tried and true! Indiana, our Indiana, Indiana, we're all for you! I-U!"

I arrived into this world screaming at the top of my lungs. Upon delivery, I had one arm above my head, my hand clenched into a triumphant fist. Perhaps it was the Donewald lineage, or perhaps it was the reverberations of the crowd I could hear and feel over and over during the NCAA basketball play-offs, but somehow I came into this world expecting fireworks, with the burning desire to let the spotlight shine on me.

I was the first child my father witnessed being born. For his three previous children's births, he had been forced to wait in the lobby with the other expectant fathers. I picture him with a cigar in his hand, although he never smoked, as each of my siblings was handed to him neatly wrapped in a baby-blue or pastel-pink blanket. Not me. From the very beginning, my dad, the conservative Christian basketball coach, saw me messy, bloody, and hollering. He took the sterilized metal clamps and snipped the lifeline umbilical cord that connected me to my mother and forever made me his. My father has always helped transition me from one life event to the next. Sometimes that involved yanking and cutting and sometimes it involved holding me in his arms to keep me sheltered from the world. What he would come to understand is that he wouldn't have arms big enough to free me from the darkness that my life would become.

My birth on November 15, 1977, made the national media two days later. It provided good color commentary as my dad coached an exhibition game against the Soviet national team: his boys at IU beat the Soviets in front of a sold-out Market Square Arena in Indianapolis. It was a big week for Dad, the entire state of Indiana, and American basketball fans. It was the season Billy Joel released the jukebox favorite "Only the Good Die Young," a song that would become an anthem for my life. But I am getting ahead of myself.

⚘

My father met my mother, Kathy, on a blind date in the spring of 1967 in South Bend, Indiana, the home of the Studebaker and the Fighting Irish. Dad was the head basketball coach at St. Joseph's Catholic High School, where he also taught economics to the junior and senior classes. Mom was an ICU nurse at Memorial Hospital of South Bend who had risen through the ranks to head of the department.

My mother was a natural beauty with a petite but strong frame and narrow face. She wore her hair in a pixie hairdo that bore a resemblance to Goldie Hawn's during the *Laugh-In* era. Her brown bangs hung above big blue eyes that were framed by long brown lashes. She wore very little makeup, just a hint of rose on her thin cheeks, a brush or two of mascara, and a glimmer of Avon pink lip gloss. She dressed in below-the-knee wool pencil skirts. Her preppy collared shirts peeked out from underneath the sweaters she would knit. She resembled an Ivy Leaguer who knew how to keep her ankles crossed beneath the chair when eating dinner or listening to the preacher in church.

She was unlike the girls my dad had dated when he played basketball at Hanover College. She exuded the subtle seriousness that comes from growing up in a wealthy, educated Boston family and ultimately working in a hospital where she dealt with life-or-death patients and their IVs and bedpans.

My dad and mom were both in their midtwenties when they sat down for dinner at a restaurant that was far out of my father's budget. He drank a Tom Collins and she sipped a scotch on the rocks. The lights were low as my mother raised her eyebrow and asked with watered-down wit, "You get paid to coach basketball?" She knew nothing about sports or his competitive, masculine world, nor did she like it. Then my father announced he had planned a small gathering that evening after dinner at his house to watch the NCAA play-offs. She found the entire encounter Neanderthalish.

"A basketball coach?" my grandmother Dorothy mocked in her heavy Boston accent no one in our family could ever understand. "Is he an eccentric man-child, or does he just not have the wherewithal or breeding to be a good lawyer, doctor, or CPA?"

Although she was in a loftier social league and perhaps out of his dating comfort zone, my dad instantly fell in love with my mother's candor, dry sense of humor, and unwavering righteousness.

Dad had grown up poor with an absentee father who had a wandering eye—he was particularly fond of pretty ladies with Marilyn Monroe's silhouette—and an unwavering dedication to never, ever leave a whiskey glass untouched.

My grandmother Alleene essentially raised my dad and his two siblings, older brother Jack and younger sister Sandy. My dad doesn't talk much about his childhood, and when I pressed him for details, he told me that they were a typical family of the 1940s and 1950s. Although they struggled financially, their lives were sled races in the snow, neighborhood basketball games, sock hops, and family dinners with aunts and uncles who filled in the gaps that were left by his father's carousing and his mother's having to work.

I've only once heard him speak about the real tragedy in his childhood, the loss of his brother, Jack. He spoke quietly and deliberately about it to my sister as I pretended to be asleep on the couch. I was about seven years old, but the tone of his voice has stayed with me my entire life.

He told her of the Christmas holiday of 1959. The snow was two feet deep along the driveway and icicles hung from the rain gutters on their old house on Sylvan Lane in Carmel, Indiana. Sometime after midnight he heard the upstairs phone ring. My father stood in his bedroom doorway, watching his mother, in her light-blue nightgown, make her way through the dark hallway and pick up the black Mountain Bell receiver to hear the horrible news: his nineteen-year-old brother had been killed in an airplane crash as he was traveling back to his naval ship. My dad stood silently as his mother collapsed to her knees, wailing uncontrollably.

I believe we all have these moments that change us forever, moments when life hurls baseball-sized hail onto the glass ceiling that is our innocence, and everything that is naive and good becomes tarnished and broken. When the devil comes to steal our hope and faith. I wonder now which was worse for him, losing his brother or watching his mother shrivel in pain and despair in the months that followed?

Thankfully for my dad, he used his juggernaut of emotions to springboard himself into the knowledge that he wanted more out of life. He found release, peace, challenge, and comfort within the confines and rules of the game of basketball. Methodically throwing basketball after basketball into a hoop has always been his therapy, and the court became his sanctuary. He wanted success and the safety of a strong household for the family—as if anything can truly make a household safe. He wanted to equip his children in the ways of the Lord and create a trauma-free environment for them, and he was determined to do so. He would break the mold of his family's disappointing, runaway male role models. He would support and nurture the people he loved.

There is an old saying about marriage: if the two of you are the same, one isn't necessary. My parents were from different sides of the tracks but complemented each other. She possessed a worldly charm that his family could never afford. He deliberately spent the first nine months of their courtship trying to impress her. He took her to lovely dinners and ballroom dancing, sent her weekly bouquets of roses, and attended Sunday service with her at church. And much to the disappointment of my mother's family, she married a basketball coach instead of a surgeon on April 6, 1968, in front of three hundred black-tie spectators at First Presbyterian Church.

Their first child, Lisa, was born almost exactly nine months later. "Were you pregnant when you got married?" I once asked my mother, hoping to find an ounce of imperfection in her as she rocked my second child, a boy I had birthed out of wedlock. She looked me in the eye and responded unequivocally, "No." Then she lifted my son up to smell his diaper and compassionately continued, "And in fact when I returned from our honeymoon, and my time of the month started, I cried to your father that at twenty-five years old, I had waited too long to have a baby." I was taken aback by her vulnerability.

~~~

My parents were God-fearing, private people who didn't talk about adult things with their children and tried to keep a protective bubble around each one of us. When my eldest sister, Lisa, was born, my mother gave up nursing to be a stay-at-home mom and basketball wife. There was no time for the man who called the plays for six-foot-two college prospects to be changing diapers, and some would have considered it downright inappropriate. But I believe my dad would have done anything that my mother asked him to do.

Although she has always stood in the shadow of my father's successes, my mother is hardly a wallflower. At five foot one, she is a powerful force. Equal parts cunning, caring, and calm, she has always been my father's right-hand woman. Nothing comes between them. Even to this day they are a united front. No job, game, in-laws, child, temptation, or catastrophe can break their bond. They lived what they taught us from the good book: "But at the beginning of creation God 'made them male and female.' For this reason a man will leave his father and mother and be united to his wife, and the two will become one flesh. So they are no longer two, but one flesh. Therefore what God has joined together, let no one separate." And no one ever did.

My mother's goal has always been to have my father's back. For better or worse. They shared a deep love for each other and God and regularly read the Bible to us kids. "As for me and my house, we will serve the Lord. Joshua 24:15" was printed on a canvas and hung above the fireplace in our house. They wanted us to be good, grounded Christians. My mother was the one saddled with the day-to-day responsibility of keeping the children in line. And up until I was born, she was doing a pretty good job.

I am the youngest of four siblings. An "oops" baby. My mom called me "her precious surprise." Each of her children had been *good*. And it wasn't until I came along that the hurricane of chaos was unleashed on them. They were used to life being stable and controllable, with their well-behaved ducklings walking neatly in a row. *Quack, quack, quack.*

First there was my sister Lisa. She has always held the role of mini-mom in our sibling hierarchy. A straight A student who was never in trouble and wouldn't dream of rocking the boat, good ol' Lisa grew up to be a schoolteacher. My brother, Bob Jr., was born one year after Lisa, in 1970.

Bob Jr. was my partner in crime. Despite our eight-year age difference, the two of us got into heaps of trouble. We both carry the crazy-competitive daredevil gene. I remember being in a red Radio Flyer wagon, tied to the back of his bike, zooming down the largest hill in the neighborhood screaming, "Faster, faster!" I was three years old. Bob Jr. followed in my father's coaching footsteps, working in the NBA and serving as the Chinese national head coach. Then there was my sister Kristin. Born in 1972, she is the sensitive and introverted one who is embarrassed by half of the stuff that flies out of my mouth. She was my parent's sweet baby girl until I came along and booted her into the ranks of the middle child. Today she's a midwife, and I would say she is the brainiest of us all.

In early 1970, the head basketball coach from the United States Military Academy, a man who was aptly nicknamed "the General," came to visit St. Joe's in South Bend. He had made the recruiting trip himself, as he wanted to see firsthand the coach who was turning out incredible defensive players.

My mom told me about the General sitting next to her during a game as she kept her statistics board on her lap and methodically jotted down the details of points accrued and passes and fouls for my father. "He's got a great defensive mind," the General told my mother, never looking directly at her. "He's getting them to play better than they are." She simply smiled and nodded, as this was something that she already knew. She also understood that having this particular man sitting next to her was no coincidence. She believed that God had a plan for our family. When my father was invited to work at the General's basketball camp at West Point that summer, she made sure he went. The two coaches quickly became friends.

The coach known as the General was none other than Bob Knight. He would eventually leave the army for Indiana University. My dad and Coach Knight's bond grew stronger over the next three years as they worked together during the summers on the west bank of the Hudson River. A few seasons into his tenure at Indiana, the General found himself at our dinner table, as he had many times before, but this time, while my mother served them lasagna, Coach Knight had come to speak to my father about his next job.

My father liked Coach Knight because he was black-and-white like my dad. There were no gray areas when it came to right and wrong. There was just good and there was evil. Winners and losers. Both men were intense virtuosos. "He's hiring you because he doesn't have to train you," my mother remembers saying to my dad as she washed the dishes that night. "He respects you as much as you respect him. I like that."

At the time of Coach Knight's job offer, my father was making $16,000 per year as a high school coach and teacher. Moving to IU meant a $2,000 pay cut and losing both a good pension plan and the insurance provided by the school district.

I had a rare moment of one-on-one with Dad recently and used it to talk about the thing that we both love and is a safe subject: basketball. I asked him why he took the job at IU. He dipped his doughnut in black coffee, smiled, and said, "I took the job because I was from Indiana. Everyone in that day wanted to coach with Bob Knight." My mom came into the room and stood behind him, adding, "With your sister, your older brother, and Kristin already born, it was difficult, but we took a pay cut to join the Hoosiers. Your dad bet on himself and the talent that God had provided him." She has an uncanny way of finishing his thoughts.

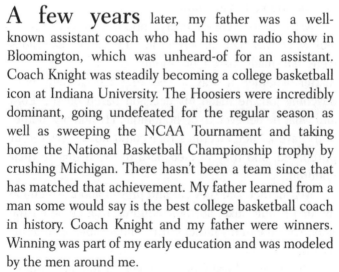

A few years later, my father was a well-known assistant coach who had his own radio show in Bloomington, which was unheard-of for an assistant. Coach Knight was steadily becoming a college basketball icon at Indiana University. The Hoosiers were incredibly dominant, going undefeated for the regular season as well as sweeping the NCAA Tournament and taking home the National Basketball Championship trophy by crushing Michigan. There hasn't been a team since that has matched that achievement. My father learned from a man some would say is the best college basketball coach in history. Coach Knight and my father were winners. Winning was part of my early education and was modeled by the men around me.

After the championship, my father was a sought-after commodity for vacant head coaching jobs. Athletic directors from around the country strolled through the tan shag carpeting in our small living room and sat on our flowered tapestry couches to woo my dad with promises of big money, radio shows, cars, private schools for us kids, and big bonuses for signing on the dotted line. He had his pick of head coaching positions, which is rare at the collegiate coaching level. He didn't want to move, as he liked the success and job security he had at IU. Make no mistake, however: he was driven. *Complacent* is not a word you would ever hear used to describe my dad. He may have been second in command at IU, but the work kept him challenged. He was always learning. He was able to keep pushing himself to the next level. The qualities that kept him successful at IU are perhaps what kept him from giving up on me despite how very uncomfortable I made him.

My parents weighed every option, grounded in God and what was right or wrong for the family. Decisions were not made based on money or stature. It didn't matter whether it was a speaking engagement or a coaching job; he made his decision based on the Lord and what he believed to be honorable. He and my mother both have a code of ethics that could not be swayed or purchased, and they worked hard to teach that to their children.

My mother said they sat and prayed about which job my dad should take, all their children in a circle on the floor, with me in my father's arms and a Bible open in his hands.

He prayed, "Lord God, we come to You and humbly ask that You guide our steps for what is honorable and pleasing to You. Let our life be not about the game or superficial details but let it be a life of goodness and honor. Lord, let every door be open that You would want open and let every door be closed that You want closed. Help us to make a clear decision for this family. Help plant us in a city to be a blessing to others. Help us to join a university family where we can make a difference on and off the court. Lord we humbly ask You to hear us and guide our plans. In Jesus' name, amen."

Then, with a clear view, they made a decision. Although there were bigger programs that had come to the table, they were moving us somewhere normal. Literally. When I was six months old, Dad took the head coaching position at Illinois State University. We moved from Bloomington, Indiana, to Normal, Illinois.

I always laugh when people at the Porn Convention or a XXX show ask me where I grew up. I just chuckle at them and say, "Normal."

chapter two
TRAINING IN NORMAL: TRYING TO LAY THE GROUNDWORK

In a recent study based on an analysis of 200 women street prostitutes . . . a majority of the juvenile prostitutes described family structures with the outward appearances of stability. Over three-fourths reported having a religious upbringing. Forty percent were raised by both mother and father. The younger the prostitute, the more educated the family.

"Pornography and Prostituion,"
http://www.123helpme.com/assets/10956.html

Just because you grow up in what looks normal to other people doesn't mean that it's normal to you.

Anny

When we moved to Normal, it had a population of fewer than 40,000 people. Being a head coach's daughter made it feel like the other 39,999 residents knew who my father was. And why wouldn't they?

During his tenure at Illinois State, he turned the program into a national sensation. In 1982 and 1983, the team was ranked thirteenth and fourteenth nationally. Everyone—from the man in a white jumpsuit who delivered our milk to the aging secretary at our elementary school—wanted to know the intimate details of our family. Details like if my parents had a fight or what my dad ate for breakfast and if he *really* practiced what he preached. After he served on the 1984 Olympic Selection Committee and had hobnobbed with upcoming NBA legends such as Charles Barkley and Michael Jordan, my dad became a local celebrity in Middle America.

Most of the university head coaches, local upper-crust doctors, and Mercedes Benz–driving lawyers lived in a swanky gated community at the edge of town. My dad and mom had different plans for the Donewald clan. Our moving trucks pulled up to a blue two-story house with a large front yard on Garden Road. The neighborhood was your average slice of Americana, where neighbors planted posies around their mailboxes at the end of the driveways and Sam, the neighborhood paperboy, would park his ten-speed to make sure that your *Sunday Times* made it to the porch.

My mother had matured in her role as a head coach's wife and had become my father's eyes and ears behind the scenes. She learned everything there was to know about basketball and became masterful at maneuvering the politics of college athletics. He trusted her in all areas of his life: personal, professional, and financial. Her intuition about people has always been spot-on. She vigilantly studied the nuances of the people around them and swiftly weeded out those who didn't fit in their circle.

She listened to and watched everyone who came into contact with my father: secretaries in the office, coaches on the sidelines, and referees on the court. She memorized the statistics of high school prospects to be his walking and talking wingwoman, and she made a point of knowing the name of every bus driver who ever transported the team and her family for away games. I swear when we would walk up the steps of the bus, she'd lean in just close enough to the driver to smell his breath and make sure he hadn't been drinking.

Raising all four of their children in a safe and stable environment was important for my parents, as growing up in the intercollegiate sports world is anything but stable. They wanted us to be able to play kick the can and ghost in the graveyard and run free until my mom would yell, "Come in for dinner." They desperately tried to keep our lives grounded and to instill in us the value of hard work and earning a dollar.

Each week my mother and my siblings would spend an entire day cleaning the house. To this day I love the smell of lemon-fresh Pledge. It floods me with emotions from a time when life was safe and joyful. Not that we didn't moan and groan while scrubbing the toilets. "There's going to be no cleaning lady following you around at college," she used to say. We all had chores. Most of the time I was too young to accomplish anything correctly, but it was the training my mom was after.

These days when I'm interviewing young women in need of assistance from my nonprofit, Eve's Angels, I almost always find one of several common threads woven through their past: an abusive, absentee, or piece-of-garbage father; molestation by a family member; or an addict mother who would leave them in the hands of purity slayers while she got high. It's easy to pinpoint why most of these women ended up on the street or the pole or chasing the cherry-flavored pain remover of the week. Not me. Oh! How I stumped the probation officers, counselors, therapists, psychologists, and religious leaders. *How did a nice white girl like you end up in the back alley?* But you see, you don't have to come from the street to end up with a degree from the school of hard knocks. I had never suffered from the abuse or neglect by father or mother that was prevalent with other women I came to share the stage with during my stripping days. I was a novelty. There were no belt whippings or scary memories of being locked in a closet. Quite the opposite. Comparatively, I came to the stage with a silver spoon in my mouth and a warm and tough cloak of parental love draped on my shoulders.

Although Dad and Mom tirelessly tried to keep us all normal in Normal, our life followed an atypical playbook. Other kids would learn the practical wisdom that stealing and lying were wrong, but we got an extra-credit course on the nuances of nondisclosure and being conscious and skeptical of everything and everybody. From my earliest memories I can recount being taught to be extremely private. The mandate was to protect and keep the family secrets—and by family, I mean us, the Donewalds, as well as the university, the team, and the bigwigs at the university—secret *no matter the cost*.

The NCAA was the Mafia without all the spaghetti with meatballs and weird Cousin Vinnie.

Out of our house none of us would ever dare repeat, mutter, or partake in disparaging conversations about the Redbirds family. We learned to keep our mouths shut and not let people too close. This was difficult when I was riding the school bus and, after any given game, win or loss, every kid had an opinion on how to coach better, recruit better, and win better than my dad. Although many times I wanted to shoot spitballs at these kids, I kept my mouth shut and ignored them. I learned to be self-contained and let loose only with a handful of adults and kids whom my mother deemed worthy. She was the gatekeeper.

My mother never went out of the house without looking put-together. Similarly, we never looked dirty or disheveled. She dressed us girls in skirts and my brother in nicely pressed pants. She made sure our hair and teeth were brushed. All of us girls had exactly the same short haircuts, as it allowed for easy assembly-line preparation when she had to get four kids ready for a press conference. I was the spitting image of my dad, and like him, the only left-handed kid in the bunch. With my full cheeks, stocky legs, and general awkwardness, the pixie bowl cut did me no favors. Eventually, exhausted from having to dry my tears every time someone called me Andy instead of Anny, my mother gave in and allowed me to wear my hair long.

The constantly lurking eyes on the periphery did something to my psyche: they made me overtly cautious and constantly wary, and the effect couldn't be undone. The activities of the Donewald clan were gossip for the local PTA, HOA, and Redbird board members. We weren't in *Us* magazine or on TMZ, but we were tabloid fodder nonetheless. I grew up in a voyeuristic world.

Thank God most of the crazy things I did were before social media, or those nude pictures of me center stage at a club in Detroit might have ended up on the timeline of some sorority chick's Facebook page. Praise Jesus!

I learned words like *ulterior motive* from my parents. I became masterful at deciphering which neighborhood girl was playing with me because she liked my Barbie house and which was told to play with me by her dad, who wanted stories about Coach Donewald to tell to his buddies at the Masonic Lodge meeting on Monday night.

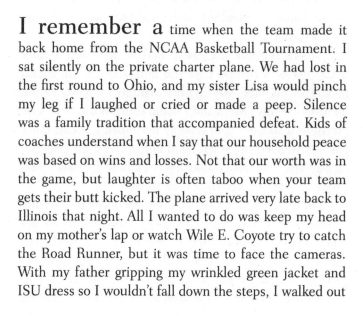

I remember a time when the team made it back home from the NCAA Basketball Tournament. I sat silently on the private charter plane. We had lost in the first round to Ohio, and my sister Lisa would pinch my leg if I laughed or cried or made a peep. Silence was a family tradition that accompanied defeat. Kids of coaches understand when I say that our household peace was based on wins and losses. Not that our worth was in the game, but laughter is often taboo when your team gets their butt kicked. The plane arrived very late back to Illinois that night. All I wanted to do was keep my head on my mother's lap or watch Wile E. Coyote try to catch the Road Runner, but it was time to face the cameras. With my father gripping my wrinkled green jacket and ISU dress so I wouldn't fall down the steps, I walked out of the plane behind my mom and I could hear the faint chanting, "ISU, ISU, ISU."

The airport was overflowing with fans cheering for what was a losing team. Although I was exhausted from two days of traveling and being paraded around to countless press conferences and, ultimately, witnessing the team's defeat, the undercurrent of adoration quickly reenergized me. The endorphins of the limelight kicked in—for all of us.

The policemen gathered around my family in a ring of safety. I felt like a tiny ball in an arcade game, being bounced from one bumper to the next until we made it from the terminal and into a police car. With the sirens blaring, I watched out the back window and waved at Gus, the driver of the team bus that followed behind us. We made it into the underbelly of the basketball arena, where hordes of Redbird basketball fans were clapping for my father.

"Go to the balcony," he called back to my mother before he was rushed past the fans shoving autograph papers in his face. My mother wanted us to go to the bathroom so my sisters and I could brush our hair to look pretty, and so she could reapply her lipstick. I had other plans. I wiggled my small hand out of her tight grip and chased after my father. Looking back now, I can see that I have always been chasing something.

"Anny! Come back here!" my mom shrieked over the commotion. There must have been enough fear in her tone that my father stopped and turned. I made eye contact with him and smiled. I ran faster, dodging garbage cans and vending machines, until I reached him.

"I have her," he called back at my mother. I jumped

into his arms and he carried me past the protruding microphones. We climbed two levels of stairs, and as he made his way to the railing of a balcony, there was a huge uproar of cheers for him. He and I stood there until the crowd hushed. They hung on his words and worshipped this basketball god as if he were as much theirs as mine.

We, my family and I, all belonged to them, to the school, and to the town of Normal, Illinois.

When I looked up at my father, he had tears in his eyes.

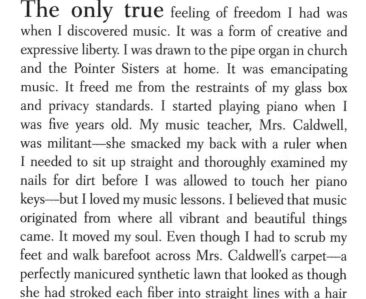

The only true feeling of freedom I had was when I discovered music. It was a form of creative and expressive liberty. I was drawn to the pipe organ in church and the Pointer Sisters at home. It was emancipating music. It freed me from the restraints of my glass box and privacy standards. I started playing piano when I was five years old. My music teacher, Mrs. Caldwell, was militant—she smacked my back with a ruler when I needed to sit up straight and thoroughly examined my nails for dirt before I was allowed to touch her piano keys—but I loved my music lessons. I believed that music originated from where all vibrant and beautiful things came. It moved my soul. Even though I had to scrub my feet and walk barefoot across Mrs. Caldwell's carpet—a perfectly manicured synthetic lawn that looked as though she had stroked each fiber into straight lines with a hair comb—it was worth it for a thirty-minute session at her baby grand. It was a time when I could just lose myself in the melodies. I would come home from her lessons and diligently practice on our piano in our basement until my fingers would play no more. Learning to play the piano was my first experience of loving the spirit of something while hating the teacher, much as I later learned about Jesus while having an aversion to church.

⋙

My primary biblical studies pushed the concept that I—well, basically *all of mankind*—had come into this world a sinner with one foot in the hole. In the church that we attended, the teaching of the Bible did not match the same Word of God my parents were instilling in us at home. The church's message was *turn or burn* and was punch-lined with doom and gloom.

I was taught to believe that I was born in supernatural liability and that all sinners went to hell. Every week after being enraptured by the old-school hymns like "Awake, O Christian" or "Keep on Praying," I was sent to the basement and taught that the way out of the hole was to climb up the good-deed ladder and follow the teachings of the Lord Almighty.

Getting to heaven meant following the rules. All the rules. The teaching of right versus wrong was ingrained into my Sunday experience fiber, like winning was on game day. As reinforcement we often studied Moses versus Pharaoh or David versus Goliath. My Sunday school teacher would make us separate the red sugar puffs from the green sugar puffs of Apple Jacks cereal to illustrate good versus evil—the red being bad.

"So not all people go to heaven?" I looked up at my ancient instructor, who had to have been born sometime at the beginning of the nineteenth century yet still squeezed into Jordache jeans.

"No, Anny. Bad people don't get to go to heaven."

"But who decides what is really good and bad? The church?" I asked, my face scrunched. Exasperated, she knelt down, eye-level with my elementary-school self, raising her brow, and said, "God, Anny. Only God."

"But didn't Jesus come to save the sinners?" I didn't notice that the room had gone silent. All the other kids were listening intently to my line of questioning. This was as exciting as Bible study got.

My teacher stood back up and noticed all eyes were on her. She proceeded cautiously, ready to squash my rebellion when the moment was right. "Yes, Anny."

"And those people with Jesus, Paul and Peter and Mary and the rest, they were pretty bad. Right?"

"Um-hm." She stood over me with her hands on her hips.

I crunched my cereal in my teeth and just looked at her as if preparing for a New Testament showdown. "So what you're really saying is they, the sinners, didn't go with Jesus either?"

My teacher wasn't prepared or willing to get into a philosophical and biblical debate with a pigtailed boat rocker. The corners of her mouth dropped into her sinking face and she placated me, "Anny, just keep separating the good from the bad. That's our lesson. Separate the good from the bad."

My father would often be invited to deliver a message on Sunday at the church, as he represented all that was pious in Normal. Coach Donewald was a faithful husband, provider, father, and servant. Plus he was rebuilding the Redbirds team in a town where the local newspaper headlines were about a power outage at Baskin-Robbins on Main Street or about a John Deere tractor that had gone missing from the chicken farm.

On those days when Dad spoke, I was able to stay with my family in the grown-up church. With the smell of musty Bibles in the air and my squishy bottom uncomfortably nailed onto the wood bench, I loved to just people-watch the multitude. We'd sit in the front row waiting for my father to begin, my mother on the aisle, my two sisters in the middle, and me next to my brother. I would have to crane my neck to sneak glances behind me at the fat lady with a two-foot beehive bun. I was fascinated with her hair.

How she got her nest that tall was a bigger mystery to me than Jesus' ascension.

In those early years, God's word was spoon-fed to me, and I wanted to know it, to live it to please Him and to please my parents. I learned that there were choices to make, hard choices, along the road of life. I learned that I could have no contradiction in my character or ambiguity when it came to how I behaved.

Relentlessly I heard: the ball either goes in the hoop or not. The idea was deep-rooted in me. There is no point accrued on the scoreboard for missing. There is no afterlife for the naughty. I knew my parents were going to heaven and I wanted to go with them. Imagine the self-loathing and fear that bloomed inside me when I realized I wasn't. When I realized I wasn't good enough. That my sin was too great and my past was too filthy to scrub clean.

As long as I can remember, the talk of a God has been a part of my life. What I came to ask later, when things started to go badly, was this: If there was a God and He was so good, why in the hell did He hate me so much?

chapter three

THE GRIND

One good thing about music, when it hits you, you feel no pain.

Bob Marley

I can lose myself in the rhythm and escape through the melody of music. Shamans call it the sacred space. Music has always been a drug for me starting at a very young age. I've always gone somewhere else when it plays, when it moves in and out of me.

Anny

At ten, I was precocious and outgoing. I loved sports and music. My athletic build had not yet sprouted up or out and I had a pretty good three-point shot: basically, I was my dad's Mini-Me.

"If you stand at the free-throw line and shoot ten thousand shots, eventually the mechanics become second nature." The ball went from Dad's fingertips and into the net—*swish!*—without the slightest hint of effort.

The rebound was mine. I dribbled the ball on our driveway before carefully planting and shooting.

"Arrrhhh!" I griped as the ball bounced off the rim, landing right in his hands.

"It becomes like tying your shoes, Little Dee." Dad always called me Little Dee, unless of course, I was in trouble; then it was Ann Nicole. Yes, I was the original Anna Nicole. "Let's go. I don't want you to be late."

"Yes, sir." I set down the ball and I grabbed my Hello Kitty lunch box and followed him to the car. When Dad said it was time to go, it was time to go.

He held the Oldsmobile passenger door open for me. A true gentleman, my dad never, ever let a woman— including his daughters—open a door. I slid into the middle of the wide front seat so I could ride right next to him. He drove me to school whenever he wasn't gone for road games, lectures, or basketball camps. The drive to my elementary school was just me and my dad, our special time.

As we pulled through the U-shaped drop-off at Fairview Elementary, everyone did a double take. The teachers, teachers' assistants, parents, and other kids would pretend not to look, but they didn't fool me. I saw their sideways glances in our direction. Of course, Dad did too, and he'd just smile and wave as if he were the mayor of Normalville. He might as well have been.

When the Redbirds won, people were nice. When they lost—which was rare—their tone changed from robust to muted. They went from smiling at me to no eye contact. But they were always talking.

Whether it was the music on the radio, the halftime shows at the arena, or my ongoing love of the piano, my fascination and passion for music grew faster than weeds after a good rain. I poured myself into the rhythmic melodies and expressed myself in fantasy-world compositions. Music provided a heightened stimulation to my sweet, predictable reality world: it gave me a realm of musical curlicues and imaginary roller coasters. My ability to disconnect and lose myself in verse-chorus-verse would prove to be a vital survival skill later in life. In the solitude of our basement, furiously scribbling down new bars and notes, I knitted together a blanket of comfort and excitement and was able to entertain myself at ten years old.

Our basement had two small windows. Through them, you could see the tips of the grass from across our yard all the way into our neighbor's basement window. During most of the winter that window would be packed with hard snow, a solid sheet of white making the basement completely void of natural light. When the spring arrived, the snow would begin to melt, and inch by inch the sun would begin to shine directly into this small, framed, and streaky box.

On Saturday mornings, I could hear Mr. Hopper from across the yard as he played his piano in his basement. Our houses had cookie-cutter layouts. From my basement windows I would have to be careful that he couldn't see me, but I could easily peep in on him.

Mr. Hopper was strange by any standard and it was the custom for neighbors to whisper about him. He almost always wore a yellow plaid woman's terry-cloth bathrobe that was stained and dirty. It looked like a

Salvation Army castaway. The fabric was so thick that it made Mr. Hopper look like a chubby woman instead of a frail man. He couldn't have been any older than my mother, yet he had wrinkles on his forehead that looked like they cut an inch into his skull. Mr. Hopper kept to himself. He would lock himself inside his house for days on end. From the neighbor's whispers, I learned that he suffered from some type of invisible brain sickness that made him prefer the safety of his own mind and basement.

"Why doesn't Mr. Hopper put on a suit and tie and go to work like Daddy?" I asked my mother, who was sweeping up my mess on the front porch. My mother stopped cleaning the dried Cheerios and looked across the street. Poor Mr. Hopper was shuffling in mismatched socks down his driveway to retrieve his letters from the overflowing mailbox. His wild brown whiskers and matted-down hair were the perfect accessories for that grimy yellow bathrobe. "He's just sad, Anny. Some people are just sad in their hearts." She went back to sweeping up my mess into her dustpan. I suppose she was trying to make his ailment understandable. But Mr. Hopper and I had a connection that my mother did not know.

On the night before they found Mr. Hopper at the end of his rope, I heard him singing and playing his piano as I practiced for my upcoming recital. His voice was booming over the pounding keys. His words were unintelligible and he was lost in the music. I tried to mimic his arrangement. I wanted to follow him through the creative forest that his bent mind had discovered to see what rabbit hole we landed in. I banged the keys frantically but I couldn't keep up. His playing became so hysterical and untamed that my hands cramped and I began to hyperventilate. Gasping, I pushed away from the piano, jumped off my bench, and ran toward the window. I watched as his methodic and wild crescendo built up but without reaching the end, then he just stopped. I nearly yelled, *Finish it!* but before I could get a syllable out, he *howled*. Mr. Hopper freakin' howled like a wolf at the full moon. My mouth dropped two inches agape. I should have been startled, but his high, guttural cry at the universe was perfectly on pitch! I stood there in shock and awe and quickly cranked open one of the windows as far as it would go, pressed my face to the hole. The cool air hit my eyelids and I opened my mouth and howled back at him. Two wild creatures spellbound in the woods of the music.

‿✑‿

The only person I told about Mr. Hopper's howling was my new music teacher, Miss Stephanie. I had outgrown the stagnant, legalistic repetition of Mrs. Caldwell, and Miss Stephanie was just the opposite: she was young and full of life and energy. She flowed across the ground as if her long, beatnik skirts were magically transporting her. Her eyes were blue or green depending on the color of her spaghetti-stringed top, and she smelled like she took baths in vanilla and mint.

One night we are sitting cross-legged in two beanbag chairs listening to a cassette tape of Carole King. Miss Stephanie played everything from Janis Joplin to Thelonious Monk for me. "Find your identity in the music," Miss Stephanie used to say, as she'd sway back and forth. "You make me feel like a natural woman," she'd sing, and say, "Let it transport you to another dimension."

I wasn't sure what that meant but I liked the way it sounded when it rolled off her tongue. Then she'd pull her thick, curly, wild long hair into a loose ball on top of her head and stick a chopstick through it and make us get to work. She made the discipline of practice freeing so that it became something I longed to do every day. She made the music belong to me just like my dad made the game belong to his basketball players.

I composed my first song that year after an hour-long session with Miss Stephanie. It was going to be the beginning of my long career in music, or at the very least the place where I could distract myself from the glaring lights that would eventually pierce my soul.

It was a Wednesday night home game. My sisters and I were in our seats opposite the student fan section. The stadium was sold out: standing room only. The fans were stomping their feet, and trumpets from the band were sounding victory. I saw three shirtless male students. They had painted their upper bodies solid white, each with one capital red letter. Standing side by side, their bellies spelled out *B-O-B* in honor of my dad. It made me laugh and feel warm inside, as they adored him as much as I did. By the second half, the strawberry-blond kid in the middle with the *O* on his

Jell-O belly was so hot and sweaty, his O looked more like a saggy U-turn sign.

Victory was the Redbirds'. I knew my dad was going to be at least another hour in the building conducting his postgame locker-room speech and press conference, so I eased out of my seat and made my way toward my secret hideout. "Hi, Jean." I waved at the elderly woman who worked security for the stadium and was positioned at the mouth of the tunnel where the team and special VIPs could trek back and forth to tidier bathrooms with our laminated passes strung from our necks.

I had come to know every nook and cranny of the new building as I had seen it go from sketch to steel. It had taken almost two years from the blueprint being laid across our dining room table to the last lightbulb being screwed into the scoreboard. I had mapped out all the mysterious places in the stadium that would come alive for me on game day and provide refuge from the noise. Anne Frank's vivid diary was in my grip; I was desperate to find a quiet corner and finish it. I had my own imaginary annexes in the new structure, and I wanted to discover one and settle into it and learn whether the Gestapo would indeed find the Franks.

We had been on a ten-year streak of winning seasons. This was my father's first losing season, and it was a losing season by only two games. The rebuilding year had wrapped up and Dad was eager to take his three returning seniors and his best recruiting class to date to the championship the following season.

My dad did not begin that season with any transparent issues with the new leadership that had come into the school. They knew my dad was a winner, had been trained by the best, and the town loved him. Maybe too much.

In the early hours of Sunday mornings before church, all things were discussed out loud in the confines of my parents' bedroom. I looked forward to these sacred hours all week. This morning I lay in my twin bed waiting to smell their coffee brewing. Once the quiet murmurs of their dialogue began, I tiptoed across the hall in my long white nightgown with my Cabbage Patch doll in hand and climbed into their bed. Snuggled between them, I was privy to the types of insider information that the media would have paid a hefty price to hear. I heard my mother whisper, "That's not right," and my father's retort, "I know. I told him I'd quit." My father stopped in the middle of their conversation and looked at me with his hazel eyes and soberly said, "You know this is *family talk*, Anny." That was code for *It's top secret*. We all understood *family talk* outside our walls could ruin our lives and my father's career if it were repeated.

He was having a few issues with someone at work. It didn't worry me. No one ever appeared stronger than my dad. And I knew that my dad had three things going for him. One, he was a conqueror. Two, everyone worshipped him. Three, he had God on his side. "The coin always lands on the side of moral values," he used to say. "There's no use flipping when you know the truth." I loved being a part of my mother and dad's sequestered recap sessions. It made me feel like a coconspirator in their club. I felt a responsibility to help protect our bubble.

Winter was giving way to spring, and with Dad's new multiyear contract, he reminded each of us that God's favor was on our family. That His grace would allow for all of our family to have stability in a wake-filled athletic sea.

There had never been any question for the Donewald family: the game was everything, and the game was safe. The game formed a positive, protective bubble for us. It consistently provided us food, shelter, vacations, and music lessons. Under it, all the players and coaches were safe too.

⟿

It was March of my fifth-grade year, and on this particular Friday, Bob Jr. and Kristin came to pick me up from school. This wasn't customary. I bebopped out of the lobby wearing my purple jeans and white T-shirt and found them sitting in our mom's idling Buick.

"What's wrong?" I asked, not wanting to get in the car.

"Get in," Bob Jr. ordered me.

"Where's Mom?"

"Just get in the car, Anny." Kristin's voice was unusually clipped.

I threw my lunch box into the backseat and parked my butt on the front next to Kristin, who reluctantly had to slide in closer to Bob Jr.

"Is someone dead?" I leaned over Kristin, wanting a straight answer from my brother.

"Oh, Jesus, Anny," Kristin said. "We'll talk about it when we get home."

My brother just kept his eyes on the road, as I stared at him knowing that something bad had happened.

"Sit back." Kristin pushed her forearm into my chest.

My brother finally looked at me. His eyes were bloodshot. "No one's dead."

When we pulled into the driveway, I barely waited for the car to be in park before I bolted into the house. Our curtains were drawn shut, which was unusual for daytime. The living room was dark except for two side table lamps. My dad sat in an oversized wingback chair, looking at his lap. My mother was across the room on our tan-and-black sofa.

"Did Nana die?"

I searched my mother's face for an answer. Nothing. Then my eyes stopped and my brain caught up with my feet and mouth.

"Why are you home, Dad?" I turned to face him.

Silence.

More silence.

"Your dad just got fired," my mother explained, but then quickly added, "but it's going to be the best thing that is going to happen to us." She tried to sound convincing.

BAM! My brother slammed the front door, causing me to jump forward.

None of it made any sense to me. I had never seen my dad sucker punched. It was as if Lex Luthor had double-walloped my dad with kryptonite. He was limp and lifeless, with only the four legs of the chair keeping him upright. His face was ashen and sunken. He'd aged ten years in a day.

He couldn't face me.

"Dad . . ."

He was devastated and shattered and shell-shocked. I looked from my mother to him. Then I did what I knew to do. I went to him and curled up on his lap. I wrapped my arms around his neck, giving him my version of emotional CPR. His arms finally found their way around my body and we just sat there hugging.

Before the evening news and while my mother cleaned vegetables, trying to act routine, our local broadcast of *Oprah* was interrupted with a special report: "Bob Donewald Fired." I stepped outside the side door and spotted a cameraman who had his lens pointed directly at me. I waved at him. My mom dropped a glass and it shattered, and she yanked me backward by my shirt collar. The media was relentless and our phone kept ringing over and over. My mother became so angry that she took our phone off the hook and refused to answer the door for anyone other than my dad's assistant coaches, who stopped by, heads bowed, hands clasped, giving their regards. It was like a wake and we, the Donewalds, were in the casket.

Eventually, the mourners and the media dispersed and my father and mother were alone at our kitchen table. Dad poured a scotch and handed it to my mother, then he poured bourbon for himself and took a deep breath. "Anny, please give us some privacy."

I knew what this meant, and normally he never had to ask me twice, but I was afraid to leave them. I wanted to be as close to them as possible. I didn't want anyone else getting a good angle on Dad and being able to shoot holes into him. I could never watch him fall from the sky and smash on the concrete again. I didn't move. He gave me a second look. Like a dog that had been scolded, I skulked out of the room toward the basement.

I stopped on the second step, sat down, and heard my dad say, "We're going to need a lawyer."

And then, I heard my father cry.

Perhaps everyone remembers a time when they see the person they believe to be the strongest, the one who loves them the most, being pushed down. Seeing them shoved and shattered. I'm not sure why, but the grief that burst out of my father is one of my most melancholy childhood remembrances. Oh, how I loved him. How I wanted to make it go away.

I stood up and put my hands over my ears. The sound of his muffled sobbing frightened me in a way that shook my core. "Please don't cry, Dad," I said. Then I looked up at the ceiling and prayed, "God, make him okay. Make my dad okay." I ran down each carpeted step to the small dingy window and looked over at Mr. Hopper's house and remembered his animal cry for help. Did Mr. Hopper have a pain like this? Was it more? Was this the sadness my mother had told me about? Would my dad end up like Mr. Hopper?

I found myself at the piano and began to play the composition that I had written two days earlier. I played it again and again, hitting the keys harder and harder. I lost myself in my enraged musical soliloquy until finally I was pounding on the keys.

Then instead of praying, I got mad. I got mad at the people who had soul-slammed my dad, and I got mad at God.

As I collapsed onto the piano keys, exhausted from my outpouring, I felt my mother behind me. She pulled my sweaty hair off my forehead. I spun around on the bench and squeezed my arms around her so tight I thought I would break her. Finally my grip loosened and I nestled my face on her breasts. She dropped to her knees and our embrace was face to face.

Mom was the anchor for our family. She was the rock that we were tethered to. She was the reason we didn't drift away and get battered to shreds on the rocky shore. She had been strong for my dad and she was strong for me now. It was then that I decided, from the healing support of her embrace, that from this point forward it would be she and I who would stand guard together over our family. Basketball couldn't be trusted. The game had failed us. The university had betrayed us. Dad was broken, and God, as far as I could tell, never showed up like He had promised me.

Life in Normal was over.

chapter four
WELCOME TO THE ZOO

*Up to 95 percent of women in the sex industry have
been sexually abused as children.*

> "Statistics of Women in the Sex Industry,"
> We Are Cherished, http://www.wearecherished.com/
> resources-2/statistics/

*With the amount of shame and secrecy that cloaks
women in the sex industry, I firmly believe that these
statistics are higher than what women will report.*

> Anny

The mourning in Normal was about
to be finished. We had been sitting shivah for a week,
letting the dead body that was my dad's firing stink up
the house, and now it was time to move on. Athletic
directors from around the country wanted my dad to lead
their basketball teams. Vanderbilt, Marquette, Western
Michigan, and Loyola University Chicago were calling.
I listened in as Dad sat through long phone interviews
talking about statistics and recruits and coaches that he
would potentially be bringing with him. I watched as my

mom would quietly enter his home office, fill up his coffee cup, and give him a thumbs-up every time she seemed to think he really nailed it. We had been kicked to the dirt and now he was showing us how to dust ourselves off and start over.

My parents would once again lean on their faith and their relationship to make the next move. It came down to the wire as Western Michigan and Loyola University Chicago both made a full-court press for him. The night before a decision needed to be made, I saw them kneel shoulder to shoulder at the side of their bed: the seeds of their tremendous faith falling out of their planters' bag onto the fertile soil of my youth. Like a small child saying his nightly devotions, my father prayed. "Lord, we trust that You are in control." His voice was hoarse and exhausted. "We know this isn't about money or esteem, so we give this to You. Whichever team calls first, we will go with them."

In the morning, my mother's door opened and the light from her bedroom momentarily blinded me. Then I could see the relief and exuberance. There was a glint in her eye as if she had just won the biggest stuffed panda at the state fair.

"We're moving to Michigan."

My gut was filled with so much preteen anxiety that I unleashed a waterworks show of confusion, anger, and joy. There were gushers of sadness. I was sorry to be leaving all I had ever known. But I was also happy that my dad had been vindicated. He—and we—had a new place where we belonged.

My mom sat down with me on the floor in the hallway, crisscross-applesauce, and let me work it out.

When my emotions had run dry, she pulled me up by the hands. I stood there looking at her hesitantly. She lifted one foot up and stomped it on the floor and repeated it with the other. I answered her silent battle call by planting my eleven-year-old feet on solid ground. "You're stronger than you think, Anny." My mom's words hopscotched across my heart. "Stronger than you think."

⮵

My father left the day after he got his new contract. The Western Michigan basketball program had been in ruins for over a decade. He was not daunted by the tremendous task of building a new team from the ground up. I went with my mother to meet my dad for several days in Kalamazoo, as we needed to find a new place to live and a new elementary school. The thought of starting over with new friends and teachers sent a host of fear bees buzzing all around me.

My mom and dad looked at house after house after house as I sat quietly in the backseat peering at all of the new storefronts. Each new thing was a new sting. From the street sign or park name that I couldn't pronounce, to the grocery store that I couldn't navigate, there was a swarm of the unfamiliar. My parents finally decided on a gray-colored, newly constructed home with teal shutters in the middle of Londonderry Avenue. Teal became my new favorite color. The house was one of the first to be built in a new development. It smelled like new paint and carpet, and the hallways with hardwood echoed. It was a fresh house for a fresh start. I got to pick my room, as I was the first of the kids to see it, and my mom promised we could paint it any color I wanted. I chose teal, of course! Our street was the only paved road for blocks, and the back of the subdivision was peppered with concrete slabs where houses would soon be erected along bumpy dirt trails. *No more howling at the moon with Mr. Hopper.* My mom pulled me close to her hip. "It's safe for Anny. I don't have to worry about her riding around in traffic." I began to embrace the future in Kalamazoo.

Once the decision had been made on location and my mom had filled out all the paperwork for Lincoln Elementary School, she and I headed back to Normal. Our marching orders were to pack it up and ship it out.

Lisa, Bob Jr., Kristin, and I boxed up our clothes, cleaned our bathrooms, and cleared out our junk while Mom rolled up her grandma's china in old newspapers and cautiously loaded it into boxes.

∾

My brother, Bob, was nineteen years old and

Lisa was twenty, so my mother made the decision to have me go with them to Kalamazoo so they could get a head start setting up our new house. I was in their custody. This had become the norm, with Lisa playing the part of mini-mom. She had become less and less of a confidant who shared sweaters and secrets and more of a watchdog. We crammed cleaning supplies, clothes, pillows, sleeping bags, and a cooler with soda and sandwiches in the car. Our guidelines were to get the cupboards and windows in the new house cleaned before the movers arrived. It would be three long days without my mother and I hated the idea of going ahead without her.

Lisa was never good at change. Between wiping away her endless stream of snot and tears, she'd take long deep breaths and sigh. As Bob drove, he would smile bravely at us and say, "It's all going to be okay." Clearly Lisa hadn't gotten the same battle stomp Mom had given me. I had the backseat of the Ford Tempo to myself, so I stretched out, placing my bare feet on the window, staring up at the ceiling. "Can someone turn on the radio?" My request was ignored. As I would not be counting down the Top 40 with Casey Kasem to pass the time, I rolled onto my stomach, curled up, and placed my head onto my arms to muffle Lisa's worry moans and get some sleep.

Unlike my sister, I was never afraid of the life outside our bubble. I believed that the dangers of the world on the nightly news didn't exist for people like us. Ridiculous, I know. I wasn't spoiled with buckets of chocolate-covered cherries or an ostentatious life on display, but my childhood had been graceful, albeit a tad militant thus far. My reality was *yes, please* and not agonizing—so my curiosity about things outside my comfort zone didn't come with anxiety.

About twenty miles before we hit Michigan, we pulled into a Hot 'n Now fast-food restaurant for fifty-cent burgers and fries and drinks, as our cooler was empty. Lisa and Bob went inside to order. I was left with strict instructions to stay in the car. As they stood in line,

I surveyed the scene. To the left, some high school–aged kids were smoking cigarettes and drinking sodas. To the right, I encountered the gaze of a man who looked like George Costanza from *Seinfeld*. He was sitting in his car smiling at me, and not because I was a Donewald kid. It was nice not to be recognized. He had his music playing and I assumed he was waiting on his wife or kids to grab their sacks of grease and goodies. I smiled back at him, thankful for his kindness. He was grinning and dancing in his seat. His thin lips and droopy cheeks were pulsating as if he were the only one in on his joke. He motioned for me to come and say hello. I watched Bob and Lisa handing the cashier their money and I eased out of our car. Mr. Costanza's eyes grew bigger as I got to his side door; he looked like our old family dentist. As I placed one of my small jelly shoes after the other, I got close enough to see in his car: he was naked from the waist down and touching himself. His face contorted, pinched together like he had just eaten a lemon. I quickly turned my head and backpedaled away from his car, feeling sickened, and hurried into our Tempo and locked the door, not wanting to look back up. Our family was incredibly modest and I had never heard of any weirdos who ran around exposing themselves to girls in schoolyards.

Bob and Lisa got in to the car. "You okay?" My brother eyed me while shoving a burger into his mouth. Lisa handed me my own bag over the dividing seat.

"This place is gross." I didn't know what else to say. I was in shock. Plus my brother was old enough to beat the living daylights out of anyone who did anything threatening to his sister's psyche.

As we pulled onto the freeway, I thought about

telling them. But how? Lisa was prudish and Bob would have whipped around, beaten the perv up, and gotten thrown in the clink for assault. The jarring, grotesque image of what I'd seen was flashing in my frontal lobe. I tried my best to block it out, make it stop. *No chance.*

I unwrapped my burger and sat there eating it, getting mustard and ketchup on my blue-and-white-striped T-shirt. I sipped cool Dr Pepper until a wave of nausea hit me. I just couldn't get that image out of my head. It kept popping up like a tornado warning on the television during a good episode of *Mork and Mindy*. The smell of spilled bathroom cleaner from the trunk filled my lungs; it was the last straw. I cranked down the window and stuck my head out. My first attempt was a dry heave. The wind blew my hair back; I lost my balance and proceeded to throw up down the car. The Tempo lurched over to the side of the road as Bob tried to help Lisa help me. It was all so repulsive and out-of-body that I never said a word.

When we finally got back on the highway, I trained my eyes out the front window. We passed a giant green sign that said WELCOME TO KALAMAZOO.

It wasn't long before our family's life in Kalamazoo had become an exact replica of life in Normal. The only differences were the mascots and the fact that no one in town cared about basketball. The first year with the Broncos was an uphill battle: there was a complete absence of fan passion. My mom, brother and sisters, and I attended all the games and sat behind the bench in the front row. The arena was practically empty, game after game. Between time-outs I would count the fans. At best, I counted five hundred by halftime. To make things worse, the arena was being remodeled. So while the new seats and flooring were being put in, my dad had to take his ramshackle bunch of boys to an airport hangar for practice.

By the second year, the team began to turn around. Supporters started to come back to the games, and enthusiasm for the team was palpable on the campus and in town. More important, we, the Donewald family, were ghosts no more: I'd walk into the athletic building and the secretaries knew me and smiled.

The student section at the game became louder and prouder the more we won. The first five hundred kids in the door were given free T-shirts. They were yellow with black writing that said BOB'S MOB. I wanted to sit with them. But I always sat in the front row, protected by my family, right behind my father. The ticket taker and usher were our makeshift guards or there to block me if I made a break for the kids screaming, "Bob's Mob! Bob's Mob!" They were amazing and I couldn't wait to be old enough to be one of them.

❧

My last year of elementary school was rougher than my mother or I could have ever anticipated. There were thirty-six of us trying to survive the sixth grade in our classroom at Lincoln Elementary School. It was a regular occurrence to see our principal in the hallway grabbing a kid at the neck or by his ear and dragging him to his office like a bad dog. Daily—or so it seemed—kids were busted for handgun possession, fighting, and drugs.

My dad and mom had taught me and my siblings to "just say no to drugs," but those conversations were the extent of my drug education until one day in math class. I sat next to a boy who had been held back two years. He wore torn Levis and hand-me-down T-shirts with yellow armpit stains, smelled of hair gel, and carried a brown paper sack with him everywhere. While the teacher had his back turned, the boy pulled a small baggie from his sack and showed it to me. "This is weed."

Another first time for me: any drug up close. Alarmed, I held up my arms like a bank teller in a robbery. Just as quickly, I put my hands back down and I looked around the room to make sure that no one had seen him or me. The teacher was still scribbling long division on the blackboard.

"I sell it for my brother," he explained as he tucked the baggie back into the sack. He didn't look like a drug dealer, but what I would come to learn is the good drug dealers never do.

These incidents weren't isolated. So, when my mother heard my teacher tell a girl to "shut up" during the winter parent-teacher conferences, she was finished with Lincoln Elementary School. I was transferred to the private Kazoo School.

❧

In the summer of 1990, our family vacationed in northern Michigan. While traveling, we stumbled upon an outdoor summer strings concert at Interlochen Arts Academy in Traverse City. The boarding school was in a beautiful setting: wooded forests with lush green trails, cabin-like residences surrounded by sweet, soft prairie grasses, and the crystal-clear waters of Lake Michigan. The thought of leaving my family had never once been appealing to me, but the moment I stepped onto the grounds at Interlochen, I wanted to go to school there. It was a few hundred miles away from Kalamazoo, but I felt it was a place where I could spread my wings and soar. There are few places in the world you immediately know in your soul that you're meant to be a part of, and that school was my place.

To get into the school took work. My last name was irrelevant at Interlochen. "You'll have to audition," the admissions administrator told me as he handed my mother a packet of forms. "We have strict guidelines for our artists." I nodded. I knew I could do it. I was in all the accelerated classes for gifted students at my middle school in Kalamazoo. Impressed with the high academic standards at Interlochen, my dad had a reason to sign off.

❧

We arrived back in Kalamazoo with just enough time for Mom to toss off her visor and Dad to put away his fun face before we all headed off to Dad's annual summer basketball camp. Boys from all around the Midwest attended, and my family and I were happy to help out.

I bebopped around the Reed Field House basketball court, listening to MC Hammer's "U Can't Touch This" on my Walkman while my dad finished running drills with the fifteen-year-old campers. While daydreaming of Interlochen, I was putting balls back onto the metal carts when my mother called me over to her seat at a table where she was sifting through registration papers that were piled high.

She motioned for me to take off my earphones. "Are you wearing a bra?"

I was so uncomfortable I wanted to crawl under her table. "Mom!"

I knew that my firm breasts had popped out overnight but I didn't want to talk about it.

"No," I confessed.

I had a bra. I was too embarrassed to wear it. My mom had taken me to a lingerie store at the onset of the summer. An older lady in a fancy dress and seamstress apron had made me remove my blouse in front of her, and she awkwardly placed her wrinkled, cold hands and measuring tape around my back and across my nipples. I thought I'd die! When I got home, I shoved the bra, still in the bag, underneath my T-shirts as if it were a dirty magazine.

But Mom was right. It was high time I started wearing that bra.

To make matters worse, my breasts weren't the only thing that had changed. It seemed like everything on me was resizing. My hips were suddenly curvy and I would go to bed at night and wake up to find another inch had sprouted out somewhere else on my body. Puberty was the pits. It was a big bucket of mortification and grossness. I remember the day I saw red goo on my toilet tissue for the first time. *Womanhood!* From now on I'd be stuck with some bulky cotton Kotex pad in my underwear while trying to shoot hoops. I wasn't naive. I had two older sisters who had acne, mood swings, and severe abdominal cramps that required heating pads and pain medicine. But I wasn't prepared for the floodgates of adolescence to open before junior high—no way! I was a rambunctious five-foot-six ball- and piano-playing tomboy now getting trapped inside a new curvaceous self.

It became painfully obvious that life was changing when the same boys that I'd played hoops with the year before, as the only girl on an all-boy team, changed their game with me. I was a scrappy inside player under the hoop and as an outside shooter rivaled any kid in town. But this summer the game morphed into something unfamiliar. The boys under the hoop weren't passing to me and shoving elbows into my shoulders anymore. Now in the mosh pit of competition under the net, I'd feel an occasional glad hand rub and squeeze my bottom.

My mother was still pensively staring at me, waiting for my answer.

"Okay. I'll wear it tomorrow," I huffed.

I didn't want to admit it, but I needed protection, and a bra wasn't the only armor I would require. In what felt like a split second, puberty had struck me like a lightning bolt, and I was going to need a muzzle, chastity belt, and new attitude by eighteen.

chapter five

WHEN THE DEVIL COMES TO STEAL YOUR FAITH

Child sexual abuse (CSA) has lifelong effects. Adults who are survivors of CSA often report a feeling of being "stuck." Their efforts to build and manage their lives often seem fruitless, hollow, or even hopeless. There can be a persistent perception that they are somehow different from others. They commonly report feeling that they are on the outside looking in or believe that they just don't belong.

"The Healing Place," adapted from *The National Committee for Prevention of Child Abuse Publication,*
1990

My cousin once told me that at some point in all of our childhoods something traumatic happens— abuse, death, disease—and that incident is when we realize the world is not as safe as we thought it was. Many times, it is at that moment, when our hearts are breaking, that the devil uses our brokenness to slither in and steal our faith.

Anny

What happened next would change my life, but it wasn't until I was an adult that I realized I had buried it so deep. I kept the secrets long enough that they annihilated me.

The still midnight air filled the darkness on the Western Michigan team basketball bus. We were traveling back from Ohio to Kalamazoo and the sleeping passengers were quiet. Even my father had his head resting against the window. I had been dozing in a second-row seat and woke up feeling foggy. I made my way through the dimly lit bus to the bathroom.

Matt was a six-foot-five, African American offensive star who had a killer ability to drive under the basket to the net. He was one of my father's favorite players, and at the time easily considered the team's best player.

Traveling with these young men had been my life, but at that stage I was transforming from an awkward flat-chested caterpillar. No longer a childlike waif, I was becoming a new creature.

What days before had been an easy fifteen-foot walk from the front of the bus to the back became a different journey altogether when I caught Matt staring at me. He was not looking at me with the brotherly appropriateness that I was accustomed to seeing from the college boys who both loved and feared my father. It was the type of look that resonates a gut feeling of *something is not right*. We all have that instinctual warning light, and mine was flashing.

It was dark and everyone else was sleeping. The whites of his open eyes shone brightly, like a predator's in the night. His long legs were spread over the aisle from seat to seat, and his gray sweatpants dangled low. My stomach sank, but I pressed on. I kept my eyes on the rear wall and stepped over his limbs. I touched the seat for balance and caught his smirk, as if I had taken his dare. I went into the bathroom and quickly locked the door. I leaned my head on the bathroom window and cool air rushed through my lungs. I stared at the oncoming headlights. A sensation rushed through me: *Just breathe. Stay put.* After what seemed like hours of waiting for the right time to escape, I mustered all my thirteen-year-old courage and came out of the bathroom. Matt's legs were now down and the aisle was clear. I quickened my pace, but he reached out and grabbed my hand.

His grasp was tight around my wrist. His other hand began to seductively rub my arm. I froze. Then the rubbing moved from my arm to my leg and he caressed my thigh beneath my skirt. His hands were strong and his arms were long and he had me trapped behind his overpowering intimidation. My mind floated above my body as if I were watching it and it wasn't me. *How is this happening to me?* In an instant, Matt had gone from a loving older-brother type to a ravenous, hungry predator.

I stood there like a puppy stands for a groomer combing out its tangles. I could not scream or cry or make a sound. Silence. Trained in silence. The humming of the tires flooded my ears. There were no words exchanged; I just looked at him like a deer looks down the barrel of a rifle at a hunter while he touched me.

Then it was over. I don't know if he was satisfied or just felt empowered by robbing the untouchable coach's daughter of her innocence. It was over, for now. I don't know how long it took; I can't remember. My implicit memory is more than my conscious memory. The gory details are now irrelevant. My body was never the same and my spirit was crushed.

As I moved away, my long jean skirt was riding sideways, with the button and zipper scraping into my hip.

How did it get this way?

I tried to process what this grown man had done to me. Make no mistake, college student or not, he was a grown man.

I got back to my seat at the front of the bus and everything looked normal. I wondered if this is how people feel when they lost a loved one in the blink of an eye but the world keeps going on around them. Sweat seeped from my pores. I wanted to crawl over my seat and wrap my dad's suit jacket around me and curl up in his arms, even though he was unaware of the torpedo that had just annihilated me.

For two more hours I sat on high alert.

When the team bus pulled into the arena, it was 2:30 a.m. The players shuffled off one by one. My dad and I sat, as he had a rule for the Donewalds: *Last one on, last one off.* As each gray sweatshirt passed me, I pressed a little closer against the inside window. Finally the bus was empty. My dad rose and I robotically stood behind him. We walked in unison across the parking lot, into the building toward the team locker room. I stopped at the door and checked to make sure that no one was behind me. "I'll be out in ten minutes, Little Dee," Dad said.

The steel door shut and I pressed my back against the brick wall and slid down to the floor and gripped my knees. I pulled my Walkman out of my purse and hit play. Heavy D was up on my mixed tape.

What happened that night was only the beginning of Matt's ongoing abuse.

∽

Parents teach their children to tell, but we never do. For me, the risk was too high. I could never be the reason my father would lose his dream, that my family's name would be dragged through the mud, or that the school's reputation would be tarnished.

I made the decision to protect the legacy that my father was building. I had heard a quote once: *Nothing takes down a team faster than the scandal of beating a dog or sex with a child. America just won't forgive you for that.*

The school, the team, the players—no one wanted this type of attention. I closed my mouth and sealed it with caution tape. The basketball world that had given us so much had now turned into the very thing that opened the door for my dysfunctional sexual appetite.

chapter six

OPENING SEASON

The experience of assault exposes the victim to the stark reality that they cannot always protect themselves no matter how hard they try. The assault is an invasion not only of the victim's physical self but also the intellectual, social, and emotional self. The experience of assault brings vulnerability issues to the fore, which can devastate self-confidence and destroy assumptions about the world and your place within it.

South Eastern Centre Against Sexual Assault
(SECASA), Victoria, Australia

For a long, long time I knew my past was insane, I just didn't understand the significance of the situations that had set it all in motion. I tried to keep putting my past in the past. Funny thing about the past is, whoever said you leave your *hit there, lied.

Anny

On the night before my fourteenth birthday, Mom and I drove up to the Bronco basketball arena to pick up my dad after practice. From there, we were driving straight to Traverse City. My interview for Interlochen Arts Academy was the next day and my dad was not going to miss it.

It's a sign! A sign from the universe that we have a green light and I'm going to drive through the intersection of heaven and hell.

For the last two months, I hadn't quite felt like myself. My mom thought it was my changing hormones. I didn't know anything about that. I just was tired all the time. I felt sick, achy, sore, and nauseous. My parents were constantly asking me if I was okay and I had become a scratched record, saying "I'm *okay*," over and over.

Mom wanted me to get a good night's sleep and be rested for my audition, so she had booked us adjoining rooms at the Holiday Inn on the water. Before turning off the lights, I kept flipping through the folded-up pamphlet that described the musical and theatrical prodigies the academy was spitting out.

That's when it hit me: the discomfort that I had been experiencing over the last two months had become a blurred line of insecurity. It had replaced the confidence that my family had instilled in me since birth.

Am I out of my league trying to go to Interlochen? Am I good enough?

Whether the answer was yes or no, what I did understand with crystal-clear vision was that Interlochen was far away from the darkness of basketball buses.

But I couldn't sleep. *"Arrrrrrhh!"* I pounded the pillow trying to turn off the error message that was replaying in my brain. At midnight, I yanked off the tightly tucked cotton sheet that was binding my feet. I tossed and turned the rest of the night, the neon clock radio monitoring my painful progress: 2:05 a.m., 3:26 a.m., 4:15 a.m.

My dad came into my adjoining room at 7:30 a.m. with an orange juice and croissant in hand. "Your mom's downstairs waiting."

"I'm so tired." I allowed my exhausted body and deflated ego to sink into the bed.

He placed the cup and pastry on my dresser and leaned against the wall, crossing his arms at his chest. "Little Dee, if you don't want to do this, you don't have to do it."

I propped myself back up onto my elbow and muttered, "It's just, I just . . ." before flopping back down, flat on my back.

Dad walked over and stood next to the bed, looking down at me. "The foundation I lay down all week, that I drill into my players on the court, is the same foundation I've laid into you."

He has a way of cross-pollinating faith and sports.

"We do the groundwork over and over so when the crowd or the voices in the player's head become too loud, when the pressure is on, and it's time to shoot at the buzzer, their body pivots and shoots from their core. They do it because they have done it over and over. Just like you practicing day after day. You don't need to worry. You know how to do this."

I love my dad's pregame speeches. This is what makes him great at what he does.

"God has given you the talent, the ability, and the resources. Now, how and if you use them is up to you. The question is—"

I wanted to tell him about the bus right at that moment.

"Do you want to go to school here?"

I wanted to tell him that I didn't want to leave him or Mom, but distance was the solution for all of us. I was afraid of everything now.

"Yes."

"Then let's go. This is your time."

⌖

Pure adrenaline took over.

I stood in front of a professor with long hair who wore John Lennon glasses and a burlap tunic. The small room had one desk, one piano, and books lining the shelves. I shook out my hands and then ran my pinky gently down the cool, smooth keys. I pulled my shoulders back, as if my music teacher Mrs. Caldwell had her ruler in the middle of my back, pushing at my arch.

"Posture is everything," I heard her say in my head.

The repetition of practice and the passion for the music took over, and from the first bar of Mozart's "Sonata Facile in C," the piece's paradoxical combination of joyous rhapsody and bone-chilling mystery was freeing and heartbreaking. I liquidated every emotion inside me and poured it all out and onto the keys.

When I was finished, the professor said, "Thank you, Anny." And that was it.

I scooted the bench back on the hardwood floor and walked out.

In the lobby my dad and mom were talking with a jazz musician who was a professor at the school and performed at the local watering holes, playing for the Traverse City locals.

"Well?" My dad held up his arms.

✎

Mom, Dad, and I walked in silence to our car, not knowing what to make of the entire experience. At exactly the right moment, a group of students passed us. All boys, all wearing tights and *Flashdance*-style sweatshirts. It made me feel happy inside and gave me some relief.

I had picked my career in music before I had even gotten my braces off, and today had seemed like the day the truth would come out. But it didn't! It was completely anticlimactic! We drove the winding road home as I replayed everything in my head from the first day I touched a piano key up until I walked out of that tryout. This was the stress champions were made of. I recounted to myself the days and months and years of practice, rehearsal, and recitals. And now my entire musical future was left in the hands of a granola-eating, Birkenstock-wearing professor who gave me absolutely no feedback. *Come on!*

Feeling dumbfounded, my dad broke the trancelike state in the car. "Anyone want McDonald's?"

I leaned over the front seat between Mom and Dad. "McDonald's?"

"Yeah." I looked at the side of his face and then—

A deer jumped in front of our car! My dad slammed on the brakes. I was sent crashing forward toward the front window. The car jerked and then skidded to the left, narrowly missing the buck in all his enormous glory.

My dad let out a string of curse words.

"Are you okay?" My mom helped me to get settled back into my seat, as Dad appeared to regain his composure. It was incredible that we'd missed it. That five-point buck should have sailed into the windshield and killed us all!

"That was a miracle," I said. "He was *huge*."

"Thank you, Jesus." My mom hammered the point home.

A sedan coming toward us in the opposite lane had a deer strapped to the roof.

"Ah. Deer season opened today," Dad said. "They're running for their lives."

I understood the feeling.

It seemed every other car we passed had some type of zombie Bambi on it. Tongues hanging out, necks bent at unnatural angles. It was gross.

"Does anyone else feel like it's the deer apocalypse?" I felt light-headed from the lack of sleep.

We followed a pickup truck into the McDonald's drive-through. The bed of the truck was open, and in it, lying motionless, was a beautiful doe. She was massive and must have been powerful, as her shoulders were muscular and strong. The truck bed had an orange tarp in it that was pooled with blood. The deer's head was flopped to the side and hanging almost out of the tailgate. She was staring at me. I'm not sure if she was dead but her eyes transmitted *the fallen*. Going . . . going . . . gone!

She was me on the bus. As much as I tried, I just couldn't shake it. I couldn't escape it. I couldn't bury it deep enough.

~

After unloading from the team bus: *I hate the bus. When I'm old enough I will never, ever ride a bus again! Is it weird that my life is always in transit? That charter airplanes and Greyhound buses are the bunk bed of my life?* I was in the lobby of a Marriott-esque hotel, a backpack slung over my right shoulder, suppressing my fear until the fear changed to goose bumps. I saw Matt lurking around. My eyes darted from the back of his head to a safe dirty spot on the carpet.

My parents, thankfully, met me so I didn't have to spend too much time studying a coffee stain on the floor and pretending I didn't see Matt. Mom went to the front desk to see if there were messages or faxes for my dad. As my father and the team manager handed out itineraries and room keys, I remained safely tucked in their shadow. We had just arrived in Toledo, Ohio, after a two-hour bus ride. We were early enough that French onion soup and cheese bread from room service were still a possibility.

My dad held out a key. As I reached for it, he pulled it back to make sure I was listening. "Back down in fifteen so we can go to dinner."

Oh, how I just wanted to submerge in a hot bath and watch television. I wanted some alone time behind locked doors. In some ways, the constant companionship of my parents and the dutiful obligations of being part of a basketball family brought a level of comfort to the routine. Now, perhaps because of teenage angst or just the need to never be around Matt, writing lyrics and music was my only distraction from what appeared to be a metaphoric prison. With the same complexity that a lion in the zoo both loathes and loves its captor, I learned to find sanity and stimulation despite the underlying tension and longing to attack and devour Matt limb by limb.

"Little Dee, here's your key. Go up to your room and come back down and we'll go to dinner."

I looked over at my mom chatting it up with another coach's wife. "I'll wait for Mom."

"She's not going up. Get going."

No, Dad! No! Can't you see I'm not safe here? I'm never safe anymore!

The elevator was filling up with boys. I rushed to jump on, as there is safety in numbers. I didn't want to be caught alone with anyone. As the doors shut, an arm came through and forced the doors back open. More players loaded in, squishing me against the back wall. I kept my eyes and head down toward the dried mud that had been swept into the corner.

I could feel him looking at me.

I didn't dare move or look up, but I knew that Matt was on the elevator and had made his way next to me in the back. I felt his hand on my bottom. I tried to move away, but there wasn't room enough to blow even a whisper between the railing and me. I stood like a toy soldier from *The Nutcracker*, with my arms at my sides.

The players were horsing around, elbowing each other and laughing while Matt began to press the bulge in his pants against me. *How doesn't anyone see me?* Or maybe they see and don't care. Maybe they could see, but this year Matt and my father were taking us to the National Invitation Tournament (NIT). We were second in the conference and anyone—player, coach, administrator—who spoke up would destroy it all. The fans would stop cheering and buying tickets, the donors would stop giving, and the dollars that build national championship winning teams would dry up.

What's one girl? One touch? One rub? One life?

He was rubbing his crotch against my hand, and instead of jerking my hand away, I pretended it wasn't there. I pretended nothing was going on, just like everyone else in that box. That this six-foot-five man wasn't pressing and rubbing his privates against me. Perhaps the concept of simple rubbing doesn't sound terrible, but it was! The shock wave of being confined with the grossness of a man's private parts *on me*: it was a powerful, violating menace, a baseball bat that had cracked my head open on the first swing. I was so overwhelmed that I was holding my breath and on the verge of passing out.

Ding. The elevator doors opened and players begin to file out onto the ninth floor.

Finally!

But Matt didn't move. Was he staying on? I had one more floor to go, as the coaches and their families never stayed on the same floor as the players. *Why isn't he moving? Don't let him stay on here with me!*

Then a player in the hallway turned back. "Man, you

gettin' off?"

Yes, he is getting off!

And he took a step forward.

I made the mistake of looking up, and he smiled at me as if saying, *We're not finished here.*

As the door shut, I heard him say, "See you later, Little Dee." Mocking my father.

I knew this was true. He had been around every corner, in the hallways of the basketball tunnel and in other hotels. He would touch my shoulder as he exited the bus. Rub my head in a hotel lobby. Over and over, every chance he had to mentally, emotionally, physically, or sexually wreak havoc on me, he took it.

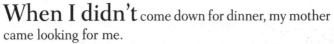

When I didn't come down for dinner, my mother came looking for me.

I was locked in my room and in my bed under the covers.

"We've been waiting for you!" She was angry.

"I'm not going."

She turned on a lamp and looked at me. "Your father and I want to talk to you about something."

Oh my God, did someone tell them? Do they know?

I rolled over. "I feel like puking."

"It's important."

Then the door in the adjoining room slammed, startling me. We both turned toward the door separating my room and my parents'.

"What are you two doing?"

My dad stood looking irate. "Let's go."

"She says she's sick."

"Really?" His inflection changed. Disbelief.

"Yes, really." I'm not sure who just blurted that out with a sassy tone.

"Did you tell her?" My father looked at my mother.

She shook her head, no.

"Tell me what?"

"You don't look sick." He was baiting me.

"Dad!"

"We have things to discuss with you."

"Anny—"

They knew. Thank God, they knew. My father was going to lose everything he had worked for and all because of me. I could tell by his mixture of trying to maintain composure and his sadness. He had his *here we go* mask on.

My mother looked at my father for approval. Then she stroked her hand down my hair. "You were accepted into Interlochen."

chapter seven
UNRAVELING

Between 66 percent and 90 percent of women in the sex industry were sexually abused as children.

—D. H. Bracey, in "The Juvenile Prostitute: Victim and Offender," *Victimology* 8 (1982), 151–60

Personally, I think the other 10 percent are just too ashamed or scared to talk about it. Because the God's honest truth is that something has happened to that little girl to make her private parts public. When a girl has that much fight going on inside, eventually something is going to leak out.

Anny

I was a walking, ticking time bomb.

"It's up to you," my father reassured me.

He, Mom, and I were sitting at the octagonal breakfast table off the kitchen. I was rolling a pencil between my palm and the acceptance letter. The news during the Toledo road trip that I was accepted to Interlochen had quite the opposite effect that my parents expected. I had retreated from excitement and possibility because of the realization that I would have to leave home.

"I can't believe I got in."

My dad stood up from the table. "We love you and we're leaving it up to you."

Up to me? Up to me?

Despite feeling upside down and dizzy, I was doing loop-de-loops in my brain. I changed my expression to reflect that of a confident girl. "Okay, I'll think about it."

"Pray about it," Mom added with a sprinkle of certainty.

I did pray about it, but not for answers everyone wanted. I prayed for a suitable explanation as to why I didn't want to go. I was mad at myself. I had worked beyond my ability to get into the academy and now fear had sabotaged me. I was mad at God for turning me into the lion who limped down the Yellow Brick Road without his courage.

You would think that my parents would have been disappointed with my lack of gusto, but to them I was never a piano prodigy in the making. I was the only child left at home, the sticky glue that kept them young.

That night, I couldn't help myself from eavesdropping. I had wandered into my parents' bedroom and overheard my mother in their bathroom talking to my father in the shower. I was straggling around pretending to make my way out, walking in small circles near their closed bathroom door.

My mom was trying to keep her voice low, but I heard her over the running water. "I just don't think she's ready," she said.

"What?" My father turned the water off and I heard

the shower door slide open.

Her voice lowered, now that the distortion of the water was gone. "She's not ready."

"She's ready for that school," my father pointed out. "She just isn't ready to leave home."

Interlochen was the escape tunnel that God had dug for me out of Kalamazoo, but I was too timid to get in it. I had a yearning to stay close to my mother. The reality of being away from her seemed a desolate and scary one, more so than being on the Broncos' team bus.

They had both seen through my performance. I tiptoed to their liquor counter and poured a clear liquid out of one of their alcohol bottles and into my Gatorade and swished them together. It wasn't bad and it made me feel nothing but out of my body and sleepy.

The next afternoon I sat with my parents over fried bologna sandwiches and justified my decision to pass up my musical dreams to stay home. I had weighed all the options and prayed for all the answers. In truth, I never heard from God, and the overarching con was leaving my mother. I iced the cake with the fact that, like my dad, I loved basketball and wanted to continue to play hoops; Interlochen didn't have a program for me. As hogwash as the justification was, the reality was I wanted to be home, and somewhere in themselves, I know, they wanted me home. There was no digging deeper into my reasoning. We all left the decision feeling, well, satisfied.

This is the point where I began to distance myself from my dreams and compartmentalize my actuality.

"Why do I have to be at *all* of the away games?" I protested as my mother and I debated heading out for a road trip. It was the middle of my freshman year at a local God-centered private school in town—a far cry from Interlochen.

"Kristin can come here!" My mom knew my sister would welcome having a refrigerator full of food, but she was still tepid about letting me stay without adult supervision.

"She'll be fine," my dad reiterated as he walked out the door.

Between sleepovers with girlfriends and my sister on lookout, I began to escape the trips on the team bus. Matt had graduated, but to me there would always be another Matt. The religious school my mother had chosen had a decent basketball program where I could excel and dominate.

Life was okay.

My first relationship with a boy happened during my freshman year. His name was Jeremy and he was two years older than me, a perfect blond-haired, blue-eyed Dutch boy. A needlepoint pillow on his family's couch said it all: "If you're not Dutch, you're not much."

They were an upper-class, strict Catholic family. Jeremy had seven brothers and sisters, and his mom never let any of her chicks too far from the coop. They went to Catholic mass three nights a week, and Jeremy was their youngest. He played football, ran track, and loved Jesus. Most of our time we spent talking about the weekend sports' highlights and tossing the basketball underneath my hoop in our driveway. It was all pretty innocent. His parents didn't love that my name wasn't

Mary Ellen, Mary Ann, or Mary Beth, but the fact that my dad was Coach Donewald was enough of an excuse to glaze over the fact that I wasn't on their pope squad.

"You're scratching me," I said to him as he fumbled trying to undo my bra underneath my T-shirt.

We were standing and kissing under the football stadium bleachers. He had just finished track practice. "Sorry, it just won't—" He tugged at it more.

"Let me do it!" I reached behind my back and just undid it. "You were gonna rip it."

Jeremy was the first boy that I had let touch me with approval. He made my knees quiver and buckle when he smiled at me. At six feet tall, he stood four inches above me and made me believe I was safe. Everyone loved and feared him. *Much like my dad on his own turf.*

Our embraces and attempts at intimacy were goofy and, for the most part, harmless. But being the good Catholic boy that he was, Jeremy felt a colossal guilt each time we made out. To relieve his burden, after every heavy petting session, we would walk to St. Something-or-other and I'd sit outside the church on the curb while he went in so he could confess.

"That's it?" I said to him as he came out.

"Yeah." He took my hand in his and walked toward his parents' house.

"Are you going to do this every time?"

"Maybe."

"I saw your priest at the Olive Garden when I was out with my parents."

"Really?"

"He looked at me funny. You didn't tell him my name or anything, did you?"

"Anny, he goes to our games. He knows who you are."

"Grrrrrreat!" I mimicked Tony the Tiger from the Frosted Flakes commercials.

He stopped. "You know what we're doing isn't right, right?"

I shrugged him off.

"Anny, I don't want you to go to hell."

"I'm not going to hell."

"I think you should come to church."

"Look, Jeremy, I get God at home. I don't need to sit in a closet in there"—I pointed at the cathedral—"to not go to hell."

He just kept walking.

"What?" I could feel my heart beginning to race with resentment.

"Nothing."

I needed to calm my inner anger down, as I was about to verbally pounce on him.

"I think it's wrong if you don't, well, love me." *Defused!*

We walked in silence together.

"I do love you," he finally said, and put his arm around my shoulder, pulling me into his body.

That was easier than I thought.

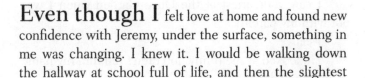

Even though I felt love at home and found new confidence with Jeremy, under the surface, something in me was changing. I knew it. I would be walking down the hallway at school full of life, and then the slightest irritation would turn me into a different person. What was going on inside me? It felt as if I had cracked. I wondered if I had a personality disorder.

I was masquerading most days trying to be Anny, but my patience had been snatched. I was still getting straight As, and at home my moods seemed to stabilize except for the nightmares. Being the last of four children has its blessings, as my parents had gone through teenage years before, so nothing up to this point had surprised them. They knew what to expect when the adolescent temperament struck.

At five foot nine with long blond hair, I could have easily passed for a cheerleader on Halloween, but I wasn't the pom-pom-carrying type. Being around men on the court my entire life, I had a toughness and testosterone level that a girl has only if she's been raised in a house full of boys or comes from the mean streets. You learn to catch the ball when it's passed to you, or get beaned with it. You know that the question "Which horse won the race?" always leads to a giant slug on the leg, followed by "Charley horse." You get used to towel snaps and noogies and rug burns. You develop a roughness. But what doesn't come naturally is true physical violence. The run-of-the-mill female doesn't have the guts to actually throw a punch or slap someone in the face. It's just not how we were designed.

Shuffling through the lunch bar in the cafeteria, talking to Jeremy in front of me, I heard a girl say to me, "Can you hurry it up?"

Her name was Juanita. She was three people behind me in the line. She was the only African American girl in our vanilla religious school. Her mother had enrolled her after she had had a baby out of wedlock. She was a giant Juno.

"Why don't you shut up?" I snapped back at her before I could comprehend the consequences coming from my smart mouth. The whites of Jeremy's eyes got bigger as he looked over my shoulder at Juanita. I just set down my tray and said calmly, "Don't get involved." My Dutch knight in shining armor was preparing for battle. After all, Juanita looked more like a dude than half the guys in our school.

Then I felt the heel of her hand on my shoulder, thrusting me forward. "Why don't you say that to my face?"

In an instant you have to decide: sit this one out, or dance?

I decided to dance. I spun around in a flash. My fist was clenched tight and I connected with a right hook to her gut.

Wow, did it feel good to hit her and unleash the wrath!

Shocked, she inhaled loudly. Her face resembled Medusa's before turning victims to stone. Her eyes narrowed and she grabbed the side of my hair and slammed my face into the metal ledge where my tray was sitting.

I thought my cheek would explode.

The crowd in the lunchroom went silent.

Amid cries of "Stop it!" and "Hit her!" I yanked her arm and raised my right knee and nailed her in the hip.

Juanita connected with two quick jabs, the first to my ribs and the second to my chin. My teeth slammed together so hard it sounded as if my wisdom teeth cracked in half.

But it didn't matter. This wasn't Candy Land. The drama was out in the open. This fight was primal, and for once, I didn't hold back. It felt good to respond to her attack even if she was the better fighter.

I felt sheer rapture in release. The silence that I had controlled and the standing still and hiding from Matt in the corner of *everywhere* came to the surface. I swooned in the ecstasy of just flailing and screaming and kicking and punching. It was a mental breakthrough and breakdown at the same time.

I was dazed, and she took the pause in the action as an opportunity to grab me and throw me hard onto the tile floor.

As I went down, she open-hand slapped the side of my head. It stung, setting my ear ablaze.

I screamed, "Get off me!" and swung furiously but didn't connect until I yanked her large gold hoop earring. I snatched it out, tearing her earlobe in two. Unfazed by the blood and the pain, Juanita proceeded to punch me in the face so hard that I don't remember anything past that moment.

I sat across from Juanita in silence. I could barely see out of my right eye. We had hurt each other. Yet I saw myself in her. Juanita had the same interior fury that

I had, hiding in the shadows. As a woman I felt both sorry for her and proud of her, as that kind of indignation doesn't come from an easy life of love and Build-A-Bear weekends.

We were waiting in the lobby of the principal's office when she looked at me and spoke. "I gotta hand it to you. For a pretty little white girl you sure got a lotta street in you."

Why this made me happy I'll never know. I was still clutching her big gold hoop in my hand. I opened my fingers and leaned forward, offering it to her. She would be the only woman to ever take me down in hand-to-hand combat. I would never again lose a fight. I remembered hearing once, *It's not the size of the dog in the fight, it's the size of the fight in the dog.* I had a lot of fight in me.

She took her earring back as my father walked through the door.

My dad clenched his jaw in alarm when he saw me. His eyes began to water. "Are you okay?"

I avoided his gaze. "I'm fine." *Rewind. Fast-forward. Repeat.* "I'm fine."

He helped me get up and we went home. Seeing his baby girl battered had left my dad speechless.

⌁

"She sure beat the daylights out of you," Mom said, changing the ice pack over my eye. She said it in a way that took the steam out of the situation. Unlike my dad, it didn't rattle her to see a swelling eyelid or purple rib. After all, she'd been an ER nurse. She was calm and cool and steady. "You're going to be fine," she said, as she tended to the bruise on my rib cage.

Two days later I resembled Rocky at the end of the beating he took in the ring with Apollo Creed.

I'm not a monster. I laughed at myself in the mirror while trying to put concealer around my black-and-blue eye, realizing that my black-and-blue outside now matched my bruised inside. Too bad they don't make internal concealer for victims of sexual predators.

Shortly after the lunchroom knockout, Jeremy broke up with me. Not that I blamed him, as I am sure at some point he waved the white flag at his priest after the sight of my devil horns poking through my halo was too much for him and his Catholic confessionals.

My family was disappointed that the relationship with Jeremy had skidded off the straight and narrow. And then, to make matters worse, I brought Scott home.

Scott's parents were divorced. He worked part-time after school to help pay for his mother's diabetes medicine. He was the first boy that I liked that hadn't been in our economic class or at the level of holiness my parents expected. He was from the wrong side of town, and my father instantly knew he was trouble. It had nothing to do with money or stature but more that Scott lacked the decency that a father demands for his daughter.

"I scout talent," Dad reminded me. "And I don't like it when a man can't look me in the eye."

Scott was shady.

His attire and general sense of style didn't help matters. Scott was thin and wiry, yet he wore oversize pants. His nails were dirty. The back of his hair was mashed down from napping. He didn't look at all like the high school jocks that had once come calling. Scott more closely resembled Eminem from 8 *Mile*, without the rapping talent.

The same instinct that made my mother sniff the team bus drivers for alcohol told her from the beginning that Scott was dark. Yet despite her sixth sense, she had missed the fact that darkness begets darkness. I was slowly becoming more comfortable feeling dirty than living up to any preconceived greatness that was expected of me.

Matt's repeated violations had left me feeling used and shameful, and now my frills had burned around the edges.

All my mother knew was that he had an energy that she didn't want around her daughter.

"No way," she said matter-of-factly after Scott had dropped me off from a night out at a school dance.

"What?"

"I don't like him."

"Mom!" I walked into the kitchen and pulled out leftover shepherd's pie.

"Anny, he's trouble. Can't you trust me on this?"

How come she can see trouble on one boy and not on a basketball player on Dad's team? Perhaps it was her picking and choosing for me that caused my rebellion to kick in.

"No, Mom. I can't trust you on this."

"Well, if you continue to see him, you're going to be chaperoned."

"I'm fifteen years old!"

My dad entered the room. "It's just how it's going to be. When he's in this house, you'll never be alone with him. That includes when we are on road trips."

"That's not fair. You let Jeremy—"

"Jeremy was different," my father chimed in.

"Why are you doing this? Because Scott's parents don't have money?"

"No! Because he doesn't have the integrity level that I demand." My father was right but I didn't want to admit it.

Jeremy had always opened my car door and spoken to me with question in his sentence. He was always checking to make sure I was doing okay. Scott, on the other hand, was the type of guy who would take the only seat left on a bench and then have me sit on his lap so he could grind on me.

~≋~

On my sixteenth birthday my parents gave me a new white Thunderbird. It was a reward for receiving all As on my report card and for perfect attendance at basketball practice. I was working part-time at the Gilmore's department store cosmetics counter and appeared to be, as Johnny Cash sang, walking the line, but I was living a double life. I had the duality of being a pretty tree that was growing poisonous fruit.

On the weekends Scott and I would go to teen night at the dance club Stingers. I had been drinking vodka for a year and a half. The drinking numbed everything. I'd take it out of my parents' liquor cabinet and pour a little water into their Ketel One bottle so they wouldn't know it was missing. I'd mix it in Gatorade or Dr Pepper and take it to school. Between periods I'd do a shot to just take the edge off.

My parents were none the wiser until one Thursday evening when Scott dropped me off well after my ten p.m. curfew.

In her typical Rock of Gibraltar fashion my mother stood in my bedroom doorway and stated, "No more school nights with Scott."

If I had been more sober, I would have retorted back, but I was afraid if I began to melt down, she'd see that it was more than a teenage crush that was impacting me.

⤳

Scott picked me up on my lunch break from Gilmore's in his mother's Honda Accord. He parked in the back of the parking lot, behind the store and next to a Dumpster. He came around to my side of the car and got in. I had already taken off my panty hose in the break room bathroom, so all I had to do was hike up my skirt and sit down.

It wasn't romantic or intimate or how I knew in my heart your first *real* encounter should be with someone you love or are married to. It was uncomfortable and awkward and my knee hurt as it was jamming between the seat and the gearshift. "Anny . . ." Scott looked at me as if I was his one and only.

"Don't say anything." I closed my eyes and reached

behind me with my right hand and turned up the radio.

I lost what was left of my innocence. I didn't do it because I was in love. I didn't do it because Scott had given me an ultimatum. I did it to get it over with. I wanted to paste over the images of Matt everywhere. My holiness was gone.

~⋧~

In May of that year, my mother found a discarded pregnancy test on the floor of my bedroom under a pile of clothes. My period had been late and I was in a panic. The test was negative but in my sloppiness I had forgotten to dispose of the evidence.

"Where is he!" My dad sped over to Scott's mother's house and marched in, uninvited. At the time, I thought he was insane. But now I suppose he was doing what any father would do if he knew a boy was having sex with his sixteen-year-old daughter.

I warned Scott that my dad was gunning for him, so we both split our houses. I hightailed it through the back door and walked four blocks away, where Scott was waiting to pick me up.

This was it for me! My parents would put up with a lot, but sex was something that was not acceptable. We didn't talk about sex. We didn't have sex. It was a sin. It was unheard of; it was a deal breaker in my mind. You have sex, you're going to hell!

I knew what God said about man and woman. I had been taught the scriptures and learned the rules. But if God cared so much about sex, why did He let perverts and pedophiles get away with snatching up girls' goodies? *Tell me that.*

⁓

I ran away.

I couldn't face my dad and I didn't want the consequences that followed. I just wanted to be away from it all. The jig was up.

A friend of Scott's had moved to Texas. The family's house had not yet sold, so we knew we could hide out in their vacant mansion. We broke in through the basement window and climbed into the house. It was eerie and cold, despite being nearly summertime. Scott had brought some pillows and blankets from his house and a few things for me to snack on. My first night in the house alone, I slept in a master bedroom closet. The closet had gray carpeting and I could close the door and feel safe and keep the draft from the staircase from hitting me. After night five, I was exhausted and starving.

I perched on the kitchen counter and watched Scott unpack a box of Cheerios, a spoon, and a bowl he had brought from his house. "Milk?" I looked at him.

He smacked his own head. "I left it at my house."

"It doesn't matter." I took a handful of cereal and poured it into my mouth.

"You've got to go home." This came out of nowhere from Scott.

"Home? I'm not going home. My dad hates you. He'll kill us both."

"What are you going to do?"

"You mean *we*?"

"I mean you, Anny."

I seethed inside at his quitter nature.

"You've got no diploma," he continued. "No car. No job."

At this point I wanted to smack him with the box of Cheerios.

"I just think you should go home."

Scott left and didn't come back. I spent that night in the house alone, only this time the fairy tale of running away and marrying Scott had become a nightmare that even he had bailed on. I was exhausted from sleeping on the floor, fighting constant hunger, taking cold showers, and nursing my wounded pride. I was ready to make the walk of shame back to my house with my tail between my legs. Honestly, where else was I going to go?

❧

"You look hungry," my mother said, as I came in the back door of the kitchen.

"I am." I stood there looking at her and wanting to cry.

I wanted to stop the merry-go-round and get off, but it kept spinning and spinning.

She was in the middle of setting the table for lunch. She went to the cabinet and pulled out a third plate.

My dad came into the kitchen. His worry was evident by the bags under his eyes. He walked around my mother, slowly squeezing her shoulder to give her a vote of confidence and reprieve, and then he stopped in front of me.

I wasn't sure if he was going to hit me or hug me. He took a calculated breath in and let it out. He put both hands on my shoulders and looked me square in the eyes, searching for the right words.

"What can we do?"

This is how both my parents are: what's done is done. From the beginning of time they have been about constantly moving forward.

Together we decided that I needed a fresh start. My reputation in the town had become trashed, and most of what people were saying was true. My parents wanted me to be happy and to flourish in school with all the God-given talent and goodness that they believed was in me.

I didn't see what they saw. But at this point I was ready to go anywhere. I just wanted to get out of there.

chapter eight
THE TRAVELING CIRCUS

In 2012, in Maryville, Missouri, after fourteen-year-old Daisy Coleman was allegedly sexually assaulted by two star athletes in her small town, the girl's family pressed charges after emergency room doctors confirmed she clearly had been attacked. The backlash and harassment toward the victim and her family was endless and included having their house burned down for telling the truth. This should have astounded and caused outrage in the town, but it did not. This doesn't surprise me. The Denver Post *ran a report on a disturbing incident in Norwood, Colorado: a thirteen-year-old boy on the high school wrestling team was bound with duct tape and sodomized with a pencil in a brutal hazing ritual. When the boy and his father—the school principal—reported the assault, much of the town turned against them and backed the attackers (two of whom were the wrestling coach's sons). The boy was mercilessly bullied, and there was a clamor for the principal's dismissal. Eventually, the perpetrators pleaded guilty to minor charges and were sentenced to probation, community service, and modest fines; the boy's family, like the Colemans, left town.*

Cathy Young, RealClearPolitics, October 29, 2013

These types of cases, where girls and boys are afraid to tell what happened to them but do—and get dragged through the streets for it—go on every single day. And keep in mind, the more popular the perpetrator, the bigger the risk for the victim. But for every one girl or boy who does have the courage to speak up, there was a girl like me, who didn't come forward until it was almost too late. If you learn anything from me, learn this: it's not your fault, it's never too late to start healing, and I'm here to help you.

Anny

In America, athletes are like gods to millions. Don't get me wrong, I love sports and I love coaches and athletes. Many, many good men and women in professional and collegiate athletics have blessed my life. But unless you've lived life under a microscope where your family's name, reputation, and father's career make headlines, it may be hard for you to understand why I didn't tell what Matt had done to me. I couldn't tell; I could barely admit the truth to myself.

I had seen how telling had worked out for other victims. The lies and gossip that were spread about the victim. The possibility of major careers ended. The university investigations, sanctions, court cases, police interviews—and who really got punished?

Whether it's someone you don't know or your own uncle, grandfather, or father, when you're a child it takes strength to tell that a grown-up touched your privates.

It took strength I didn't have. Running away was my answer.

At this point everyone believed that I was a gifted student who was bored. Bored, and out of my boredom came my new rebellion.

I was always moving in five different directions at once. My brain never shut off. I couldn't quiet the voices. *Tick-tock-tick-tock.* I was constantly reshuffling the deck and moving on to the next task before anyone knew I had completed the first. The persistent state of busyness helped me to not look backward.

I was playing musical masterpieces, competing on the basketball court, and sailing through my academic classes, but personally no one could understand why, with such a buttoned-up family, I was figuratively lighting myself on fire. I suppose if I had told anyone that when I was thirteen, a man had assaulted me for the whole basketball season, it might have made more sense. Maybe if they had understood that, they would have had some sympathy for me and my desire to throw gasoline on myself.

The pressure I felt to be silent, *real or imagined*, to protect my family and the university, was too much for me to carry and remain calm. I still couldn't tell them, even with Matt gone. I needed to be away from the university.

I was acting out in ways that may have seemed normal for a rebellious teenager: drinking, nightmares, shutting down, running away, becoming sexually active.

But it wasn't rebellion. It was self-destruction. I was hiding shame inside and it was eating me up like a parasite that tries to chew its way out.

~⊗~

Leelanau claimed to be a boarding school that catered to kids who were exceptionally bright, but it actually seemed to me to be a dumping ground for the exceptionally challenged. The campus was set on the stunning bank of Lake Michigan. Nontraditional educational stylings were offered, along with average sports programs and extracurricular activities such as skiing and snowboarding, canoeing and fishing. It was basically summer camp for parents who could afford to send their kids away during the school year.

"When can I go?" I asked my mom.

Leelanau didn't feel like a fit, honestly. I wanted out of the entire state. But my parents believed it would be academically "enriching" and still close enough that they could retract their leash on me as needed.

During a school counseling session, a group of young women who worked as what I can only label "life coaches" tried to determine where my strengths and weaknesses actually lay. I found most of the questioning ridiculous and fairly simple to undermine.

The positive was that attending Leelanau was indeed a second chance to breathe, but it also gave me license to break the rules. Despite my façade, I wanted to be better, to be healed, and to be less angry, but at Leelanau, tucked beneath the maple trees and surrounded by pinecones, I had the privacy to do what I wanted and a gang of other misfits to do it with me.

There were too many kids popping out of their own skin from all around the country for my lack of enthusiasm to stand out. They were both medicated from prescriptions and self-medicating from street drugs. Unlike the ethereal Interlochen, where dreams skipped across the lake easier than a smooth stone, this place was gloomy.

My room had a broken window frame, which allowed easy after-curfew access to my dorm room or "cellblock." Before long, everyone was using it to sneak in and out. We referred to it as a doggy door, as Snoop Dogg was always rapping in our space.

My roommate, Susan, who wore jean skirts and Pink Floyd T-shirts, would roll joints for the other dope smokers at school. No one could roll a tighter blunt than her. Lying on my top bunk, I would watch as kids would come in and out of our room with their little nickel bags and she'd get paid a buck a joint to roll them. It wasn't that she needed the money; it was so she never had to buy her own weed. She pulled a bud or two off each customer's supply and stashed them in a back compartment of her cosmetic drawer.

Susan's boyfriend was a guy everyone called Swifty. His real name was Calvin. He was British and moved between classes by dodging around people in the hallway. That's how he got his nickname. The guy was fast. I believed he'd make a great basketball player with his height and ability to maneuver around the obstacles in front of him, so I made him my project and trained him to shoot. His brown, neatly trimmed hair, preppy shirts with ironed-up collars, and Topsiders completed his potential as a basketball ideal.

The first time I smoked marijuana was with Swifty. Susan had rolled a joint and the three of us snuck out the doggy door and cut down through the woods, over the property line, and sat in an abandoned canoe on the shoreline. Within two minutes of my inhaling marijuana, the world became a *Saturday Night Live* skit. Nothing was off-limits. My God, did it feel good to laugh. To be in another world far away from any galaxy that I had ventured before.

After the weed began to wear off and the craving for chili dogs and Ding Dongs set in, the three of us trekked back to the school grounds and into the kitchen area of the main student building. I put a bagel in the toaster and Calvin started fondling Susan. *Gross.* They were an oddball couple. He looked at me over her shoulder and it made me uncomfortable.

"I'll catch you later," I said, grabbing my bagel and two oatmeal cookies.

"You can join us," he said.

Susan glared at him irritably.

"I'm joking!" He kissed her, pacifying her insecurity.

"You're an idiot." I couldn't suppress my true feelings.

I took my munchies and ambled out of the room and down a hallway.

There it was, the music room. And inside, an old familiar love that hadn't forgotten me. I looked behind me, and then around the corner, and seeing no one, I proceeded to place my warm hand on the cool doorknob. Unlocked. I quietly entered, shut the door behind me, and slid onto the blue cushioned piano bench.

With my cookies on the top of its black shiny back, I tapped my knuckles on the keys, checking the piano's tuning. My anxiety curled up into a ball like a kitten next to me, ready to listen to me play. I began again.

⊷

Swifty and I had just finished shooting hoops in the indoor basketball court. He was getting better but he didn't like being beaten on the court. Although my fundamentals and shooting were better than his, he dominated me by size and speed. He'd dribble around me and lay it up but it never went in the hoop. When I would get an opportunity to break free from his persistent fouling and plant my feet and release the ball, it was all net.

I could tell his ego was wounded as we walked back to my room. "You play like a dude on the court," he said.

"Relax. I've spent my life on a court with men."

"Whatever, Anny." He shoved me a little too hard with his forearm on my shoulder.

I could tell he wasn't playing. I shoved him back.

We got to my dorm door and he stood back for a minute and then said to me, "Open it."

He acted as if I was his servant and he lived in Buckingham Palace. "You're a moron, Calvin."

"Do it," he barked again.

"You're a psycho!" I went to grab the handle and he blocked me.

He then reached for the handle and held it open. "Calm down."

He's nuts.

We got into my room and Cypress Hill was playing but Susan was gone.

"I bet she went to the canoe," he said. "She's never good at waiting."

I sat down in the desk chair and took off one sneaker.

"You want to come, smoke one out?" He held a joint.

Immediately something cautioned me *no*. But numbing sounded good. So instead I said, "Lemme put on my boots."

"You don't need them. You'll be fine."

≈

Even though I knew that the ground from the dorm to the lake was still frozen and had pockets of slippery ice that could be treacherous, I put my sneaker back on and laced it up.

Swifty and I spent twenty minutes looking all over for Susan. She was one of those girls who, off her meds, could easily be found upside down in the frozen lake. Her naivety mixed with anxiety was an ideal fit for my eagerness to control and willingness to pounce with anger. We were a teenage, dysfunctional Laverne and Shirley.

I was huffing and puffing, grabbing on to tree trunks to steady myself, heading downhill. The air coming out of both Swifty's mouth and mine bore a resemblance to steam rising off a hot spring in the chill of winter. "Let's go back," I said finally.

"Okay," Swifty said, but then he turned around. "Hey,

let's smoke half and save half for her."

He stopped and handed me the joint. "Here, hold it while I get my matches."

The first match dropped onto the snow. Then the second one got going. He cupped his hand around it and I took a long inhale to burn the cherry.

"Here," I said, holding the smoke in my lungs.

He took the joint but didn't smoke it. I exhaled.

"That's good." I referred to the weed. "Sweet."

"Take this. I got to have a whiz." He handed it back. He walked about ten yards away from me, his boots crunching in the snow, and then ducked behind a tree for privacy.

I took another hit of the joint. I felt dizzy.

"You doing all right?" Calvin's voice sounded weird. His English accent was sucked into a drainpipe and swirling downward.

I waved my hand in front of him. "I see three of you." I waved my hand again. "I see three of my hand." I started to laugh as Calvin grabbed me and pushed me backward. The back of my arm clipped a tree branch and I stumbled. I couldn't get my bearings.

Did he just push me or did I fall?

Then he was scooping me up, but he wasn't getting me off the ground—he was pulling off my sweatpants.

I swung wildly at him. "Get the hell off me!" I slurred.

"You're not so good on your back." He grunted as I felt him penetrate me, sending my torso forward on the ice. It hurt so badly.

His face looked white and blurred as he tried to kiss me. I turned my head to the side. The cold ground on my cheek took my mind off the fact that he was pumping on top of me. I couldn't do anything. Tears poured from my eyes uncontrollably from the ripping pain.

This is what happens when you're wasted. You can't fight. You have no control. Even if you want to run away, you can't.

When he was done, he sat on top of me with his knees on each side of my hips. My head was spinning. I kept trying to focus my eyes.

He put my pant leg back over my sneaker and yanked me to my feet.

"You know you wanted to do that."

I was so out of it I could barely put one foot in front of the other. I followed Calvin's voice and trail of footprints in the snow until I made it to the school.

❧

I didn't move from my top bunk for three days other than to go to the bathroom. I skipped school and lay motionless, sleeping. People would come in and out of the room, but I would just roll over to face the wall.

How did this happen to me? Again?

In my head I could hear sounds like a vacuum cleaner. Something was sucking my sanity out of me. *Is this a nervous breakdown?* I couldn't hold it in any longer. I called my sister Kristin, swore her to secrecy, and told her what had happened.

Within four hours my father and my sister were at the school packing my room.

My father had driven up directly after practice. Four

hours up, two hours packing, four hours home. My mother had stayed back to get my room ready, or maybe just to process what had happened to her baby.

Dad had never missed a game in his career. He played with a bucket next to him so he could throw up in it when he had the flu. He played through fevers and births and deaths. He never let one thing stop him from being on the court when the whistle blew, until now. Now he would not go on the road to coach. Instead he would stay home and try to protect his daughter from what had already happened.

I rested on our couch as my sisters and brother came home and in muted tones inquired, "Is she okay?" I was a breathing corpse on the couch, and each pitiful look made me feel more lifeless. The only voice I heard raised was my mother's, when she sat in my dad's office with the door closed, across from our family lawyer and a police officer. They were both preparing to press charges against Swifty and sue the school.

"I want to go to the game." I sat up and addressed my dad as he came out of his office looking at his watch.

"I'm not going. I have it covered." He shook hands with the police officer who had stood beside him at countless press conferences or alongside him when he walked the tunnel before packed games.

"We got it, Coach," the officer said when his depressing eyes fell on me.

I've got to get up and out of here.

Neither Mom nor Dad believed I was in any emotional or physical shape to travel. And my dad wasn't prepared to leave me. I could see a crack in my mother's rocklike stability from hearing me describe the events, and I felt embarrassment for having to admit the drug use. It was layer upon layer of humiliation, topped off with my being the reason that my father would, for the first time in his career, let his assistant coach call the game.

"Please, I need to get out of here."

Both my sisters came into the living room, where my dad and mom were standing.

"You need to rest, Anny." My mother eased down in her chair.

"No, I want this over. I want to move on." Then I turned to my dad. "Please, can't we just go do something normal? Can't we go to the game?" My dad looked at my mom.

"Just go, Dad," Kristin said.

"We can drive together," I appealed to my dad. "We'll make it there in time."

I couldn't be the reason behind Dad not coaching. I couldn't be the one who tarnished his perfect record. I needed to protect him, again. The media would speculate the worst and at some point the truth would come out. At least this way we would stand united.

We drove in silence to the game at Loyola Chicago. During dribbles and dunks and whistles and time-outs my father never let me out of his peripheral vision. He sat me on the end of the bench between two assistant coaches. My guards. It would be the only time in history that I sat on the bench with my father during one of his games.

Word spread about the rape. Within thirty-six hours the small town knew everything.

We decided to not press charges. No one, including me, wanted to keep reliving it.

❧

Life was officially not friendly. Honestly, the God that my parents had prayed to didn't seem real, and if He was real, He had forgotten about me. I would have to stand on my own feet and take care of myself. *What a joke.*

I wanted to carve out everything and everyone from my past. Scoop them out like pumpkin guts and roll them on old newspapers and send them to the dump. I decided to drop out of high school altogether and go to college. I took the ACT and scored high enough that after my father pulled a few strings at Western Michigan, I was able to take three classes starting with the winter semester. Six credits. The caveat for attending the school was that when I turned eighteen the following November, I would get my GED. I was putting all the rape and dysfunction behind me.

Once again my family had saved me.

Trying to regroup and reboot, I went to work at McQueenie's Bakery. It was a scene straight out of the eighties television show *Alice*. I wore a pink apron, my coworker Trish had big hair like Flo, and another employee, Carol, would have been Vera. My coworkers were two decades older than me, but I, at seventeen years old, was the one who felt washed up.

I served glazed doughnuts and hot black coffee to lonely businessmen and service workers. During their breaks from the nine-to-five slog, I listened to their complaints and nodded attentively to their troubles. These seemingly endless therapy sessions I provided to the guys across the counter were priceless training for later in my life.

Carol was always quoting catchy phrases out of a book called *The Celestine Prophecy*. It was like spirituality for dummies, but I liked it. When she finished reading it, she handed it to me.

"I promise you, Anny,"—her bright-red nails stood out against the greenish-blue hardcover with white lettering—"everything happens for a reason."

"That's comforting." I squinted my eyes.

It was comforting. I began to completely submerge myself in that book at night in the safety of my parents' house. Although it was not the Christian hardcover they would have preferred, the sight of me reaching for anything with uplifting lessons was a sign of hope for Mom and Dad.

I took my green neon highlighter and traced over the words, "We must assume every event has significance and contains a message that pertains to our questions . . . this especially applies to what we used to call bad things . . . the challenge is to find the silver lining in every event, no matter how negative."

Really? Every event?

I shut the book with a thud. I wanted to believe it with every underlined word, but it just didn't seem possible.

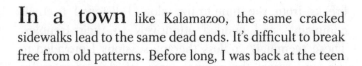

In a town like Kalamazoo, the same cracked sidewalks lead to the same dead ends. It's difficult to break free from old patterns. Before long, I was back at the teen club, Stingers. I would dance alone with bulky sweaters on top of my overalls, as if clothing atop clothing could protect me. One night the DJ was spinning a song called "Hey Mister." I was a little buzzed on Boone's Farm wine and my inhibitions started to seep out. The warehouse-style club wasn't packed yet, as it was still early. There were vacant platform cubes around the dance floor where girls and boys could dance. When the song ended, Montel Williams was up next. No one was really talking to me, as my attitude screamed, *Leave me alone!* I stepped up onto one of those cubes to get away from it all.

On top of the pedestal, I lost myself in the groove of a shoulder shake, then a hip gyration. It was pure synergy: the combination of alcohol, loud music, and dancing alone was the best diversion from my life that I had ever found.

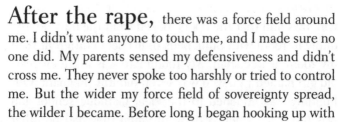

After the rape, there was a force field around me. I didn't want anyone to touch me, and I made sure no one did. My parents sensed my defensiveness and didn't cross me. They never spoke too harshly or tried to control me. But the wider my force field of sovereignty spread, the wilder I became. Before long I began hooking up with Scott again and breaking my curfew.

In the beginning my parents turned a blind eye to the fact that I was fifteen or twenty minutes past my evening curfew. But they did have their limits. Three hours late, it turned out, was too far. When I rolled through the door at three a.m. on a Friday night stumbling, mumbling, and sweaty, my dad had seen enough.

"You will not come in this house after midnight."

After I yelled a robust series of obscenities, I scampered to my room and locked the door behind me.

The next day, I ran away again.

My parents weren't about to spend five sleepless nights worrying about me this time, so they had me arrested.

"I can either take you home or I can take you to a halfway," the syrupy, gray-haired policeman said when he found me outside my friend Beth's house. Beth was a high school friend who had told her newly divorced dad that my parents were out of town and I needed somewhere to crash.

"If you take me home, you're going to be looking for me tomorrow."

Welcome to the Ark, the Ritz Carlton of halfway houses. *Not.*

Minus the 400-thread-count sheets on the mattresses, and despite the fact that there were no windows and that the doors locked from the outside, the dimly lit room with bunk beds didn't seem different than my room at Leelanau. My roommate was a fifteen-year-old girl named J.C. who was seven months pregnant. Our building was attached to the local Catholic school and was the place where kids went when they had no other place to go. A last stop before the clink or living in a box outdoors. I was an oddity, as everyone in that place, including me, knew I had somewhere else to go.

"Why would you choose to come here?" J.C. asked me as she tried to straighten her afro in the mirror. "You must have some big ol' problems, girl, with your designer overnight bag in this crack house. You know you're in a shelter, riiiiight?" Her gum popped in her cheek.

I wished I knew what made me choose this instead of my home. I scrutinized her with blankness on my face. I didn't have an answer.

The best I could decipher was that I was out of control and driven by circumstances, and I had a flair for the dramatic. I had become a champion at being a monster. But more than those fantastic qualities, I was livid with everyone. Particularly my parents. And I had no idea why.

Because I was on twenty-four-hour suicide watch, the drill sergeant woman who ran the night shift was assigned to rifle through my gear.

"I'm not going to kill myself," I scoffed. "I may kill you, though." I lowered my voice to get a reaction out of her, but being a militant, special forces type, she didn't flinch.

"Hand it over." She made me give her my razor.

"Seriously?"

"Yes."

My parents came every day, but I refused to see them. The only person that I saw from my family was my sister Kristin. She had finished nursing school and was an RN. Mind you, the only reason I really had any desire to see her was that my period was late, again.

Kristin had brought me a small plastic cup to pee in, and the next day she came back with the results. "Please go home," she begged. I just stared at the positive paper. I had received an A on my pregnancy report card. "You've got to get your life together."

"What? This isn't together?" I motioned around me.

"Anny, if not for you, for the life in your body."

Life in my body. Ironic, isn't it, how God would put something as clean as new life inside what I perceived to be polluted?

I couldn't admit defeat. I was too strong to be weak.

In the last year, I had slashed at my parents with every verbal barb I could. I had taken out all my hostility on them. Maybe I blamed them. Maybe I blamed myself. Yet the fact remained that they were the only people on earth who would keep on loving me, no matter what I did. I knew I had been given more opportunities than anyone else in that halfway house—more than most kids in this country—but we had all ended up exactly the same. I was penniless and uneducated. I had been used and abused and now was a teen-mother-to-be.

~

"Yaaaahhhh! Help!" J.C. started screaming when she saw me lying on the bathroom floor surrounded by blood.

Ms. Drill Sergeant came flying into our community bathroom, where she found me in the fetal position in a bathroom stall, lying in my own clotted dark-red liquid. Her eyes darted around my body for incisions, abrasions, and wounds, but there were none. My blue pajama bottoms were in a ball next to my body. I had fallen from the toilet in pain. A few more girls came into the bathroom. "Call nine-one-one," Drill Sergeant said to J.C.

Kristin came to the hospital to get me. She knew I wasn't dying. But she knew something had died. She pulled open the curtain in the emergency room and just stared at me.

"I can't even keep a baby inside of me. I am so screwed up."

She leaned down and hugged me. "Let's take you home."

There comes a point when you have to admit that your way isn't working. This was that point. I needed the structure of high school. I needed to be around kids that were clean and sober.

For my senior year of high school, I attended the prestigious Lake Forest Academy in one of the wealthiest, old-money suburbs of Chicago. Originally an all-boys' academy, it was founded in 1857; the girls' school, Ferry Hall, opened in 1869. The academy has a history of producing America's top collegiate students. It's a springboard to Harvard, Yale, MIT, and Vassar.

As we pulled onto the grounds, I remembered looking at their alumni page, which listed everyone from musicians like Page McConnell, the keyboardist for Phish, to CEOs of major corporations like Tim Armstrong from AOL. There had been media personalities, politicians, and pundits. It was an eclectic group of overachievers. The main hall had white marble floors, a formal dining room, and a study room with windows that overlooked what I could only imagine might be an English garden with rosebushes and Japanese maple trees.

The girls on campus were wearing skirts and blouses.

The boys all had collared shirts and ties. "We dress for success," the headmaster said to my father. After the interview process with her, I was officially enrolled in Lake Forest Academy for my senior year.

The beauty of being in Chicago was that no one knew what I had been through. It was another fresh start. I could pretend the last three years had never happened. My own internal destruction, mistakes, and pain were enough for me to try and regenerate my faith in God and myself.

I was committed to releasing all my anger and inhaling the rich atmosphere of accomplishment that enveloped LFA and its students.

I quickly made friends with a group of upwardly mobile girls, and one boy who was from Central America, Marco. My best friend became an angelic Southern voice to me. She was black, two years younger than me, and her name was Anna. Her thirst for knowledge was electrifying. "I'm going to be the first female president," she threw out to us as we studied in a think tank group on psychology. No one said a word, as Anna *could* possibly be the first female president. Those types of high expectations were normal. The school had limitless constructions of learning. People weren't there looking for financial rewards; they were committed to changing the world. From global warming, global hunger, global this or global that, the idea of change was epidemic, and I had caught their disease and wanted to be part of a cultural revolution of difference makers. We were all engrossed in possibility and change. I soaked up every drop of encouragement and expectation of greatness like a dry sponge. The students held out a mental and scholastic high-jump bar for each other and lifted one another over it.

My Lord, how I needed these people. They breathed life back into me.

Between playing basketball and the piano, my heart began beating relief and bravery again. I'd found favorite nooks to read C. S. Lewis—not to hide, but to elope with theology at its most mind-bending. My mom had mentioned C. S. Lewis in our house, but until my studies at LFA, I'd just dismissed his books as more confusing religious grandiloquence.

From the moment I walked into my first classroom, I knew that my spinning top had stopped. My music teacher was empathic to the nonverbal but instrumental voice that poured out of me and onto the keys. She looked like Meryl Streep and took a special interest in making sure each of us felt confident. I rebuilt a musical repertoire of my forgotten musical queens like Carole King and the soulful Etta James. I saw myself again as a creator and a creation. A dreamer and a dream. I dared to let my passions bubble like root beer over the top of the ice-cream float that was LFA.

Anna was an old soul, always pondering what-ifs at me: "Where are you going to college?" She sidled up beside me dressed in a Roman sheet for a toga party.

"I'm not really sure I want to go to college."

She stopped so suddenly that her golden-leaf headband lurched forward onto her forehead.

"You need to think about your future, Anny." She was one of the few people I ever heard speak like that who wasn't over the age of thirty-five.

"I'm not like you." I wanted to tell her I had been in

survival mode for the last four years and had lost grip of my possibilities.

"Girl, you're going to rule the world. What world that is, is going to be up to you."

She was a special operative of God with all her positive energy.

"Don't be fooled by the people who stand in your way. They are inconsequential to the endgame."

Honestly, what kind of fifteen-year-old talks like this?

"All right already."

"Oh, I'm not done with you yet. Let me tell you something that my grandmother told me. There are people on this planet that have a God-given life force. It's a spirit life force that is stronger than others. They see things brighter. They feel things deeper and they experience life fuller. It is a literal power that can be wielded for evil or good."

I stood there looking down at this black girl preaching at me in her toga.

"Now you're one of those people." She poked me in the arm. "And so am I!" She turned and started walking. "So what are you going to do with it?"

I skipped a step and caught up with her.

"Well, since you have this president thing covered, maybe I'll just . . ."

We stopped at the door of the party as people passed us going inside.

"What?" She tightened the gold rope around my side that held my sheet in place.

"I'm going to do something. . . ."

I had no idea what.

⤠

Graduating from Lake Forest Academy was both the concluding chapter of my youth and the beginning of a bright future. The experience had been an answer to my prayers.

My mother, father, both sisters, and my brother sat in the third row inside the gymnasium for graduation. The rain had spoiled the traditional ceremonies in the formal gardens but it had not dampened my spirit. We girls wore white dresses and the boys had white-collared shirts with ties, blue blazers, and khaki pants. Ms. Goldenson, the inspiring headmaster, gave the commencement speech. She was distinguished and polished and had an elite strict nature to her.

As the music played, I began to cry like a blubbering baby. Like a bride walking the aisle to the groom, I felt the wait was over. I had made it out of high school and the nightmares were over.

When they called my name and I walked across the stage, I knew that my mascara had left dark smudges down my cheeks, but it didn't matter. Nothing mattered in the past. All that mattered was that it was over. Almost in slow motion I made eye contact with my father. His face was filled with relief and pride. I knew that my parents too had the same astonished feeling that Tiger Woods does when he hits an amazing shot into the hole and does the *yes!* right-armed uppercut swish movement. We had all done it together.

I had made the decision. I was choosing hope and the future. It says in the Bible that God knows the plans He has for you. At that point I really believed Him. I believed the words my dad had told me over and over, "'For I know the plans I have for you,' declares the Lord, 'plans to prosper you and not to harm you, plans to give you hope and a future.'"

I really believed it.

chapter nine

HIGHER EDUCATION

Ten percent of students know classmates who engage in sex work in order to promote themselves financially, with 16.5 percent indicating that they might be willing to engage in sex work to pay for their education.

"Sex Workers in Higher Education," *Daily Sundial,* December 12, 2011, http://sundial.csun.edu

Although many sex workers claim that the sex industry is "putting them through college," how many of us have you really seen on campus? Sure, maybe the first semester . . . but not much longer.

Anny

There was never talk of my attending any university other than Western Michigan. I do not recall even having an opportunity to explore schools that were on the West or East Coasts. My entire entourage of family and friends naturally assumed I would follow in the footsteps of my siblings and be the fourth and final of the Donewalds to be handed a rolled diploma with red ribbon from Western Michigan.

It was decided that I would move into an apartment. So in June, my mother and I rented a flat in a delightful three-story building away from the party scene, a fifteen-minute drive from school and twenty minutes from my parents' house. My new neighbors were serious graduate students and newly married yuppie couples.

My apartment was small but gave the illusion of being spacious thanks to the light that broke through the front windows in the morning. The furniture delivery guys had a rough time trying to fit the tan-and-black-striped couch through the front door, as the turn from the elevator to my front entrance was just an inch short of the space needed. With the legs removed, they squeezed that baby inside, leaving just enough room for a matching chair and the two barstools that Mom set up outside the galley kitchen. My sister Lisa donated a little wicker table with a glass top. I slid it into the corner next to the kitchen, where it was perfect for doing homework. My bedroom was down the short hallway and across from the only bathroom. It had a shower, toilet, and pedestal sink. All a girl needs.

As a move-in present, my dad gave me an electric keyboard. I put it on its stand in front of the main room window, and when I wanted to play, I pulled a chair out from the kitchen, sat down, closed my eyes, and began to channel my inner Billy Joel.

Those first two weeks alone in my very own apartment—well, they were heaven. My paperwork was completed for the coming school year. All I had to do was stay out of trouble for the summer and prepare for the job going forward, which was to get through the next four years drama-free with dean's list honors.

But by week three in Kalamazoo, the ho-hum-dom had started to kick in. Left inside my own mind, my internal dialogue would swing violently from wanting success, joy, and independence to demanding punishment for mistakes and shame that I thought belonged to me for ping-ponging from school to school and incident to incident. I was internally conflicted. On one hand I loved my life and believed I deserved happiness; on the other I was still dealing with unresolved anger and torment.

I saw myself in the mirror as perhaps a fallen angel.

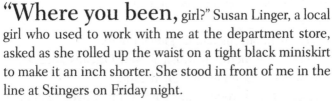

"Where you been, girl?" Susan Linger, a local girl who used to work with me at the department store, asked as she rolled up the waist on a tight black miniskirt to make it an inch shorter. She stood in front of me in the line at Stingers on Friday night.

"Around," I said, as we made our way into the club.

I had finally peeled away a layer of my cocoon, had some vodka, and gotten out of the apartment. I had to shake the dust off.

I knew most of the townies assumed I had been shipped off to yet another boarding school last year, as I had been in the gossip limelight just a tad too much. But the truth was I didn't want them knowing where I had been, and didn't want them to steal my hope that I could be a good Lake Forest graduate. I wanted to dwell in the achievement of having made it through high school in one piece. Or at the very least, that my pieces had been glued back together.

In the middle of Stingers, I saw a girl that I recognized from Kalamazoo Central High School dancing hip-hop with a guy with movie-star good looks and scene-stealing abilities to rival those of Dwayne "The Rock" Johnson. He caught my eye, his green eyes and gleaming white teeth set off by his smooth, latte-colored complexion. He was big and muscular and well dressed. We first made eye contact when he rounded the floor heading to the bar. His smile opened wide. He was the most handsome black man I'd ever seen.

"Do you want to dance?"

Wordlessly, I joined him, and by two a.m. there wasn't a dance move we hadn't covered.

"Who are you?" I asked him, as the lights came up in the bar.

He held out his hand. "James Lucre."

He had a meltingly musical New Orleans accent. As if he wasn't charming enough already.

"Can I walk you to your car?" With crowds of people pouring out around the club, I felt protected enough to let him escort me. I was still leery of men, but the flame of my sexual appetite quickly got reignited within one week of meeting James. By July, James was sleeping over at my apartment every night. Let's just say I was making up for lost time.

He knew who my father was, as he played football for Western Michigan. He had been a redshirt freshman the previous year but was planning on starting this coming football season as wide receiver. He was fluent in French and from a decent middle-class family that could trace their roots back to the slaves in Louisiana.

Like me, he had big dreams and had no intention of

ever being anyone's commodity. He was no dummy or hood rat. We spent many nights talking about being that "power couple." But I suppose bad company distorts good character. We were teenagers left to typical human devices and neuroses.

We started off just drinking small amounts of alcohol together. A beer at a party or maybe even a Gatorade vodka. A few of his friends from the football team got wind that his new girlfriend had her own pad, and before long my sweet Pottery Barn–style bungalow became the hip after-hours hot spot. We swiftly escalated from playing house to a never-ending late-night party complete with seedy characters, drinking, drug use, and loud music.

Old habits die hard.

The situation went downhill faster than I could have imagined. Before the end of July, I was falling into my old hard-core partying ways, and the town gossip grew louder and juicier. "Look out, she's back and she's dating a black guy!" the ladies in my mom's book club no doubt would say before she arrived. Or "I hear she's partying again!" a neighbor would toss out to another over the hedges in my parents' neighborhood. Or "That Anny always was and always will be trouble." "Goes to show ya you can't have it all." I can imagine it all too well.

I received two formal noise complaints before the third, and final, complaint was hand-delivered to me by the building superintendent. Mr. Knox stood about five feet tall, had a Polish accent, and stuttered from time to time. He wore a tool belt that I was frankly astonished he could carry, as he couldn't have weighed over 130 pounds. That belt had to have weighed more than him.

He was a gnomelike character, marching around stammering new rules for the building.

As I was checking my mail in the small lobby one day, Mr. Knox came out of his office holding a small red envelope with APARTMENT 3B written in black Sharpie on the front. Mr. Knox stuffed all his "infraction" notices into those same red envelopes. Red envelopes were always bad news.

"Miss. Donewald." He spit out my name one word at a time. His disgust with me was apparent. I knew he didn't think I belonged in his quiet building. "This isn't n-n-no frat house." His face crunched trying to get his words out. "You know what I m-m-m-ean?"

"Yes, sir, I know. I'm really sorry; we'll try . . ." I took the envelope and turned to walk away. But he wasn't finished.

"And there's another thing. Your lease says you live there alone, not with a b-b-b-oy."

I wondered if he noticed how much bigger I was at five foot nine than him, because if he had I am sure he wouldn't have said "boy" the way he did. It was not the stuttering but the way his eyes squinted with obvious repugnance.

"Mr. Knox, my rent is on time, and I will do everything I can to keep the noise down." I could feel my familiar antagonism starting to bubble.

Settle down, Anny, I thought to myself.

"Well, I'm sure your father wouldn't approve of you being a"—he looked over his shoulder behind him, then said—"n-n-n-nigger lover."

In one rapid, fluid movement, I reached down and pulled his flashlight right out of his tool belt and held it under his chin like an out-of-control police officer.

"I will pull that twisted tongue out your mouth with my bare hands if I ever hear you use that word again."

I had backed him against the metal mailboxes. I towered over him and contemplated cracking his jaw with the heavy black flashlight. *Wow, it didn't take long for the angry key of my mind to unlock the control room door.*

"I may be Coach Donewald's daughter to you, Mr. Knox, but I will slit your throat. You know what I m-m-m-ean?" I wanted to crumple and shove that red envelope into his mouth.

I just stared down at him, daring him to move.

James walked into the lobby. "What's up, baby?"

I took a step backward, stunned that my animalistic instinct to ravage was still so close to the exterior.

I held out the flashlight to Mr. Knox.

"Thanks for letting me borrow this."

I sounded like a stoned Barbie.

That night, James and I had a bunch of his friends over for an after party. I got more wasted than usual and didn't wake up until one p.m. the next day. My head pounding, I pulled on my underwear and James's Broncos football T-shirt, and walked into the living room.

Clouds of stale cigarette smoke mixed with the scent of spilled bong water and the sour tinge of vomit. There were two overweight guys still passed out on the floor. One was using the other's calf as a pillow. I picked up a couch cushion and inspected a burn hole on the front of it. There were shoe prints on the coffee table. *How did those get there?* Oh, my hazy memory of people dancing on my tables started coming back. The entire night had gotten out of hand.

Having the football team use my apartment as *the* after-hours scene was a bad idea and one that was going to continue if I didn't put a stop to it. My handsome boyfriend, oblivious to the debris that surrounded him, stepped over a four-foot graphics bong that was lying on its side—no need to pick that up!—and scratched the back of his head as he made his way to my refrigerator. I watched as he pulled out a half gallon of milk and proceeded to down it from the carton.

I could see my future. A trapped, knocked-up housewife in a small town with no education and a husband who would probably trade me in for a newer, hotter model.

As deeply as I had, in my mind, rooted my victory plant to grow, two months of life in the Zoo had pulled it out of the ground like a wimpy four-leaf clover. I recognized it would be four long years if I stayed in Kalamazoo.

I had to get out.

❧

I reached across the table for a dumpling with my chopsticks. "Is there any way that I can *not* go to Western Michigan?" I solicited my mom and dad at Ming's, a Chinese restaurant.

"Why?" my mom asked, but I was sure she could tell from the bags under my eyes from late nights of partying why I wanted out.

"Honestly, I think I'm going to die here." I sipped my water. "I am not sure why but coming back here is making me strike a match and detonate myself."

"Where do you want to go?" My father shook the ice in the bottle of his green tea.

"IU."

He sighed.

They both watched me, wondering if this was another charade or if I was indeed preemptively asking for assistance.

"I know it's late, but I need your help to get in." My dad knew what I meant.

"I'll make a call," he said.

That call was to the General, Coach Bob Knight.

～

Indiana University is about 250 miles from my parents' house in Kalamazoo. The campus is stunning, with its historic buildings and large limestone archways, and it's massive compared to Western Michigan.

Indiana University pulsated with life, especially Kirkwood Avenue, where all the cool restaurants and trendy bars were located. On my first day of school I found myself blissfully frozen in place outside Ballantine Hall, just underneath the giant red clock, watching the students pass to and fro, letting their collective positive energy wash over me.

It was the tail end of a Midwest summer, and relief from the sticky heat was nowhere in sight. I smacked a mosquito off my thigh. They were everywhere, no doubt launching their multipronged attack from the shallow pools along the banks of a stream called the Jordan River that flows through the heart of the campus.

There were many religious names and references at Indiana University, as the school had been originally built sometime in the eighteen hundreds as a seminary.

My first order of business as an Indiana University freshman was to meet with the General, Coach Knight. The condition for my late admittance to the school was that Coach Knight would have to take personal responsibility for me and be my academic adviser before they would enroll me. I would be required to meet with him weekly so he could evaluate my grades, attitude, and attendance.

Sitting outside his office, with my ankles crossed and back straight, trying to look like the good Lake Forest Academy graduate that I was, I watched Coach Knight's secretary slice envelope after envelope with her steel letter opener. She was seriously dangerous with that thing. I wasn't too nervous, as I knew him, but this was a different type of appointment, one that required me to put on extra roll-on so my pits wouldn't shvitz on my first day.

He came out of his office radiating the same intense presence as my dad did. His notoriety didn't give me pause, nor did his six-foot-five frame, but I felt a responsibility to perform for him. I knew that he already had enough burdens and demands on his plate, so I was to play the part of the good girl.

"Are you behaving?" He smiled at me as he sat behind his desk.

"Yes, sir."

"Not going to miss any classes?"

"No, sir."

"Okay, then, see you next week." He stood up.

"That's it?" I looked up.

"What were you expecting?"

That was a good question. What was I expecting? I don't know. The rules. The expectations. The fifth degree.

"No, this is fine. Thanks." I stood up and walked toward the door.

"Do you need basketball tickets?"

"Um, sure, thanks."

"Sally?" he called out to his secretary.

"Yes, Coach Knight." Sally came scurrying into his office.

"Will you put together season tickets for Anny?"

She looked me up and down as if inspecting my ponytail for lice. I'm not sure she had any idea who I was or why I was there.

"Thank you." I smiled.

"Behave yourself. I'll see you next week."

This was the extent of it. Ninety seconds of do the right thing because you already know what happens to people when they don't.

My dorm roommate, a girl named Terry Smith, was laid-back enough. She was a local Bloomington girl who had gone to LFA with me, so we had an immediate connection. A tall, thin girl with shoulder-length, stringy brown hair, Terry loved basketball and introduced me to everyone on campus. It was good for both of us, except she kept dropping Coach Knight's name every time we met someone new. Poor Terry had braces in college. She was constantly double-checking her teeth in the small mirror that hung on the wall in our nine-by-nine room with bunk beds. There was always something green, dark brown, or mushy that had to be freed from her mouth of silver.

Terry and I would go to eat or hit a couple of campus parties here and there the first month, but for the most part I was sticking to myself. James had come up one time the first week in October to visit me. We spent the night in a bad motel, had sex, and realized the flame was gone. In my heart I wanted to leave him in Kalamazoo. For the most part, I had a very limited social life at the start of my freshman year at Indiana University, and that was just the way I wanted it.

~≋~

As the leaves finally began to change colors, my body also began to change. I felt physically exhausted. The newness of school had worn off, the routine was steady, and I was passing Coach's weekly assessments. Perhaps my body had been on a high mode for so long it was finally coming down. That's when I tend to get sick. Perhaps we all do.

I was dragging myself to class, barely able to make it out of bed, and falling asleep during lectures. I needed sleep but I didn't want to skip classes and let Coach Knight down or make my parents regret spending their money on a Big Ten party school, but I just never seemed rested.

I was just enjoying the slow and refreshing pace of being an ordinary girl on campus and having the opportunity to go to class under the radar like every other freshman. I knew IU would be the same type of educational opportunity as LFA, where possibility would be replaced with achievement for me. All I needed was the time.

≈

Terry and I had just finished playing a friendly game of basketball and were walking back to our dorm room. As we passed the Showalter Fountain outside the IU Auditorium, I lowered myself onto its concrete edge to rest. Terry sat down next to me.

"You look pale."

"I feel dizzy."

"Have you eaten today?"

I just rolled my eyes at her, as obviously if I'd had any food in me, I wouldn't have gotten my butt whupped on the court by her. I was lethargic and out of breath.

"You know there's a legend about this fountain?" she said, giving me time to recuperate. "The fountain depicts the birth of Venus."

"Really? What would that be?"

Terry seemed to know everything about everything on campus, which at times was unbelievably aggravating but tonight was helping me to reenergize.

"Well . . ." She took a deep breath and got bug-eyed. "When IU won the NCAA basketball championship in 'eighty-seven, a bunch of students stole all the fish from in here." She pointed at the water. "And then . . ."

"Is this going to be gross? 'Cause seriously, I may hurl."

"No! Anyway the fish started turning up in random places all over the campus. All except for one. They say she's never coming back until they win another championship."

"Poor fishy." I stood up. "I need to eat."

Making our way in the salad bar line in our student dorm, I poured a huge spoonful of ranch dressing onto a chef's salad and then someone turned the lights out.

Nighty-night.

"Anny!" Terry clapped in front of my face.

"Whoaaaah. I'm on the ground, aren't I?"

People were standing over me, as apparently I had passed out between the salad bar and the soda dispenser.

"I'm okay."

"You're not okay." Terry looked worried.

"Here's some juice, baby." A cafeteria worker handed me a glass. "Do you have low blood sugar?"

I just nodded yes, as I didn't want any other questions, nor did I want anyone calling Coach Knight or anyone else. I wanted to remain unidentified.

"*E. coli!*" Terry said, looking at me that night as I hurled into our toilet.

"You need to get yourself to the student health center."

I shuffled my way back to my bottom bunk. Between vomiting and the dizziness I just wanted to sleep. I pulled my green flannel sheets around my body and the forest-green comforter over my head.

"You know there was a huge outbreak of *E. coli* in Illinois this summer from lettuce. All you eat is lettuce. Seriously, one girl had to have a bucket of blood removed from her brain."

"Terry, can you just stop!"

"Will you go to the health center?"

"Yes, if you'll stop talking about brains bleeding."

She climbed up onto her top bunk.

"It's no joke, it can kill you."

"I'm going to kill you if you don't stop."

The next day I sat in the student health center with a baseball hat over my ponytailed greasy hair. Wearing my IU sweatpants and a T-shirt, I was listening to Tupac rapping about his nerves being wrecked and his hands swollen from "Picture Me Rollin'." I lay back across the table waiting for the nurse to come back and tell me that I had *E. coli* and at any moment my ears were going to start pouring blood.

The sound of the metal rings sliding across the metal track that held up the curtain dividing the patients startled me. I took off my headphones as the nurse yanked the drapes shut. I studied her face and fully expected her to tell me at the very least that I had a flesh-eating virus.

"You're pregnant."

My dreams censored, my hopes are gone . . . Tupac rolled over in my head.

chapter ten
CONDITIONING

Compared to the general population, women in the sex industry experience higher rates of drug and alcohol addiction, STDs, sterility, miscarriages, abortions (many of them forced), vaginal and anal trauma, and more. Psychological effects include developing clinical depression, personality and dissociative disorders, suicidal tendencies, post–traumatic stress disorder (PTSD), and complex PTSD.

"Statistics of Women in the Sex Industry," We Are Cherished, http://www.wearecherished.com/resources-2/statistics/

In the adult sex industry there is a term called conditioning. Basically it's a flesh-peddling pyramid scheme. It's building a business based on your recruits' business. Pimps and owners of clubs have girls, those girls bring in other girls, and everyone makes more money. It's a sex-industry Avon party. The best way to bait young women is by offering them a sense of acceptance and belonging

to the "cool" crew. The second is money and the
third is drugs. Conditioning is a triple-X sorority
rush: Kappa Kappa Sex-a-Gamma. I was about to
be courted.

Anny

I am not sure what called me to the doorway of a small building in the center of the IU campus. Across the green from the chemistry building and surrounded by trees, the cottage looked to me like a place where Hansel and Gretel would hide from the witch. And yet, the Beck Chapel was *the* place for local lovebirds to get married on campus. I found myself standing at the doorway eyeing the rows of old wooden pews, lined up one after the other, leading to where the preacher might stand on Sunday.

I had no interest in God now, yet here I was. The only other time I had stepped foot in this nondenominational church was on September eighth. It was the morning after Tupac was shot in Las Vegas. I loved 'Pac. His words were poetry to me.

When I saw the news, I made my way to the only church I could find to send up a few hallelujahs to the big man on Suge and 'Pac.

Today, I walked in and out of the church like a zombie, trying to collect my thoughts about being pregnant. *A mother, me?*

I left the church, climbed over the three-foot stone wall, and entered an old cemetery adjacent to the chapel.

A few students were heading inside Foster Residence Center but they never noticed me ease down on the cool ground in Dunn Cemetery. I sat between two headstones that leaned to the left from the earth shifting beneath them over time. My back was against a woman's name that I couldn't quite make out. I stared blankly at the chess piece–shaped grave markers from the eighteen hundreds. It was a place for the dead, and it was where I felt I belonged as I compulsively killed every good thing in my life. I felt a sadness that was six feet deep at the realization that I was not able to be responsible for another human being. I felt pity for my unborn child that she had drawn the short straw and gotten me for a mother.

I was six feet deep in my own dark hole.

⬠

"Come home," my mother told me on the phone. "We'll help you. Just come home."

Maybe it's my parents' God that has given them a phenomenal sense of resilience when it comes to me. Through everything that gouges me, they keep trying to cohesively nurse me back to health. Their faith in me is the biggest mystery of all.

With my clothes and a few boxes of papers and books shoved into my trunk, I returned to Kalamazoo with my tail between my legs. The baby in my body was proof that I hadn't actually gotten out of anything. I couldn't run away from my past. I wasn't able to be polished up and made new anywhere. I was the same old messed-up Anny. I was still a troubled girl. "Take this." My mother handed me a prenatal vitamin that my sister Kristin had given her. Kristin, who was working as a labor and delivery nurse at Bronson Methodist Hospital, had dropped off vitamins along with pamphlets on prenatal care and a copy of *What to Expect When You're Expecting*. That book is a more frightening read than the novel *The Silence of the Lambs*.

I was home twelve days when the certainty of my impending life began to crush down on me. I began to realize that decisions were being made without me. *I* hadn't decided to leave college. *I* hadn't decided to return to Kalamazoo. *I* hadn't made the decision to have the baby. *I* hadn't decided to keep the baby. Nor had *I* made the decision to not put it up for adoption. *I* certainly wasn't making any decisions about my own life, *I* clearly was capable and just not doing it. My parents were making all the right moves for me. They were trying again to save me. I had no idea where their strength came from to keep on yanking me up and shoving me forward.

There was to be no talk of an abortion. Abortion was not an option. My parents are the people who drive around with the Pro-Life sticker on their car. They were pro my baby's life, pro my life, and pro salvation.

They just assumed I would have this child and they would help me raise it. They weren't mad or overwhelmed. They were just them. "We'll handle it and get you back on the road of life." My mother always knew the right words to say.

But what life? This isn't my life.

I waited until my dad had left for work. I couldn't face him. Dressed in jeans and a sweatshirt, I stood in the kitchen watching my mother make coffee. She turned and looked at me as if she could read my mind.

"I can't have this baby." And then I walked out of the house.

❦

I walked alone to the clinic in town, and this was my mistake. I hadn't asked a friend or my sisters to be a coconspirator with me. I knew it was murder, but I also believed it was my only choice. I couldn't let my parents raise my child and I couldn't raise this child on my own.

It's the only way, something wicked taunted me, egging me on.

❦

In a small, sterile changing room, I slipped out of my jeans and sweatshirt. I placed the Planned Parenthood paperwork and consent forms at the bottom of a wooden locker and set my purse on top. I carefully folded each piece of clothing as if every crease of my jeans was another nail in my unborn baby's coffin. I slipped my arms through the hospital gown and placed my underpants on top of my purse, along with a giant Kotex they had given to me for afterward.

"You're going to bleed a lot," the nurse had warned me.

I turned toward one of the lime-colored walls and began to cry. I touched my stomach and whispered, "Baby, I don't know what else to do. If you will come back to me later, I promise I'll have you no matter what. No matter what my life looks like. No matter where I am or what I am doing, I promise if you come back another time . . . I won't hurt you." I sobbed with my forehead pressed against the cool concrete.

The TLC song "Waterfalls" was playing on the radio in the procedure room as a doctor in a white coat and glasses entered my room. He picked up my chart off the counter and began to look it over.

"Please relax. Just lie back . . . Anny." Absorbed in my paperwork, he didn't even look at me.

"I feel really sick."

His face changed. Something had caught his attention.

"Are you related to Coach Donewald?"

Are you kidding me? I wanted to scream.

I just nodded, *yes*.

He pulled on his latex gloves. The nurse oozed some clear jelly onto an instrument.

Then the cold speculum was eased inside. I flinched.

"Keep relaxed," he said. My hands gripped the sides of the table. I stared at the ceiling with a poster of a rainbow on it as tears poured out of my eyes onto the paper sheet that lay beneath me. The pain at first was gut-sucking, and then my entire belly began cramping.

"Do you go to Western with your dad?"

I turned my head to the side, so I wouldn't have to look up at him.

He was trying to make small talk about my dad, and all I could hear was a humming and sucking noise.

"No," I answered, digging my nails into the padded table.

"Is your dad here with you?"

I am not sure if he was struggling to comfort me or if he wanted my dad's autograph after this torture ended.

Maybe to him, this type of procedure didn't matter. It was routine. But not to me. Then I began to feel woozy from the pain and the Valium and having to be conscious.

"I'm trying to keep him out of my disasters," I lied.

In the recovery room, as I was lying in my clothes with a blanket over me, the nurse brought me another Valium. "Do you have a ride home?"

"Yes," I lied again. "My sister is coming."

My soul felt as barren as my womb. I walked out of the building and got into my car and put my seat back. I cried in my seat until I fell asleep. It was almost eight p.m. when screaming sirens woke me up. Groggy, I put my keys in the ignition as the fire truck raced past me, punctuating what I had just done.

When I got home, my dad was on the porch in a chair. I walked up the driveway and stood looking at him.

"I'm sorry you're feeling so sad." And he reached out for me.

I just walked into his arms and began to weep. My dad stood there with his body slightly moving from his silent cries. He was heartbroken for me, for the grandchild he would never know, and for the deep wound he knew I had carved into myself.

He didn't believe in my decision to have an abortion, but he hadn't stopped believing in me.

My father has a great capacity to love.

I enrolled in Western Michigan for winter semester. In addition to my classes, I was working in the athletic department as a temp secretary during the week. I answered the switchboard and made endless copies and binders and mailings for all the coaches. On the weekends I placed baskets of greasy fries and burgers on patrons' tables at the local Billiards joint. And I was given another chance at life on the straight and narrow: my parents moved me into a one-bedroom apartment in the student ghetto.

I was on my own financially, paying my own bills and no longer dragging my parents into my drama or having them foot the bill for my failures. If I was going to screw up my life again, I wasn't going to have them pick up the tab.

I worked endlessly and stayed away from my parents and siblings as much as possible. To me, I had leaked battery acid of shame onto the squeaky-clean Donewald reputation. Something was clearly wrong with me. My elder three siblings were flourishing and my parents were overachieving local heroes. Other than the job for school, I didn't associate with my family, and I let them off the hook of having to associate with me.

My roommate Libby had her own troubled history, and I was in no position to judge. Together, we kept each other comfortably numb, drinking and smoking marijuana. I sailed through my classes and managed to skip all family holidays, vacations, and Sunday get-togethers. I saw my dad only when I was at work in the office.

I kept out of trouble picking up shifts at the Hunan Garden, a Chinese restaurant, and occasionally still picking up shifts at the Billiards. Lying on my couch, absorbing its moldy Salvation Army smell and the stench of egg rolls still on my clothes, I puffed on a blunt as someone pounded on our apartment door. I just lay there as if no one was home, but the banging continued. When I finally pried myself up and opened the door, I found two blondes, clad in fly nightclub attire, wearing white patent leather heels. They were fiercely angry at my roommate and they were holding a broken beer bottle.

Their names were Serena and Jill and they had come to *talk* with Libby, who was conveniently missing. They were not messing around and had come to settle a score with Libby that I knew nothing about.

Despite the pot smoke cloud still hanging in the living room air, I did what any good ponytailed Midwestern girl would do and invited them in.

It may sound crazy, but my thought processes weren't clear. In my state, I felt all hostile issues could be resolved with the peace pipe. After all, it was working for me, wasn't it?

꿈

Serena and Jill were a handful of years older than me. They looked like cheerleaders gone wild and made dancing in strip clubs seem glamorous. After the Libby situation got worked out and she moved out, Serena and Jill started bringing me fun trinkets and presents from their latest shopping excursion—sexy leather pants and halter tops—so I could dress like them when we went out to drink and dance and smoke.

"How do you guys afford all this stuff?" I asked Jill as she handed me a Gucci bag.

"It's easy money, Anny. Honestly, it's just like Stingers,

only you take your clothes off." She laughed. "I mean, at least we're getting paid for it."

"And babe, it's not all gross dirtbags. These guys have Porsches and live in mansions."

No way. I looked at myself in the hallway mirror. The Gucci bag looked like it belonged slung over my shoulder.

I was constantly being introduced to friends of Serena and Jill—nine women in all. Like big sisters who actually understood me, they would show up at my apartment to treat me with a spa appointment or take me to brunch at some fancy restaurant where we'd drink mimosas and smoke cigarettes. With them, I wasn't so lonely. They had made me their pet project, but it was not out of the kindness of their hearts, as I thought, but because they were investing in their future. They knew I was a coach's daughter and if lured into their lair, would be the ultimate crown jewel in their female dig for dancers. They were all exotic dancers at a club in Lansing, about ninety minutes away. They brought me into what I thought was their circle of cool sisterhood and money.

"Why don't you try it?" Jill asked me one night.

"Look, it's an amateur night," Serena said. "I'll even pay for everyone's cover charge. There's no way with all that"—she did a finger snap like Elle Woods's from *Legally Blonde*—"you're not going to be amazing at it."

In my mind I thought, *Hell no! I'm not like you.*

Turned out, I was.

⇌

I took the stage for the first time at nineteen.

The club was dark. It was not just the lighting; the atmosphere had a seeping sense of doom. *Run!* I felt something inside me telling me to get out. Maybe it was my dad's voice in my head, but I was impressed and infatuated with the girls who brought me—my new friends—and felt I couldn't chicken out at this point. I was no quitter.

A completely nude blonde woman was on stage. Hanging upside down in six-inch stiletto heels, she had one leg wrapped around the steel pole, and the other leg extended out. Crowds of jocks were yelling as if it were their hometown football game. I'd borrowed shoes and a dress from Serena, who showed me the way to the dressing room to get ready. It looked like a dingy walk-in closet, with lockers lined up against the wall and a mirror adjacent with chairs and a counter.

There were already some other girls in the room. I looked around to take inventory of my competition. A few of them looked like they knew what they were doing, while others sat in chairs looking at nothing, smoking cigarettes. No one spoke. I looked different from them. I was five nine, 120 pounds, and firm all over. I was not cheap or desperate. I was just in it to win it.

After I changed clothes, I went out to surf the crowd and find my friends. They were sitting at a table sipping mocktails, as alcohol isn't served at all-nude clubs. I scanned the crowd and saw—front and center—a boy I used to date in high school. He was ogling the blonde on stage—who was now doing a handstand—with his friends. I knew he would recognize me. Again, I had the impulse to bolt, but I figured I was already dressed, so there was no turning back. Honestly, what could he say about me that wasn't already being said?

Serena had given a fake name for me. When I danced, I would be Bailey, not Anny. And so it was that with R. Kelly's "Freak Tonight" blasting over the speakers and every fiber of Anny's body tied up in knots, "Bailey" took the stage. For the first few seconds it was no different than the dissociation I felt when standing at the back of the team bus as a little girl when Matt began to run his hand under my skirt. I just stood out of my own body.

I closed my eyes and thought, *Just block out all the noise from the crowd like an NBA player does at the free-throw line.*

I began to dance, trying to copy what I'd seen the other girls do when it had been their turn; I just imitated them and focused on the music. I began to pull a sleeve off my shoulder. If I had thought for one second about *what* I was doing, I would've bolted out of there and hidden under my bed for the rest of my life.

My stomach was tied up in knots. I pulled down the other sleeve, and then the whistling and howling started. I closed my eyes and swung around the pole and let the music peel off every last piece of my clothing until I was completely exposed.

Then the song stopped and I realized I was kneeling at the front of the stage. I shook my head as if I had just woken up from a bizarre dream. I tried to stand up in the shoes but they were wobbling. I smiled at the boy I knew up front. Embarrassed for me, he looked away. I got to my feet and ran to the dressing room.

After all the amateurs had their turn at dancing, the DJ called us back to the stage. I didn't want to go, but the girl behind me gave me a little shove. "Cattle call, baby. Get out there."

On stage, we stood in a line, naked except for our heels, awaiting judgment by the crowd of hungry men. One by one, we paraded around the pole, and our worthiness was determined by the rowdiness of the men's applause.

It would've been horrifying had I allowed myself to feel anything in that moment. I had gotten so good at blocking out my feelings and stashing them away into little compartments in my mind, I simply opened another drawer in my pretty little pain dresser and shoved my emotions in.

I couldn't see anything but the glare of the stage lights when the DJ announced the winner.

"Baaaaaiiiiilllley!"

And the crowd went wild. It was a rush, and yet it made me so very sick at the same time. Serena and Jill ran to the front of the stage and cheered for me.

"You were awesome!" Jill blew me a kiss.

"I knew it. You rocked it!" Serena yelled.

I did some mental acrobatics to convince myself that this was a good thing, not degrading; that their applause meant I was affirmed, not disrespected. I was unknowingly taking a plunge into something that would affect the rest of my life.

I won two hundred dollars for less than two minutes of work.

It was the moment my life changed forever. It was the night I started to dance for the devil.

chapter eleven
INITIATION NIGHT

The United States has the most strip clubs in the world with 2,778. The next closest is Canada with 275. If the numbers in the tables are accurate, or even close, the irony is self-evident that in spite of the United States' professed public commitment to family values, Americans lead the global community in the number of strip bars available for "gentlemen's entertainment."

Bernadette Barton, *Stripped: Inside the Lives of Exotic Dancers*, New York: NYU Press, 2006

For a young girl, two hundred dollars for stripping pays for a lot of ramen noodles. But you don't believe that one amateur night will turn you on to a career in the sex industry. It was only supposed to be one night.

Anny

Heading to Lansing with Serena and Jill, we stopped at a liquor store to pick up Bacardi LimÓn and Squirt for the drive.

Jill took a swig from her coffee mug and explained

why we were driving so far from home. "You don't want to run into a customer when you're eating apples in the produce aisle of your corner grocery store."

As they sipped their vodka Squirts, the girls went over Stripping 101 with me. The more they talked, the more nervous I became.

"What else?" I said, pulling onto Highway 69 north.

"Keep the stage name Bailey. Never, never give them your real name," Serena continued. "And give Bailey an identity. Make her a character."

"Like Minnie Mouse?"

"Exactly." Jill lit a cigarette and cracked the window.

"Can't I just say I'm in college?" I looked in my review mirror at her.

"Just don't say where. Make the customer feel like you're a nice schoolgirl just doing this to pay the bills."

I am a nice schoolgirl just doing this to pay the bills.

"We all have personas," Jill expounded. "I am the private-school girl. I have the plaid skirt and white knee-high socks to prove it. And Serena is the dominatrix."

"Shut up!" Serena blew smoke at her.

"What's *that* entail?" I switched lanes to get out from behind a big rig that was blocking me from the open road.

Jill pretended to have a man's voice. "*Ma'am, please slap me. Ma'am, please step on my testicles.* It's some freaky dark stuff now. Too dark for me."

"It gets creepy when they want you to choke them." Serena held the cigarette in her mouth and made a choking action with her hands.

"No way." I was trying to act cool in front of them, but I wasn't.

"Girl, I am all good jumping on some guy's junk for eight hundred dollars an hour if that's what makes him happy."

I almost spit out my drink.

"She's serious." Jill put her hand over the backseat to high-five her.

"That's so wrong." I just shook my head.

"And so hilarious at the same time," Serena added.

"But I could probably do that." I sipped my roadie, realizing that stomping on some man's privates sounded easier than taking off my clothes again.

The girls at Déjà Vu in Lansing were trained hustlers. They knew how to milk every single dollar out of their customers. It was one of the biggest moneymakers for the national chain, always jam-packed with a VIP waiting line. The club was nationally known, set right in the middle of the city. It's what we refer to as a *party club*.

❧

Every type of club across the country has its own brand and own style of clientele and dancer. There are the *skank clubs*: dingy places fronted by gravel parking lots littered with dented cars. They attract cheap men who don't mind bringing their own beer in forty-five-ounce cans and ogling chubby nudies.

One step up the stripper ladder and you have the *blue-collar clubs*. They're frequented by workers in pay-by-the-hour manual labor trades, who park the family station wagon around the corner, pay five bucks to get in the door, and then plop down and want to talk for hours, practically for free, giving up just thirty bucks for the entire night. These men are what the girls refer to as *sitters. Don't be a sitter. It's just rude and cheap.* Trust me when I tell you, most dancers would rather be having a colonic than have to make chitchat with a *sitter.*

Then you have party clubs like Déjà Vu. In the party clubs, everything is loud and fast, with two-minute songs and not a lot of discussion going on between the client and the dancer. If a guy is talking in a party club, he's doing it nestled in the VIP room, where it will cost between four and five hundred dollars an hour. Party clubs are frequented by twentysomethings paying for first-marriage bachelor parties with Daddy's green American Express cards. A dancer can tuck twenty dollars in her G-string for a two-minute lap dance that makes a horny twenty-five-year-old think she actually likes him.

Lastly you have the *white-collar club* or the *gentlemen's club.* Here men in Armani suits come to have meetings while rappers, actors, hedge fund moguls, and wealthy suburban couples get their kinky on while drinking Cristal champagne and high-end cocktails. The dancers—wearing see-through cocktail dresses and gold thongs—look like they stepped out of the pages of a Victoria's Secret catalog. The clients in these clubs do a lot of talking. A girl who is skilled at luring clients into her web becomes a naked therapist. There's no touching and barely any dancing. While a dancer drinks Cakebread chardonnay and downs one of her clients' Vicodin, he will divulge his most intimate complications about his marriage, mistress, and kids in college. Girls can easily walk out after a night in a gentlemen's club with over two thousand dollars for four hours of listening, lying, and the occasional lap dance.

These clients seem to be the most deviant, as they come in to own these women, but they don't realize they are pawns in the short con. Women in these clubs know more personal trash on them than their wives, therapists, and priests or rabbis combined. The problem for dancers becomes this: to be abundantly successful in a white-collar club, you have to be so out of touch with who you really are, and how you got there, that you deceive yourself that you're not so caught in a snare of enormous piles of cash and top-line drugs that there is no real way to get out. Particularly for the ladies that have been doing it for over three or four years: those girls are their own prison guards.

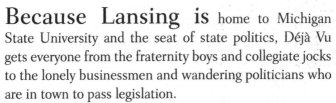

Because Lansing is home to Michigan State University and the seat of state politics, Déjà Vu gets everyone from the fraternity boys and collegiate jocks to the lonely businessmen and wandering politicians who are in town to pass legislation.

Déjà Vu is housed in a huge white building. With multicolored lights flashing skyward as if it were Grauman's Chinese Theatre on Hollywood Boulevard lit up for a Sony movie premiere, it has an almost holy feel to it.

"You can do this, Anny," Serena said as we pulled into the parking lot. They had too much invested in me to let me chicken out now.

"Valet!" Jill jerked my steering wheel to the left.

I pulled my car up to the valet. A college kid who couldn't have been older than me opened my door for me. I smiled at him.

"Hit him up good later with some green." Serena slammed my car door.

An overly large black, bald man wearing a crisp white shirt, black trousers, and Déjà Vu logo on his leather jacket escorted us into the club.

"Ben, meet Bailey," Serena said.

We shook hands as he rushed us through a novelty shop where vibrators and condoms and handcuffs were hanging on the wall. I dug my nail into my leg. *Be cool, Anny.* Something inside me was trying to spin me around to leave. *Whoops, U-turn. I don't belong here.*

I looked down a long, dimly lit hall.

"What's down there?" My voice was shaky.

"Peep alley," Jill clarified. "Keep walking."

I must have looked confused, as Serena added, "It's a peep show area where dudes go in these little rooms, pull open a curtain, and watch girls dancing while they get off."

"Euggghhh."

"Exactly," Serena said over her shoulder at me. "You're not going in there."

We stopped at the DJ booth. "Bailey, this is Regan." Regan leaned over and took a CD Jill was holding out. "Play this for her in rotation, will ya? She'll go after me."

Then she handed him another twenty dollars.

Everyone is getting paid in this place.

"Welcome, Bailey." Regan shouted over the wall.

"Make sure and check in with him when you get

here. I gave him your R. Kelly song and LL Cool J. Make new stuff up if you like. Tip him good or he'll shine the brightest lights on the cellulite around your thighs and cheeks."

"Don't be doggin' on me," Regan said. They did a knuckle bump. My head started to spin with all the information. I was beginning to feel a panic attack coming on. I wondered what would happen if I did just walk out of there. Would they stop me? I didn't want to let them see my fear. I wanted to fit in with them.

"Nice to meet you," Regan said.

I walked away, trying to keep up with Serena and Jill. Ben was behind me. They had this XXX initiation relay team streamlined.

"Stay away from him. His girlfriend's a dancer and he likes the newbies." Ben leaned over my shoulder, throwing me an information bone.

We got toward the back of the club, and Ben opened a door to the dressing room.

Serena handed him some cash. "Thirty minutes or so," she said, as we went into the dressing room.

"Never, ever walk out of this building without a security escort." She sounded serious.

"And take care of them," Jill added. "They are life support when you need it."

The dressing room was overly bright and white, with a long line of benches that faced a wall and a counter with a long horizontal mirror. Behind us was the door to the main floor and a few stairs that led you up to the stage when it was your time to come out and perform. Around the other wall was a bunch of lockers. We all had our own private locker. There were also two bathroom stalls and a tanning bed. Each girl had her Caboodle set up on the counter in front of the mirror. At the end of the mirror was another full-length body mirror.

I was trying to take it all in. To learn but not to appear, well, scared to death. We all walked back to the lockers.

"What? You thought this was going to be *Striptease* with Demi Moore?" Serena started taking off her 501s.

"Always check up in your business for toilet paper and strings before going out there."

This was no joke.

"For you." Serena handed me a gift basket from her locker. It had a sticker on it that said *Bailey*. It had a pair of four-inch new platforms, a cute organza baggie of silk G-strings, body spray, hair spray, and a flat iron.

"Thanks." I looked at the G-strings.

Jill's locker had pictures of her kids in it, a bunch of one-dollar bills, and business cards from lonely men.

I changed into silver mini-mini hot shorts that glowed in the lights, and a bedazzling sequined bikini top and my new four-inch heels. I had my G-string on.

"You look fabulous." Jill fluffed up my wild, long curly hair.

I turned around, scrutinizing my legs and arms. "Honestly. You look great." She kept on encouraging me. "Make rounds on the floor asking guys if they want a lap dance."

"Lap dance?" I had no idea what that meant.

"Sit!" Serena shoved me onto the bench and then preceded to stand in front of me, shake her tight buns and fake smile at me. "Fifteen dollars gets him just your boobs."

"He can touch my boobs?"

"*No!* He gets to *see* them. The customer can never, ever touch you. Now, on boob lap dance you can touch him, like this . . ." She began to grind her bottom on the top of my thighs and my lap. "For twenty bucks he gets full nude. *But* you can't touch him. No grinding naked. Got it?"

No, I don't got it. But I just nodded my head yes.

Jill told me, "You'll see me on the front stage—it's little—then Regan will call me to the main stage. When I'm on the main stage, you go get on the front stage."

My brows furrowed.

"Just follow my lead. Watch where I go, what I do, and how I do it in stages. Just do what I do. Do what you did on amateur night." Jill was so convincing.

"You'll do one main stage dance. Collect your money on stage and then get off for the next girl. The rest of the time, work the floor. There's at least thirty-five girls on rotation, so you'll probably only dance the stage one or two times."

Ben opened the door to the floor and I heard Biggie singing, "I don't know what they want from me . . ." I closed my eyes, letting Biggie serenade me for a second.

Then we walked onto the floor and I heard, "Bailey. Bailey. *Bailey!*" Serena yelled at me in her black leather miniskirt catsuit.

Jill pulled my arm. "*Bailey.*" She put her face right into mine. "Your name is Bailey."

I looked around at the purple and red velvet-lined room crowded with half-dressed women and men everywhere. "Yeah, yeah . . . Bailey."

I was no longer Anny.

chapter twelve
TAKING THE STAGE BACK

Americans spend eight to ten billion dollars per year on the sex industry. This includes the consumption of strip bars, peep shows, pornography rentals, phone sex, sex acts, sex toys, and sex magazines.

Bernadette Barton, *Stripped: Inside the Lives of Exotic Dancers*, New York: NYU Press, 2006

"Power" for women in the sex industry is a counterfeit idol, compliments of the devil, and it becomes too adhesive for you to put it down or shake it off. Yes. Pun intended.

Anny

As I stepped out of the dressing room and walked toward the floor of the club, a bouncer was yanking a topless and screaming stripper named Laci by the arm.

"Someone took my purse!" Laci piercingly slurred. "Someone stooooollllle my money! Where's my money?" She was grinding her teeth.

Serena tried to get me out of her way but she slammed right into my chest. "You got my money? Huh? Do you?"

I just shook my head no and Jill soared in. "No one took your money, Laci."

Laci spun around, nearly falling over as the bouncer grabbed her up, jerking her off her feet, and slightly dragging her into the dressing room.

Jill stood between me and the closed door. "Never lose sight of your purse. Girls in here get all jacked up on booze and drugs and they lose their money. Watch your wad, Bailey."

The place was thumping and pumping from the vibrations of the speakers. Toward the front of the club there was a small stage, or rather what looked like a midsize four-top cocktail table to normal human beings, only this one was made of steel and had a pole going through the center of it. A girl was spinning around the pole with her right arm up high and her leg holding onto the middle like a cobra. "Front stage." Jill pointed at her. "Don't take your clothes off."

"Think of it as a commercial." Serena drank the last of her cocktail disguised in a Gatorade bottle and tossed the empty container into the garbage can.

Regan the DJ came over the loudspeaker. "Maaaaiiin staaaaaage is Taaaasha, boys." He stretched out every syllable and started playing the song, "Girls, Girls, Girls." Tasha, a fierce and toned redhead, had slathered herself in glittery lotion. As she marched down what looked like a runway for models with a pole set dead center, the guys sitting around the lip of the stage with one-dollar bills dangling out of their mouths began hooting and howling.

Tasha peacocked her way down the stage, slowly peeling off layers of clothes, bending, strutting, and shaking everything that would gyrate up and down and side to side. By the time she got to the end of the runway, she was on all fours, rising onto her knees and pressing her breasts together to snatch the bills in her cleavage. The guys were rowdy but she was able to calmly steal their money. Toward the rear of the club and near us was another stage exactly like the one at the front.

"That's the backstage. It's a rotation. Work the floor until you see me go from the front stage to the main stage. That's your cue. You go get up there." She pointed at the front stage.

Jill straightened her plaid green and blue pleated skirt. She looked like Baby Spice from the British pop band Spice Girls.

"Gather up your money off the stage, and go back to the dressing room and clean off with the baby wipes."

"You'll be sweaty and want the guys' saliva smell off your skin," Serena threw in.

Jill kept instructing. "Make sure and redo your makeup, count your dough, and go back to the floor. Easy."

None of it sounded easy.

I could see the precision of the club structure. The owners were well organized and had streamlined the sale of sex. The girls working the rotation were like pretty yellow ducks in a floating river at the county fair, and all the men were aiming and shooting at them.

Regan said, "Gentlemen, get our favorite. Two for thirty."

What does that mean?

"Get picked or up there." Jill gestured to the main stage, as she bolted.

Dancers jumped up, working the guys. "Wanna dance? Wanna dance?"

Then the red police lights on the ceiling went off. Sirens blared. "Two for thirty," Regan enticed again over the loudspeakers.

A nondescript man said, "I'll take a dance."

He sat down on the couch looking at me.

The girls with men on the couch started wheeling and dealing. "Hi, I'm Penny . . ." I saw to my left. "Hi, I'm Sugar."

Then I saw Jill in front of me. She motioned rubbing her fingers together—

Get the money.

The negotiation: "Hi, I'm Bailey." I was awkward. "I need—"

He just handed me thirty dollars and said, "I like a little meat in my face."

I turned around and put my back to him. I was repulsed. I made eye contact with Jill, who was an inch off the lap of some loser who looked like he was winning the Kentucky Derby. She motioned with her hand over her mouth, fake yawning. *Sucker.*

My eyes momentarily explored the other dancers. Most were superb actresses. Oscar-worthy, each one of them in their own way.

I took his money and put it in my little purse.

"Ladies up." Regan's voice echoed.

I followed Jill's lead. She took off her shoes. I took off my shoes. She climbed onto a small table in front of her client on the couch. I climbed up on my small pedestal and steadied myself with the pole. Even in my bare feet I felt clumsy. The girls who weren't picked for a private lap dance made their way to the stage like they were boarding trains to concentration camps.

Drums began to beat, then Steven Tyler began to sing his song "Rag Doll."

I closed my eyes for a minute and just listened to the music. "Hot tramp, Daddy's little cutie . . ."

The man looked up at me, and then I began to replay in my head the entire allegro from Mozart's "Sonata Facile." The dance between intimacy and destruction at the same time. I was lost in the rapture of it, and then my foot slipped off the table and instinctually I caught myself on the pole and tried not to look stupid. Steven Tyler slashed into my thoughts: "Baby, won't you do me."

Jill had gotten off her perch and was lap dancing. I copied her.

I had my rear leaning over him, and then I tried to turn around, but he grabbed me by my hips and wouldn't let me stand. He slammed me onto his lap and started grinding against me through his pants. He was stronger than I was; I couldn't go anywhere as he shook and then finally finished.

That was the first of what became many sexual assaults in the club for me. Nothing new for dancers. It comes with the territory like a saw injury if you're a woodcutter.

Where was Ben and security? I ran toward the dressing room and flung open the door. I headed to the locker room.

I want out of here. This is too much for me.

I stopped at a bathroom stall, as I thought I was going to throw up. I opened the door and a dancer they called Cinnamon was snorting a giant line of cocaine off the toilet paper dispenser. "Shut that!" she yelled at me.

She had been working in the clubs a long time and

looked the part: long, beautiful hair, tattoos, the shoes, the outfit . . . and an expression on her face that was hard as nails.

I had tears streaming down my face.

She looked straight at me and lit up a cigarette. "Listen, babe," she said, "you've got two choices. You can sit here and hide, and wish your daddy would've saved you and your life didn't go this way and you didn't end up here. We *all* wish we didn't end up here. None of us planned this. But you're wasting time." She took a long drag and exhaled the smoke. "So your other option is to be here, dry your face, fix your makeup, and get out there and make some money. You might as well do that. You're already here." She put out another big fat line. "Here"—she motioned to the line of cocaine—"you'll feel better."

I took the rolled twenty out of her hand.

"Plug one nose hole," she instructed.

I leaned down with her rolled twenty-dollar bill and snorted her white powder.

She turned around and walked out. "Go make some money."

What I should have said is, *My dad does try to save me, over and over. If he knew I was in this place, he'd burn it to the ground and miraculously save me. So why am I here? Why?*

That was the first night I did cocaine. Drinking was no longer enough.

Cinnamon was right: I *was* already there, and not just physically. This was what I had chosen. I decided I had to stop feeling sorry for myself if I was going to survive. The mental roller coaster about my decision to jump into the sex industry was playing with my emotions in a way I didn't know how to control, and Cinnamon had seen right through me. Time to toughen up.

❧

For the first month everything on my entire body hurt. My feet, my thighs, my back, my belly . . . there wasn't an inch of me that didn't ache from being in those shoes and doing sexual aerobics for eight hours straight. My social life had changed, my sleep schedule changed, and worst of all, I was doing things on a regular basis I never thought I'd do *at all*. My inner circle had shrunk; all my friends from school were gone. At home, I felt like a marathon runner ever night after a race, and the only relief I found was in my bathtub at seven a.m. trying to ease the physical and emotional pain and come down from the high of the night's drug du jour.

After the tub, I'd crawl into bed, and when I woke up at three in the afternoon, I felt like a lost, compromised little girl. The moment that regret would hit me and I'd start to think about it, to really question what I was doing, I'd numb the pain by lighting up a joint, doing a line, or pouring a drink.

At month two, every ball I was trying juggling at school had hit the ground. It wasn't possible to keep my work and school life going simultaneously.

I left the club at 5 a.m., once I had paid everyone out, and I wouldn't walk through my door until after 6:30 a.m. On the weekdays, I'd be home around 4:30 a.m., and on Monday, Wednesday, and Friday I had an 8 a.m. communications class. At the start of the week, I dragged my ragged self into the lecture hall, but by Friday mornings I hadn't sobered up enough to make it through the courtyard of my apartment, let alone onto campus. It wasn't long before I stopped going to my morning classes at all. By the time the alcohol and drugs ran out of my system, it was well past 1 p.m. Regular life was no longer an option.

The sex industry is its own culture entirely, with its own values, schedule, social mores, and rules. It didn't take me long to get sucked into the culture of the sex industry and out of the culture of suburban America.

⤫

"I'm dropping out of school."

I told my dad over the phone. I didn't want him wasting his money. It took him all of one hour to show up at my apartment. I was still buzzed and couldn't look him in the eye, as I was afraid he would be able to tell I was high on coke and weed.

"When was the last time you slept?" He tried to touch my face, but I instinctively blocked his arm.

I treated him like a customer.

"I'm working at night." I turned my back on him. "You want something to eat?"

"What exactly are you doing?" He stood in my living room and I could feel the anger in his voice building.

I pulled out a wad of cash from my pocket. "We can go out. My treat."

I am acting like a monster. Stop it!

He looked puzzled, as if I were a stranger, not the daughter he had raised. But I wasn't his daughter anymore, I was Bailey now.

"Are you on drugs?"

"Right at this second? Technically, no."

I saw his face grow cold. "Ann Nicole. Do not mess around with me. Are you dealing drugs?"

"I'm not a drug dealer. I'm a stripper."

He took a step back, as if he'd just been stabbed in the heart.

"You're what?" His voice lowered to a growl.

"I take off my clothes"—I pulled out the cash again and waved it around—"for money."

He turned around and walked out of my apartment. His well of unconditional love had officially run dry.

I went into my bedroom and took out a small glass vial from my top drawer. I poured two small mounds of cocaine onto an antique mirror that had belonged to my grandmother. I got out the American Express card from my wallet and separated the pile into four fat white lines. I tightly rolled up a twenty, plugged one nostril, and leaned down toward the mirror. With the bill as a straw, I snorted hard and made the first line disappear into my nose. Then I did a second line with the opposite side. When I came up, a rush hit me—I'd come back for the other two lines later—and I shook back my long hair and looked at myself in the mirror.

Excellent blow, isn't it, Bailey? There's that voice again.

Is it me, or the wickedness that lives inside me now?

⬿

I was hanging out with other strippers in a group of five or ten girls. We traveled like a very hot, angry she-wolf pack. Everyone now called me Bailey, and thanks to a ten-pound weight loss and regular visits to Beach Tan, the metamorphosis was complete. Anny had been buried underneath piles of acrylic nails and buckets of vanilla-scented lotion. Bailey was a rock star on tour. Bailey was tough: she released me from Anny's anxiety and fear with a sneer and a flip of her blond hair extensions. She had stacks of money, unedited cheers and applause, booze, drugs, and the VIP treatment in the club.

On our nights off from dancing, the she-pack went on recruiting missions in either Lansing or Kalamazoo. After an apartment preparty where we'd drink and smoke weed, we'd pounce upon a nearby college nightclub and mingle with the Sigma Nu boys while we sized up the Kappa Kappa Gammas as potential dancers. You can tell the girls that want to get high. They fantasize about dancing and living an alter ego lifestyle. It's not the prettiest one, or the wildest one; it's always the silent girl in the middle. I can spot her like an injured rabbit in an open field.

We were always looking for new girls to recruit for the club.

My entourage was the cream of the crop as far as strippers in Michigan. We were a total misfit group of racy girls in trendy clothes driving BMWs, and everyone began to recognize who we were. Moreover, everyone on the campus at Western Michigan began to recognize me, particularly the male students. They had been up to Déjà

Vu and the rumors of Coach Bob Donewald's daughter the stripper were no longer gossip but an honest fact.

Making things worse, my girls, like me, weren't mild-tempered. They were prone to brawling. Whenever someone grazed or sassed them, the moment too quickly escalated into a fight. I'd just roll my eyes as I'd watch the bouncer shoving through the crowd toward us, and I'd flash a hundred-dollar bill so that instead of tossing us to the curb, he'd get us out of there before the cops came.

Strip girls look delicate in their tiny clothes, high heels, and firm bodies, but they are WWF street fighters. Maybe our fuse is shorter because of some childhood meltdown or all the drugs we're on, or maybe it is the fact that at this point in our lives we all have an *I don't care about anything anymore* attitude. But it took very little egging me on for me to turn and slap someone upside the head, and not in a funny way, in a way that would break their jaw.

None of my siblings ever hit me. My parents never *had to* spank or belt whip us like the stories I would hear in the locker room, but my desire to uncork my inner street fighter was as great as my desire to get high.

I had been dating multiple guys in both Kalamazoo and Lansing. I manipulated them as easily as the targets in the club. One night at a bar in Kalamazoo, I saw a football player that I thought was my local boyfriend—I use that term loosely—about to kiss a cheerleader from my dad's team. I walked up to the bar where they were sitting on stools and reached over his shoulder, grabbing her by the hair, and pulled her head toward mine and spit directly in her face. She screamed and recoiled backward.

I dropped her hair, looked at him, and said, "Why you got to make me do that?"

This was one of the lowest things I've ever done to another woman with the exception of recruiting dancers.

The next morning my mother came to my apartment without my dad. News of my spitting in the face of the local cheer-fever girl had clearly made it to our family dinner table.

"Anny, we love you." My mother sat across from me on the couch. Then she paused.

"But?" I interrupted her.

"No buts. Nothing will ever make us stop loving you. But you're not *you* right now. You're not *right* right now. You need help. Help we don't know how to give you. So"—she sighed—"we're not going to pay for your car, your insurance, or this apartment unless—"

I laughed out loud, wondering if she knew I was making hundreds of dollars a night.

"Unless you'll see a therapist."

"You want me to see a therapist?"

This is the course of action she and my dad have plotted out for me? Therapy?

"Yes, and if you go, you can keep living in this apartment and we'll help you with your car. But you need help."

The therapist was more for her than me. A last-ditch effort. I almost felt pity for her because she didn't know what to do with me. I mean, *she* was always the one who had the secret GPS for my life, but Bailey was behind the wheel now and she had driven this girl *way* off the road.

I agreed to go. I knew I was becoming sadistic, and

working in the sex industry wasn't the norm for girls like me. I also knew that somewhere under the calluses that were growing on Anny, I loved my parents.

Therapy was more a gesture to calm them than it was a tool intended to help me.

~≈~

I rolled into the small office on the third floor of a five-story building in my sweatpants and flip-flops. If I wasn't in the club, I couldn't be bothered to spruce up.

I reclined on the nice Jewish doctor's couch and felt the need to light a cigarette.

"Please, no smoking," she politely asked me from behind her huge oak desk that looked like she had just Pledged it off for me. Her office was neat, sterile, and tidy, just like her.

"Dr. Bernstein, you have very pretty hair. Can I see it down?"

I was just messing with her in a sexy way that I am sure made her uncomfortable. But she was pretty for a forty-something, suit-wearing psychiatrist. Can you blame me?

"Thank you, but I like to leave it up. It gets too warm when I wear it down. Your hair is naturally curly?" she asked.

"Yep. Sorry, I haven't washed this mess. I don't really get made up unless I'm dancing." I fluffed up my untamed, thick mop.

I looked at the framed picture on the wall of a dense forest with orange, yellow, and red fall leaves on the trees. At the bottom the word INSPIRATION was printed. So you knew what to feel when looking at the fall colors, apparently. She probably bought it from a motivational workshop that doctors attend on long weekends in Chicago. The place was very impersonal.

"Tell me about dancing."

"I guess we're getting right to it?" I eyeballed her.

"You started there. Is that okay with you?"

"Sure." I was flippant and had done a line of coke in the car, so I was chatty.

Here are three problems with doing cocaine: The first is that it wreaks havoc on your bowels, fast. The second is that the chemical smell seeps out of your most personal body parts. The third is that you get verbal diarrhea, to match the first. Why this happens, I have no idea.

"Why am I a stripper?" I repeated her. "Well, the money's good."

"Then it's about the money?" She stilled her pen.

"Now, I guess."

"You guess?"

What did she want me to say? Serena and Jill made the most sense to me? That dancing was empowering? It was.

"I like being in control." There, that would give her something to chew on for a minute.

"Control of who? Yourself?" She wrote something on her white legal pad between two tan leather covers.

"Men. I like being in control of the men."

"Is it control if they are paying you?"

I sat up, slipped off my flip-flops, and crossed my legs.

"Ya. I mean, sure, I take off my clothes, but most

girls do that for free on Friday night on Michigan's campus. The guys in the club, those guys can't touch me. I'm in control. I'm not some victim."

Too much. Too much. Too much. Too much!

Silence hung in the air.

"Have you ever been a victim?"

"Everyone has been a victim at some point."

"Yes, I am sure that's true in some fashion. But you're talking about controlling a sexual environment."

"And pop goes the weasel." My defenses came out.

Don't let her inside, Bailey. There was that voice again.

She watched me, not saying a word.

"Look, it's not what you think. I get up on stage and people love what I do. It rains money on me. Why is that a problem?"

Someone help me, I sound like a monster again.

She rose up from behind her desk, walked to her bookshelf, and pulled out a book by Sigmund Freud.

"Have you heard of repetition compulsion?"

"Sorry, no."

No! I haven't heard your psychological babble. And my blow is wearing off and I really, really need another line.

"I need to pee. Do you mind?" I eased up.

"Of course. Here's a key. It's down the hall to the left."

Fully clothed, I sat on the toilet and dug through my purse until I found my little vial of drugs. I turned one hand upside down and carefully dumped a little bump into the underside curvature of my pinky nail. I put it to my nostril and snorted. I did the other side and then one more for luck. I came out of the stall and stood in front of the sink.

What the hell does she know? The dark side ridiculed me in the mirror.

I washed my hands, put on lip gloss, and felt blissful again.

"Sorry." I tossed my purse on the couch and sat back down.

She was now in her wingback chair to the left of the couch and in front of the window.

"Repetition compulsion at its most basic is when someone has trauma in their history, and they put themselves in a similar situation, almost trying to wrap their mind around what happened to them. They'll do it over and over."

"I promise you that I wasn't a stripper in some previous life."

"We saw a lot of PTSD victims from Desert Storm. They were really struggling with repetition compulsion. To the point where they were putting themselves in life-threatening situations."

"Look, I appreciate your degrees, and what's that . . . Freud?" I referred to her book. "Neurosis ABCs? But I'm not a war victim."

"You don't have to be. But you do seem—"

There was beat of silence as she waited for me to finish her thought.

"How would you describe yourself?" She finally broke the long silence.

"Angry." *Arrhhh! She tricked me.*

"That's honest." She leaned forward, almost pleased that I was fuming. "So let's put the anger and job together."

I gazed at the clock on her wall. Time was almost up.

"Victim? Isn't that what you said?" She looked at her notes and reread, "You're not a victim anymore."

I crossed my arms. I had participated in her psychoanalytic formulations for forty-nine minutes. That was more than enough. *Ticktock, ticktock.* I glanced at the clock again.

"Women who are sexually abused often choose the sex industry as a career without knowing they are suffering from this compulsion."

She was on to something, but the truth was Bailey was a stage celebrity and wasn't going away without a struggle. Serena and Jill understood me, and in tiny spurts during a dance, I felt in control and wanted.

"But what really happens is that the women are retraumatizing themselves, over and over and over. The power is an illusion and the truth is sexual exploitation of the girl at whatever age she was when she started feeling unsafe."

"I am angry. You're right. But I'm not exploited."

I started to think about all the sexual encounters I had had and realized that none of them were loving.

She looked at her clock. "I just want you to think about it and I want your mind to be clear when you're thinking."

"My mind is clear."

"Anny, I know you're on drugs. Your hand or foot hasn't stopped moving since you walked in my door. You're not fooling me. The fact that you stayed the entire session and didn't escape when you went to the bathroom actually tells me that you want help."

Wow, the nice doctor just went straight up on me.

"This is a prescription. It will help you calm down.

Less anger. But I want you to try and be sober. This is serious medicine but I think it will help you."

She ripped the prescription page off its pad.

I felt a sense of relief and panic. Relief that possibly this woman did know *something*. Maybe she could help me quiet the voices in my head and the way I feel when the drugs wear off. And I felt panic. I didn't want to go any deeper. I was done with this.

This was the dichotomy of my search for reason.

Half of me comprehended that I was spiraling down Dante's Inferno, and the other half was enjoying the ride.

chapter thirteen
NEW LIFE

Eighty-nine percent of women in the sex industry said they wanted to escape but had no other means for survival.

Melissa Farley, "Prostitution and Trafficking in Nine Countries: An Update on Violence and Post-Traumatic Stress Disorder," Prostitution Research, www. prostitutionresearch.com

Creating a new life doesn't mean the old one is gone.

Anny

November is one of my favorite months. The smell of sweet wood fires drifts from fireplaces and tickles my nostrils, college basketball is kicking off, and the leaves are changing. My birthday is in November too. The arrival of the month always lifts me up: *A new year of possibilities.*

Regan, the club DJ, and his girlfriend, Tandie, picked me up at my new apartment on west Main Street. Gone was the ghetto student housing with its Salvation Army furniture. In were oversized shabby chic white couches, crisp white linen drapes, and designer ivory beanbag chairs with large orange polka dots. The place was modern and clean.

One night when I was really high, I had decided that I had chosen white because it was the color of purity and those big orange spots represented the way I managed to ruin everything. They looked like vomit had spewed all over the beanbags.

At thirtysomething and overweight, Regan was sweating profusely from his forehead from carrying the provisions for my intimate birthday preparty up two flights of stairs.

I opened the door and was greeted by his huffing and puffing. "Here," he grunted, dropping two cases of beer on the floor.

"He's going to have a stroke," Tandie teased.

She had also put on a few pounds and the club manager was riding her hard about losing the extra roll that had attached to her middle.

"I made him take the stairs. He needs the exercise."

"Do you wanna drink?" I held out a cocktail to Regan.

"No, we need to jam."

"Okay, okay . . ." We were carpooling to Lansing.

I went into my bathroom, loaded my makeup, body spray, and baby wipes into my Caboodle, and did two fat lines of cocaine before heading out the door with them.

Halfway to Lansing, Tandie wanted to make a pit stop at Walgreens.

"Come in with me?" she asked.

"You're not going to rob the place, are you?"

Something about her tone told me that she was up to something stupid.

I do have some stealing standards.

"No." She slammed her door.

We headed to the girl products aisle and stopped in front of boxes of home pregnancy tests.

"Are you for real?" I asked her.

"I'm late. Three weeks." Now I understood why she hadn't wanted to go alone.

"I'm late all the time. Between partying and getting my days and nights mixed up, my cycle is a total mess." I tried to sound reassuring.

She bought an EPT, and we went into the bathroom at the back of the store.

"Honestly, I think all this weight is because I'm pregnant."

She did have a point about the weight. But I figured it was because Regan loved to smoke weed and she had fallen into the late-night munchies trap with him.

"Take one." She handed me a test strip, as they came two in a box.

"I don't want that." I tried to give it back to her.

"Please," she begged, "just do it with me."

"Fine."

We went into our respective stalls. I pulled a protective sheet out of the wall dispenser, placed it on the seat, took down my jeans, and proceeded to pee on the stick.

"If it's a cross it's positive." She was reading the box. "If it's a line it's negative."

Duh. Been there, done that.

I set the test on the toilet paper dispenser, pulled up my pants, and kicked the handle with my boot to flush.

"You're freaking out about nothing." I washed my

hands as she stood nervously holding her test.

Then she started crying.

"Oh no . . ." I didn't want her to have to go through what I had done. *That baby that lived inside me would be a toddler now.*

She began to hug me. "It's negative. Thank God." Relief tears.

I wanted to peel her off me, as this type of embrace makes me feel uncomfortable. *This girl bonding was a bad idea for me. I need to get out of here.* I pushed her away. "You're a freak."

Guilt for what I had done seeped under the door like a poison gas and I felt like I was choking.

As I walked out the door ahead of her, she called out to me, "Wait."

❧

I worked an eight-hour shift completely sober. At five in the morning I cleaned out my locker and drove home with Regan and Tandie. I slept the entire trip. I woke up starving and needed to go to my parents' house and I didn't want to be hungover or high. I knew they were upset that I had stopped seeing the shrink, but I didn't need their money, so what exactly was the point of Dr. Bernstein?

She had gotten under my skin and that's not a place I allow people to go.

❧

"You look clean," my mother said, setting down a plate of ravioli for me.

"You made my favorite."

"I didn't know if I would see you tomorrow," she said.

My father came into the house through the kitchen door, and when he saw me, instantly his load seemed to lighten, but he still remained guarded. No matter what I had done, I believe that having me with them, even in small doses, gave them pockets of relief.

"Little Dee."

"Dad."

"You okay?" He set his briefcase on the counter and went around the kitchen island and kissed my mother. "Smells good."

"Yep." I leaned into my bowl.

Dad sat down at the table in front of his waiting place setting. My mother served up both of their dishes and relaxed into her seat.

My father bowed his head. "Lord God, we just thank you for this food. For the health of our family. For blessing us every day, and for letting Anny be home for her twentieth birthday."

We all said, "Amen."

Everyone began to eat.

"Do you want to come to the game tomorrow?"

My dad's team was playing Michigan. They were a powerhouse program that had survived a national scandal, had fired their coach, and had interviewed my dad. He didn't get the job. Michigan was a Big Ten school and they were expected to blow us out.

"Are you going?" I looked at my mother.

"No."

My mom had grown tired of the road games and travel. I think we all wore her out.

"Just me?" I set my fork down.

My father stirred his pasta. "You can bring a respectable friend if you want."

I knew that meant someone wearing clothes, so I guess that was no one.

"Okay. I'll come."

They looked at each other, surprised. I had declined every other invitation to attend games, family milestones, and Sunday dinners this past year.

"I wanted to give you some good news," I began slowly. "I'm not going back to working as a, a, dancer."

My father never looked up at me. If he didn't look up, then the fact that I was a stripper would slide under the table.

"And I am going to try and go back to school."

At that point he looked up, set down his fork, and asked, "Why?"

His voice was skeptical and he was growing passive-aggressive.

He has every right to be skeptical. They both do.

I took a long drink of my milk, trying to formulate my reasoning, but there was no fancy hypothesizing about this decision.

"I'm pregnant."

As I went to sleep in my apartment that night, I replayed my mother and father telling me that they thought the baby was a good thing. They were honestly excited for me. It was the answer to their prayers. Well, maybe not being pregnant, but a reason to stop stripping and partying. They saw it as a sign that I would put an end to the mess I had gotten myself into and hopefully return to the person I used to be.

But who was that?

I touched my stomach, remembering the promise that I had made to my unborn child when I had the abortion. *If you come back, I won't hurt you. No matter what I am doing, no matter what my life looks like, I'll have you.*

The following night I drove slowly and alone to my dad's game in Ann Arbor, Michigan. There was black ice on the road everywhere. I switched my music from Master P rapping—or rather, cursing—about gangstas' Bs and rat traps from his song "Plan B" to my new fascination with Seal. His cover of Steve Miller's "Fly Like an Eagle" was about people like me, being out of my mind and trying to soar higher. I sang along, "Time keeps on slippin', slippin', slippin' into the future." In my heart I prayed that I would have a baby girl, as I had a heightened perspective on the sickness of men, the degeneracy that can exist in them. I knew a girl would be my get-out-of-jail-free card. She would give me a legit reason to get out of the industry.

Tip-off had passed by the time I arrived in Ann Arbor for the U of M game. My dad was engaged in the game, but as I walked down the stairs of the arena, I noticed him look over his shoulder, twice. He never looked at the crowd during the game. *Never.* He was like a masterful Zen Buddhist quieting the noise of the world. But tonight there was someone he was looking for. Someone who was late, and that someone was me.

The last time he turned around, I was in my seat behind the bench. He didn't looked back again until Western Michigan had upset the darlings of the basketball world. He had beaten one of the biggest teams in basketball. Postgame he met Coach Ellerbe midcourt and the two men briefly shook hands. The emotions I felt almost made me cry. *Why had I let myself disappear from him?*

I was escorted into the tunnel and waited for my dad to do his victory speech in the locker room with the team. He came out of the locker room and headed to the media room with security and me by his side. Though he was ecstatic, he never showed it. In public he projected the perfect blend of stoicism and charisma.

During the press conference I sat in the back of the room watching him in front of the various microphones shoved at the podium.

"We did what we were supposed to do, and we won," he said.

The press needled him as if they wanted to see him jump up and down like Augustus Gloop in *Charlie and the Chocolate Factory.*

What they didn't know was that his message was for me.

Just do your job, Anny. The rest will take care of itself.

I knew his words were for me because I had heard them many times before.

Dad had the team manager drive my car home, as the roads were slick and he didn't want to endanger me or my unborn baby. Not on his watch. Not anymore. In the first row of the bus, I sat next to him. Just him and me. Where had the time gone?

He wrapped his arm around me as if saying, *I am happy you're back.* I just put my head on his shoulder, melted into his body, and fell asleep.

It was a reprieve from real life.

I soaked up being pregnant. After the initial month of morning sickness had passed, I marveled at the potential of brand-new life growing inside me. I did my best to calculate the date of my last period to determine the father of my baby—it was either a customer I had met while high on cocaine at work or Kenny, the college football player from Western Michigan whose cheerleader date I had spat on in the local watering hole in Kalamazoo. Both were African American. I was up front with both men; I didn't have enough sense *not* to be. I didn't *care* about either of them; to me, this baby was *my* baby, and not having to "share" the child was a better option for me. I let them both off the hook, but Kenny didn't want to go away.

I had eased back into my life—prestripper, precrazy, predestructive—and was sober. By January I had enrolled back into Western Michigan and was taking part-time classes and working in the athletic department for money. The girls from the club would call to check in on me, but I wanted to erase them. I wanted Bailey dead, but she wasn't going away without a fight. For now, I had just put her to rest, with baby hormones.

Just pretend that the entire stripper chapter never happened, Anny. You're pretty good at pretending. Then I heard Bailey's laughter.

For the first six months of my pregnancy, Kenny the potential baby-daddy was popping in and out of my apartment checking up on me with more frequency. Although I wasn't sure if he was the father or not, he was making sure that I wasn't slipping back into my partying ways and getting high. He was showing up and actually being nice to me. He was becoming a bit of a fixture in my apartment, and it was nice to have someone to share the experiences with instead of being alone. He would get to feel the baby kick me or see the pictures of the ultrasound when I went to the doctor. As much as I didn't need him, I was growing to want him around. Sharing the pregnancy experience with him opened a piece of my heart that I thought I had closed.

We were going to my dad's games and I was yelling and screaming like always, cheering him on. No one could really tell that I was pregnant and I wanted to keep it that way. I was still small, and when my belly finally popped out, I began wearing baggy sweaters to hide the inevitable.

It was a freezing February morning, and snow and ice covered the parking lot where my Ford Explorer was parked. As my boots crunched in the snow, my belly began to cramp. It would tighten up in a spasm and then stop for about fifteen seconds, and then start again. It hurt so bad that I went back inside my apartment, as I knew something wasn't right with the baby. I called my sister Kristin.

"Is there blood?" Her voice was calm.

I went into my bathroom and checked my underpants. "Yes."

"Can you drive?"

"I think so."

"Meet me at Bronson." And she hung up.

Bronson Methodist was the same hospital where I had miscarried the baby when I was in the halfway house. I hated that hospital, but Kristin worked there as a nurse in labor and delivery and she would be able to fast-track me.

At twenty-one weeks pregnant, I was admitted to Bronson with preterm labor. They put me on various drugs to slow down my contractions. I didn't want to lose this baby, but maybe it was my punishment. Maybe God was torturing me for torturing Him. Maybe the drugs I did before I knew I was pregnant had somehow caused this to happen.

Calm down.

My second night in the hospital, after Kenny had gone home, I was beginning to relax as nurses were coming in and out and checking all the wires hooked to my body. I was listening to my dad's game as he played Miami of Ohio in the conference tournament. It was the first half of the game when suddenly the announcer said, "Something is wrong with Charlie Coles." I didn't know who Charlie was, but he was important enough that everyone stopped playing the game. "He's collapsed onto the court. Medical personnel are rushing toward him."

I reached around my bed looking for a phone.

"People are all around him." The announcer's voice got hushed. "If you're listening at home, we should all take a minute and pray for him."

I called my mother from my hospital bed. "Who is Charlie Coles?"

Charles Coles was the head coach of Miami of Ohio. He had had a heart attack; they were rushing him to Bronson.

Welcome to Bronson, Charlie, I thought as I heard sirens approaching.

Basketball coaches are an insane breed. No matter the level—college or pro—the hours, the travel, the sacrifice: it's a lot. Coach Coles was no different. As they wheeled him off, he insisted that his team keep playing.

When my dad came to the hospital to visit me that night, he also went to see Coach Coles. Dad told me that he had a tube in his throat and couldn't talk but apparently he could write, as he demanded a piece of paper, and his first question to his wife was "Did we win?"

They had beaten my dad, but it wasn't the last game that season for the Western Michigan Broncos. A couple of weeks later, my father was sitting in his recliner in our family's living room as I relaxed on the couch. Doctor's orders: bed rest for me. I had been in and out of the hospital for fourteen days and was spending more time at my parents' house than my own apartment, and although I missed playing house with Kenny, I felt safer with my mom, a former nurse, in case I had any more baby emergencies. Dad and I were watching the television, where they were announcing the list of the universities that were chosen to go to the NCAA Basketball Tournament.

"You're going," I said.

He was silent.

"Western Michigan to play Clemson," the reporter stated.

He turned to me. "I can't believe it. I can't believe it."

"I told you, Dad!" I started to get excited.

Our entire house went nuts, then Dad looked at me and said, "Settle down. Stay down." He wanted me back on the couch. *Always the dad.*

The entire university was abuzz with Donewald and Bronco fever. He had taken another underdog program and put them on the map. I begged my family and doctors to let me attend the tournament in Chicago. I had been doing schoolwork from home, and I was stable, for the most part.

Even though Kalamazoo was a small town, word of my pregnancy had not gotten out. So the sight of me, nearly seven months pregnant, walking with my mom, brother, and both sisters to sit behind the bench during the first round of the NCAA finals was shocking. During the first time-out, the Broncos cheerleaders took the court and I saw the girl whom I had spit on.

I felt instant cramping in my belly. Guilt pains, I suppose.

Western Michigan beat Clemson that night and went on to the second round, only to lose to Stanford, but to our entire family, it was victory to have my dad's hard work and winning reputation back in the national spotlight.

On June 29, exactly one month early, during one of my twice-a-week hospital stress tests to evaluate how the baby was doing, the doctors informed me that the baby didn't seem *right*. I wanted to have Kenny there, but he had gone to Pittsburgh to see his family. The doctors' voices were sullen as they told me the baby was in duress and they were going to induce me. For six hours the labor pains wrenched through me. Kristin, my nurse, and my oldest sister, Lisa, coached me through the night, trying to get the baby out. By ten a.m., after they had broken my water and my contractions were twice the standard duration, I couldn't muster even cursing through my oxygen mask. The doctor was between my legs and Kristin watched behind him.

"Push," Kristin said to me.

I was absolutely exhausted.

"Now. Push again. Good, good. Now relax."

"Okay, Anny, I need a big push now."

Lisa squeezed my hand and a supernatural adrenaline rush hit me as I tried to sit up and push as hard as I could.

"Crowning. Here that baby comes. Again, push."

I pushed three more times, and the doctor let Kristin take the baby out of me.

Screaming like a siren filled the air.

My parents both came into the delivery room to see their grandchild.

My mother said, "Oh Anny, this baby has an old soul."

I named her McKaylah Rain. She was a dark-skinned, perfect little girl.

For the first time, I fell in love.

chapter fourteen
RETIREMENT AND REINVENTING

> *Researchers have found that stripping distorts dancers'*
> *perceptions of money and sexuality; encourages them*
> *to blur their personal boundaries about previously*
> *unacceptable sexual acts; teaches them to develop*
> *contempt for men; reduces their sex drives; and causes*
> *problems in their intimate partnerships.*
>
> Bernadette Barton, *Stripped: Inside the Lives of Exotic*
> *Dancers*, New York: NYU Press, 2006.

> *The temporary relief from pain and the high from*
> *controlling men only feeds the destructive and heinous*
> *lie that you're winning, when in reality you're killing*
> *yourself over and over.*
>
> Anny

With two-week-old McKaylah,
I was in my apartment with Kenny. He was now a
semipermanent fixture and had missed McKaylah's birth
by only an hour as he tried desperately to get back to me.
He wasn't worried about whether she was his child or not:
he was ready to accept the responsibility of fatherhood.
I was enamored with him for the sole reason that he

wanted to help me. Approaching his junior year, Kenny was attending summer workouts with the team and working part-time at Target unloading trucks. His dream was to play football professionally.

At night he would wake up with me when I would pump breast milk, and I would give it to him to feed McKaylah. With his muscular arms holding her tiny body against his bare chest, they were a Calvin Klein ad in *Vanity Fair* magazine. Her flawless cappuccino skin was the perfect blend of his African American ancestry and my French forefathers.

Watching him love her was intoxicating.

I had exactly what I wanted: a new family, and reconciliation with my old family.

I was in motherhood bliss.

On a Sunday morning, 'Kaylah was napping and Kenny went out to get us both sandwiches for lunch. Finding a rhythm in my domesticated routine, I was sorting piles of dirty laundry, the whites with the whites and darks with the darks. I checked the pockets of Kenny's jeans and found an extra ten-dollar bill. Bonus! *Finder's fee*, I laughed to myself. Then, there was another piece of paper. In loopy, girlish handwriting was a phone number. My stomach sank.

I went to my phone and dialed the number.

❧

Heartbreak makes stripping so much easier.

I was livid some moments and weeping from insecurity

the next. I didn't confront him, as I was afraid I would lose him. Who would want me now? Ex-stripper turned new mother at twenty. I would never be good enough to find a decent man.

What was I really thinking? *This* man was going to really love me? *He* knew I was soiled. *I* knew I was soiled. Was I hallucinating that he was going to get into the NFL and marry me? That he was going to bring his stripper baby-momma home to meet the family in Pittsburgh?

The facts were simple: Like all the guys I knew, he just wanted a piece of the coach's daughter, and he wanted to get a little extra action on the side. He was no different from the men in the club who had their suburban wives and stuffed hundred-dollar bills between naked women's breasts.

The life I was pretending to have was a lie, so why not make it a good one?

I tried to accept the fact that while I wasn't Kenny's only girl, I was his main girl.

What now?

You know where you belong. I could always count on Bailey to remind me.

The knowledge that Kenny was intimate with other women made the transition from our playing house to my prancing on stage much easier and faster than I ever would have expected.

He walked in the door from work early on a Friday night. I was rocking out to MC Breed, "Gotta Get Mine" with Tupac, ironing my hair and putting fake lashes on.

He eyeballed a line of coke on my dresser.

"What?" It sounded like a snarl. "I'm going to pump and dump."

"Where are you going?" He leaned his back against the door and crossed his arms.

"The club. Someone is going to have to make real money to pay for this." I gestured around the room. "What? You thought my daddy was going to take care of us?"

I let Bailey do the talking.

To me now, he was a man in the club. I put on my short-shorts and looked at my butt in the mirror.

Still tight and still a size two. Bam!

My breasts were swollen with milk to a 34DD.

Bailey still has it and is ready for action.

I leaned into 'Kaylah's pink and white wicker bassinet and sighed at the sweetness of her fresh baby smell.

"I love you, baby girl," I swooned.

By the time my eyes met Kenny's, all the emotion had drained out of me. "She has a feeding in three hours. There's breast milk in the bottles and two formulas," I said coldly. "I'll be back before dawn."

My dream of having a normal family and a pure life had been crushed. I lacked the self-confidence and self-respect to kick Kenny to the curb. I lacked the vision and higher purpose to restrain myself and stop dancing. I accepted my defeat. I just wasn't sure I was going to admit it to my parents.

Happily ever after was officially over for me.

Serena rode with me to Ypsilanti, Michigan. There was an amateur night at a club there that paid three hundred dollars for a couple of hours. I was officially back to work.

I told myself I was doing it for the money.

But the reality was I danced because on stage, in the club, was where I felt most in control.

❧

I danced on and off at Déjà Vu during the year that followed. I was what they called a freelancer. I had to pay the club an extra fifty dollars every shift to dance, because I wasn't full time. It allowed me to stay in school part-time and not draw any suspicion from my family, but dancing gave me extra cash, which I stashed in shoeboxes under my bed. I wasn't going to let the industry inhale and swallow me whole this time. Kenny stayed with me because I was making good money and, well, because I was a Donewald. His junior year, he tore his ACL in a football game. By his senior year, his dream of ever playing in the NFL was over.

I no longer saw Kenny as my boyfriend or my partner. I saw him as my positive enabler. "The Manny," I labeled and renamed him. He was more of a male nanny than a companion to me. I was, for the most part, steering clear of drugs and alcohol. I wanted to be a success for 'Kaylah. She was my life now. It was just she and I . . . and the Manny.

The Manny kept running around with other women, and I kept running back to the club for adoration. He was a big player, but Bailey was bigger.

It was beyond dysfunctional.

Was this the closest thing to love with a man that I was going to have? The men in the club worshipped me when I danced, but they didn't want their fantasy girl changing stinky diapers and lactating. And there wasn't going to be a *normal* good guy who was going to be able to get over the fact that I was a stripper. I had trapped myself.

It was a slow night in the club and I just didn't want

to be there. I wanted to be home. I had a midterm coming up and I felt the tug of motherhood calling me home. Something felt wrong. I left and came into my apartment at 12:30 a.m. It was dark and quiet except for the faint sound of the Manny, snoring. I set my bag down gently by the front door and I checked on 'Kaylah in her bed. She was fine. My next impulse was to simply sleep. Hoping to crawl under my sheets and get three or four hours of rest, I stood looking at my bed and saw the Manny asleep next to another woman.

Normally he wouldn't have been so stupid. He'd have had her out of my house before midnight, knowing I'd be home by three or four a.m.

His dark afro contrasted with my white pillowcase. He was crashed out with a naked college girl. I wondered how many others had shared my bed while I was working. I didn't think my heart could feel anything for him, but it was heavy and I wanted to cry. Just cry it all away.

How long are you going to put up with this? Bailey hissed inside my head.

I picked up the phone to call my dad, and something snapped inside me like a rubber band that got stretched too far. Instead of dialing my parents, I hammered the receiver into the Manny's skull and cracked it wide open.

Blood poured onto my bed.

"You shot me!" He awoke grabbing the side of his head, screaming at me, and then proceeded to shout every curse word known to man.

"You're bleeding everywhere." The chickie looked at me nervously.

"I wish I would have shot you." I now fully

understood crimes of passion and how women or men can kill their cheating partners from emotional overload.

"Call nine-one-one!" he said to the chickie. "Call nine-one-one."

"Call nine-one-one, call nine-one-one." Bailey mocked him like he was a baby.

Then I fake jump-juked at her with my arms stretched out like I was coming for her, then stopped and just laughed. "Boo!" she retreated, cowering with my covers pulled up around her body.

"Get out of my house!" I punctuated my marching orders with obscenities.

I calmly went to the kitchen, pulled out a cigarette, and lit it. I sat in my chair, with my feet on my table, and started counting my money from the night. When the police officers arrived, they asked me why I had hit him. I crushed out my cigarette in the ashtray and simply replied, "Because I couldn't take it anymore."

Inside the squad car, after being cuffed, I questioned the officer as to why he had to arrest me and started to plead my case.

"Be lucky I'm only charging you with a domestic," he said. "That's a misdemeanor. I could've charged you with assault with intent to do bodily harm, which is a felony."

I sat back and got quiet.

I went to jail for a domestic assault charge.

My daughter never woke up and my brother came to take care of her; I think he was really there to take care of Kenny, but Bailey had done that for him.

I spent seventeen hours in a jail cell, which smelled like sweaty shoes and curdled milk. My dad came and picked me up the next morning after Kenny dropped the charges.

"You have a daughter now." It was all my dad could say to me as he dropped me off at my apartment. He had gone from passive-aggressive to angry, and he was late to give the eulogy at a friend's funeral. *Great timing, Bailey.*

"I know," I shamefully replied to him as I shut the car door.

Kenny moved out after the incident. I saw him occasionally when he came to visit 'Kaylah, but after I had skull-whacked him, he comprehended that I was more dangerous than him. He moved back to Pittsburgh.

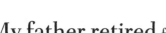

My father retired from coaching in the spring of 2000, and my goal was to retire from dancing as soon as I could finish college. A college degree was my light at the end of the tunnel. This time I was really, really quitting drugs. I had too much homework to do, and I was raising 'Kaylah alone. She was walking, talking, and full of two-year-old energy. At night I would wrap my arms around her in my bed and spoon her tight. I would press my hand on her chest and feel her heart beating in my hand. The world, my world, expanded and contracted with her every inhale and exhale.

Her big hair and eyes and constant inquisitive babbling made her the perfect distraction from the darkness of the clubs. She was an easy little girl who was filled with joy, and her joy made me joyous. I plugged my dark soul into hers and she kept me alive and motivated. She was the light. No matter how much

I had screwed up myself, I wasn't going to screw her up.

I worked once or twice a week, just to buy diapers and formula and keep food in the house, and put a little extra in the shoeboxes under the bed.

Sure, I was a stripper, but I was taking care of 'Kaylah and getting my degree. I balanced the depravity with domesticity.

When I'd go to the club, I would hire a babysitter, dance sober, get my money, and get out. The culture of sex for sale was not a shock wave to my system anymore.

That's when you know you're really screwed up.

During my last week in the club I ran directly into one of the largest financial donors for the university. He knew me, and I knew him. All I could think was that he was going to tell my family that I was dancing. He still had ways of getting messages to my father. Although my actions couldn't jeopardize my father's career anymore, this man could sure jeopardize me and 'Kaylah. He was going to blow my cover. My parents had no idea I was living a double life again. They believed I was getting As in my classes, cocktail waitressing, taking 'Kaylah to the park, and being a decent mother. Which for the most part, I was.

My fingernail gently ran through the donor's ginger-colored hair and said, "I'm Bailey. Would you like a lap dance?"

He was momentarily stunned but quick to play along. This little game ignited his fantasy flame. He wasn't special. It worked on him as it worked on all the others. *Sick, cheap-trick old geezer.*

"Yes, Bailey, I do," he gulped.

Bailey lap danced for Mr. Big Donor all night long. Bailey tied and twisted him up in his own personal perversion. He would never be able to tell anyone who he had seen, where he had been, or what had been done to him. She shoved his own dark suit sock of sin into his mouth and electric-taped it shut.

It was all under control.

In August 2001, I received a postcard in the mail saying, *Congratulations, Western Michigan University Graduate. Your diploma will be arriving shortly.* I had fulfilled my requirements for my degree in family and consumer science. I skipped the hoopla of the graduation ceremony for a private shindig with 'Kaylah.

"We did it, pumpkin. I graduated."

She clapped her hands at me. "Yay! Mommy!" My three-year-old little celebratory wingman.

The lease on my apartment was up that summer, but I hadn't planned past graduation about what to do next. I did know I wanted out of Kalamazoo. I had several thousand dollars from the club and had stopped dancing; I kept my promise to myself. Time to go legitimate. I didn't have any lifestyle to hide from my family. I put my furniture in storage, and 'Kaylah and I went to stay at my parents' house until I could find a proper job.

My daughter loved being with her grandparents. They had retired to a house on a lake in the country. She could swim, go on their boat, and be a normal country kid outside. They showed her both a male and a female role model that loved each other, and she had me. It was a good place for her. They had built an addition onto their house that stood as large guest quarters that gave us privacy on their mini compound but still attached us to them. It was a physical residence that metaphorically mimicked my life. They were happy to have us and I was happy to be there.

Here was my snafu: What exactly do you put on your resume if you've been a stripper? Hobbies include pole tricks? I hadn't had a steady job (other than at the school in the athletic department) for three years. In Kalamazoo, there wasn't a legit person who was going to take a chance on me. Not anymore. I needed a new city.

I contacted my old friend Aliyah. We had met back during my suburban boarding-school days at LFA. She now lived in Chicago. She had her undergraduate degree from Northwestern and was cocktail waitressing at night and interning at an advertising company during the day. I asked her if I could stay with her for a week, check out the city, and try to find a job. I was coming off a high of completing college and keeping it together, and I felt like I could do anything.

Convincing my parents that I was willing to start at the bottom and work my way up wasn't easy. Yes, I believed I could be a normal graduate with a degree who was having a tough time finding a gig in Kalamazoo, but they didn't support my moving to Chicago with my daughter.

Living in the country and having their help with 'Kaylah had made me peaceful and given them their daughter back. They didn't want to lose me again.

They had been along for the ride during the series of

train wrecks that had gotten me to this place, and they wanted more stability for me, for 'Kaylah. They wanted me to be realistic with my daughter. They wanted me in Kalamazoo so they could help me with her. Their desire came from a place of love, but all I heard was their trying to control me again, and naysaying.

This only challenged me more.

The fact was, I was a twenty-three-year-old living their sixty-year-old lives. They were simple, kind people who played cards and board games and knit. They didn't watch cable television or have big fancy parties. So much of their life had been spent in the public eye that they cherished the quiet and tranquillity.

I wanted more out of life than the "golden years."

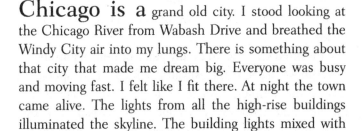

Chicago is a grand old city. I stood looking at the Chicago River from Wabash Drive and breathed the Windy City air into my lungs. There is something about that city that made me dream big. Everyone was busy and moving fast. I felt like I fit there. At night the town came alive. The lights from all the high-rise buildings illuminated the skyline. The building lights mixed with streetlights and car lights created a magically colored playground.

Aliyah lived on the South Side of Chicago in a diverse neighborhood called Hyde Park. Her flat was two blocks away from where Louis Farrakhan, the Nation of Islam leader, kept a swanky pad on a corner lot.

My first twenty-four hours in the city, I pounded the

pavement, putting in over fifteen job applications. I tried to get any job that would get me out of Kalamazoo, be it waitressing, cocktailing, being a hostess, or working at the Gap, it didn't matter; I just needed a starter job. My only stipulation was that I wanted to work at night so I could spend time with 'Kaylah during the day. At night a babysitter could stay with her while she slept. I wanted to be with her. I wanted to raise my daughter.

My second night at Aliyah's place, she convinced me to go out on the town. She took me to a few hip-hop clubs and we danced and drank and laughed until four a.m. It felt good to blow off some steam and just be a twenty-three-year-old having fun in a club. At sunrise we went to a downtown breakfast spot called Tempo. She and I reminisced about high school and life as we gobbled up stacks of maple pancakes and bacon. I never told her about my dancing. I just didn't want anyone to know. I didn't want people associating me with stripping, or my dad, or any of the shame that I kept inside.

I wanted Chicago to be my place of new beginnings.

Almost asleep on Aliyah's couch, I desperately missed the simple presence of 'Kaylah. My heart ached for her and with every second that passed, I knew Chicago was where she and I were meant to grow up. It was a place where no one cared who I was, or stared at me because I was a coach's ex-stripper daughter with a biracial baby out of wedlock.

When nothing materialized at the end of Friday, a sense of dread hit me, as I knew the timer had run out on my week of parole.

I called my parents that morning to check up on

'Kaylah.

"She's perfect!" my mom cooed.

I made the mistake of telling her that I had filled out applications all week for jobs and my heels were blistered. I shared my frustration and depression that nothing had come to fruition.

"Just come home. We'll figure something out." She tried to turn on the GPS for my life again.

Instead of feeling relief, I got angry.

"I just need a couple of extra days."

She sighed. "Okay, Anny," and hung up the phone.

Two more days of eight-hour searches and nothing. I had no idea that every girl in the Midwest caught Chicago big-city fever after college.

Sunday morning, when most people are finding hope in churches around the city, I was at my most desperate. I didn't want to go back to life in Michigan except for my daughter. I had to get her and get out. All of a sudden Kalamazoo felt like a leash around my neck that was getting tighter and tighter.

I had heard of a strip club in Chicago called Crazy Horse Too. It had a reputation of being one of the best gentlemen's clubs in the country.

On my way out of town I thought, *Maybe just for a little while to get enough money.* I could tell my family that I was cocktail waitressing so they wouldn't worry.

It would only be temporary.

~⊷~

Crazy Horse Too was a ten-minute drive

north of Downtown on Kingsbury and North Avenue. It looked like the Temple of Artemis: a white building with various carvings of Greek naked goddesses set between pillars in the front. Giant Greek-style lettering read CRAZY HORSE TOO and underneath was written A GENTLEMEN'S CLUB.

I pulled my Explorer up to the valet stand, where a young Hispanic man wearing the establishment's signature red jacket and black pants said, "Welcome to the Crazy Horse."

Parked in front of the club were a Mercedes, a Jaguar, and a Bentley. I chuckled. The valets always parked the best cars out front to advertise the caliber of their clientele.

In my platform boots, black jeans, and short sexy tank, I pulled open the exterior doors only to find another set of doors with a doorman wearing an all-black suit standing guard.

"Welcome to Crazy Horse. May I see your ID, please?"

To dance or to even enter the establishment, you had to be at least twenty-one years old, because they served booze. There are no underage girls or clients in the place. No exceptions. I showed him my license. He smiled and handed it back. I walked toward the check-in desk where a woman in her forties, also in a nice suit jacket and white blouse, sat behind a large lobby-type counter.

"Welcome to Crazy Horse. It's twenty dollars."

"I'd like to speak to the manager, please."

She picked up a walkie-talkie.

"Mr. Mike, could you please come to the front?"

"Thank you."

"No problem, sweetheart."

In a finely tailored suit, with silver and black hair, Mr. Mike came through the doors.

"How can I help you?" His teeth were perfectly white and straight when he smiled. He was handsome, with character lines.

"I want to work here."

His blue eyes scanned my outfit and he sniffed. "We're not hiring."

Play it cool, Bailey said inside me.

"Mike, is it?"

"Yes."

"Mike, I'll make you more money than anyone in this place." *Whoa! Slow down, Bailey.*

"You think so? 'Cause this isn't Iowa."

"I'm not from Iowa, I just graduated from Michigan. And before that I graduated from Lake Forest Academy."

"A debutante girl who wants to try dancing?"

"Not try. I am a top moneymaker at one of the largest clubs in Michigan."

"What's your name, debutante?"

"Bailey."

"Okay, Bailey. Let's have a talk."

I followed Mr. Mike through two black curtains and into the club.

Big. It's big and bloodred.

There was red furniture, red carpet, and red walls. Where there wasn't red, the place had gold framing everywhere. Gold railings, gold-backed chairs, gold table trims. I gazed at the huge octagon stage at the center. Two sets of stairs leading up, with more gold handrails. It resembled a high-end burlesque showplace, not any strip club that I had even seen before.

Mike made a quick left, went up five steps, and pulled open a heavy door to the VIP room. He held it and waited for me to pass. Inside was mostly empty. It was too early for the place to be going yet. Girls were just getting to work for the first shift. The VIP room couldn't have held over thirty people. Fifteen customers and fifteen dancers. There was no smashing people in here.

"Have a seat. I'll be back to chat."

"Thank you."

"Would you like a drink? I'll have someone bring something for you."

"Sparkling water, if you have it. Perrier would be terrific." I tried to sound sophisticated.

He left and I looked out the two-way mirror onto the club below. A dancer in a black, silky, floor-length dress with slits up the side, cut to her belly, was parading on the stage. She wasn't really dancing, more sashaying.

She's not working very hard, Bailey thought.

She made the turn at the end of the stage and peeled off a shoulder piece of her dress. I scrutinized her moves. She was now almost naked.

She was down to almost nothing, even though her G-string, by my previous standards, was ginormous. This was not the dental floss that other clubs required. She could have been a naughty public relations executive dressed for the annual Christmas party in her skirt suit and garter belts. Her breasts were all the same color, with something covering her nipples, giving the illusion that she was plastic and not real.

The dancers around the room were all clad in *haute couture* stripper gowns. They were flawless, pulled from the pages of the Victoria's Secret catalog, not the Kappa

Kappa Gamma strippers that I was used to working with at the party clubs. I could see a dancer in a gold lamé jersey dress drinking champagne on a couch listening to her client. Her long, tan legs were stretched out and demurely crossed at the ankles. There were no poles or cheesy tables to climb onto here.

These women weren't flaunting but flirting. It was a completely unusual vibe.

Crazy Horse dancers were dressed like invitees at a black-tie event at the annual Adler Planetarium fund-raiser with the mayor, or like monied bond traders whose dresses were cut just a tad too low. They were finely manicured American Girl dolls, not the cheap Barbies from Target.

Time for Bailey to switch gears. Time for Bailey to go from cheerleader to socialite committee member. *That's easy enough.* I knew how my mother's fancy friends behaved. I had always understood the rules. I just never followed them.

Mike came back into the room. He handed me my glass of sparkling water.

"Thank you." I took a polite sip and set the water down on a coaster.

"Five hundred dollars an hour for a VIP to set foot in this room with one of my girls."

I tried not to look impressed. "What's an average take-home pay?"

"One-thousand-dollar minimum after payout."

"Sounds like one of my parents' nights out." Bailey was smooth and steady, drinking her bubbly water.

"You're from where?"

"The Midwest. But we traveled everywhere. I bounced

around at a couple of boarding schools. I'm settling into Chicago."

I crossed my legs at the ankles. "I can only work weekends. Nights."

Bailey knew she had the job.

"Girls don't tell me when they work."

"I'm not a typical girl."

"You went to Lake Forest Academy?"

"Graduated from LFA, and college, and yes, I did cotillion." Okay, cotillion was a lie.

"Are those real?" He was asking about my breasts.

"Everything about me is real."

"I'll give you Friday, day. Saturday and Sunday nights."

"I can start next week. I need to tie up a few loose ends."

He just laughed at Bailey's assuredness.

"How about you come in tomorrow? Tie those loose ends up faster."

"I need to get my daughter."

His face changed, almost shocked.

"I'll be back next week."

"Okay, debutante. I'll see you next Friday. Be here an hour before your shift at eight."

I stood up and held out my hand. "It was nice chatting with you, Mr. Mike."

Bailey could be good.

He took my hand in his. "Well, you've got the talk down. We'll see about the rest."

I walked out of the VIP room and looked over the place and thought, *These girls have nothing on me.* But that was Bailey, not me, doing the talking.

I drove back to Kalamazoo, believing it would only take me a few months to make enough money to get going in Chicago. To keep me and 'Kaylah afloat until I could get something that paid me for keeping my clothes on. If I worked two nights a week, I'd have the rest of the week free to land something better, more respectable. I didn't want to go back to dancing for good; it was just a means to an end.

I was getting so good at lying to myself.

❧

McKaylah and I were just finishing breakfast at my parents'. The phone rang over and over and over. I was chasing her around, trying to tug off her pajama top and get her into the Chicago Cubs T-shirt that I had bought her.

Again the phone rang. "Hello," I answered out of breath.

"Anny!" My mother sounded frantic. She was never frantic. "Have you seen the television?"

My first painful thought was that my father had died. "No, Mom. What's going on?"

I scrambled up the stairs with 'Kaylah running behind me.

"I'm on my way."

"On your way? What's going on?"

Then I saw the World Trade Center on the television. They kept showing an airplane flying into it. It didn't seem real. It looked like a movie.

"Mom?" I was still holding the phone. "What is happening?"

"Our country is under attack."

McKaylah began to cry. "What's happening, Mommy?" She couldn't possibly understand the magnitude of the event. I didn't understand it.

"I don't know, baby girl."

I pulled my daughter onto my lap. I made her face me and not the television. With her legs straddling my hips and her arms tight around my neck, I just held her as close as possible.

When the second plane hit the other tower, it was almost prophetic for my life to come. Just when I thought the disaster was over, it was about to get much worse.

I started dancing in Chicago at Crazy Horse three days after September 11.

chapter fifteen
DECONSTRUCTED IN CHICAGO

*Some strippers have been in it for decades. The median
age is between 23 and 24 . . . but some strippers slug
it out WAY longer than that. The five-year mark is
usually the point of no return of stripping . . . get out
then, or buy stock in a company that manufactures
nine-inch heels.*

Sam Greenspan, "11 Eye-opening Statistics About
Strippers," 11 Points, http://www.11points.com/Dating-
Sex/11_Eye-Opening_Statistics_About_Strippers, 2011

*It did something to my psyche when I viewed my
self-worth according to my sexuality, which became
measured by dollar bills.*

Anny

Our orangish-red and crème, peke-
faced longhair Persian cat, Stella, complemented the mix
of sophisticated lush fabrics and Restoration Hardware
decor in our pre–Second World War brownstone building
in Chicagoland's Hyde Park. I paid for the place in cash:
thick stacks of hundred-dollar bills as the deposit, first
and last month's rent, plus an extra three hundred to

grease the manager's palm and make sure everything in our new home was installed and up-to-date. Working at the Crazy Horse Too, I was flush with cash, and I still had my days free to spend with 'Kaylah exploring the city.

McKaylah and I had VIP passes to our new favorite spot: the Shedd Aquarium. We walked past the large windows inside, showcasing Lake Michigan's vibrant and extraordinary beauty: sapphire-blue water sprinkled with golden sunshine and the white sails of small leisure boats. We touched and learned about the aquarium's thousands of aquatic animals during a few shows and meandered through every exhibit from the coral reef to the jellyfish. 'Kaylah's giggles while feeling a starfish for the first time and watching the beluga whales consumed me. My shoulders relaxed and my lungs expanded fully when I was with her. As we exited, I squeezed her hand extra tight and smiled; I knew that we were finally home.

On Friday before work, she and I would enjoy a mellow morning of French toast and bacon and a leisurely stroll through the park before I started to mentally transform into Bailey for the night. At three p.m. my babysitter, Eliza, a lovely Polish fifty-year-old woman, would come in the door with a baked lamb dish with boiled eggs and a beet salad for McKaylah's dinner. She always had her Tupperware filled with sauerkraut, meat, potatoes, or savory sweet cheese curds and cherries. When I finished flat-ironing my hair, the physical and mental transformation was nearly complete. I grabbed my Caboodle and purse as I kissed 'Kaylah good night.

"Mommy loves you."

"Hug, hug, hug!" she would demand.

I would take her in my arms and squeeze her so tight I might have broken her in half.

"Biggggggggerrrr."

"You bigger," I answered, as she embraced me back.

"Be good for Pani Eliza." I turned to Eliza. "My shift is from four to ten, but I may stay a couple of extra hours." Because I'd been making high dollars in my six-hour shifts, Mike usually kept me on an extra two hours for the regular, big money clients who rolled in late.

Eliza took 'Kaylah in her arms and kissed her cheeks.

"Nei ma problemu. Don't worry. She's *mój anioł."* Despite Eliza's heavily accented English, I always understood that McKaylah would be well taken care of while staying with her jubilant Eastern European "grandmother."

When I pulled up to the Crazy Horse Too valet station, I tossed my keys to Chuck with a wink. Pressing a twenty in his palm as I breezed in the doors, I passed Big Bill the doorman and Nadia, one of the Russian ladies working the desk, on my way to the dressing room. Once inside, I saw that Maggie, our house mom, had already settled in. Her small table was stocked with various sundries and an enchilada casserole for the ladies to eat. Good house moms in gentlemen's clubs have everything a girl could need, from body spray to Ibuprofens to dinner. At the end of the night most girls, depending on if they ate or not, would tip her out around forty dollars. It's a pretty decent haul when you multiply this by, on average, sixty girls. I think Maggie used to be a dancer, but she'd gotten too old and found a niche and satisfaction in this new role.

The club was already crowded and girls were getting ready in silence. There was no camaraderie here with the dancers. It made me slightly miss Serena and Jill, as at least I knew those two had my back if something went wrong on the floor. The ladies in here only had their own backs. Unlike Déjà Vu, where dancers mocked their clients, no one in here dared talk trash about their regulars, as at any time the girl with the locker next to you could use your words against you and steal your guy. The currency was too bulky and the hours invested were too many to toy around talking trash. A girl with a regular could cash out over two grand from one client for four hours of chatting, listening, conning, and very little dancing. It's cold, conniving, and cutthroat, but that is how you make the real money.

Pauline, a dressmaker, was set up in the corner. With her fabric samples spread about, she took a dancer's hip measurement for a new gown. Pauline came into the club twice a week with new designs to sell the girls and made them specialty high-end runway stripper knockoffs.

I opened my locker and pulled out the deep purple, slinky floor-length backless dress that was next in line on my rack. I had different dresses and catsuits that I alternated during the week. Each night I took home the one I wore, handwashed it, and brought it back. At any time I had five to ten killer frocks to work in.

We all had to have our makeup professionally applied, and there were already two girls ahead of me waiting for the makeup artist. From liner to lashes, they didn't skimp here. I decided to get my pasties started while I waited.

The club was filled with top-shelf, overpriced booze that was meant to gouge the men. Illinois state law has a no-nudity clause for establishments that serve alcohol. Crazy Horse Too complied with the law but still kept things, ahem, titillating, by requiring every dancer to cover her nipples, making us look like nonhuman Barbie dolls. We all did this by painting liquid latex over our most delicate parts and creating one skin color for our entire body. Because I was allergic to the latex, it irritated my areolas so badly I had extreme pain, dryness, and sometimes bleeding.

I could see twenty other girls like me getting ready. No one was speaking other than to exchange a polite "please" and "thank you" and "pass the liquid laxtex." I'd become more and more aware of their lack of spirit with every mechanical air kiss and faux "how are you?"

Being sober in there was arduous, as I was no longer disoriented and could perceive the numbness of it all. I saw the stains and bruises and deadness. As much as these dancers were raking it in and storing it in mini vaults, you'd think they would be full of life, but they weren't. This place had turned them into self-protective, robotic moneymakers and manipulators who had learned how to exist without any real connection. I was noticeably different from the other girls as there was still a hint of life inside me. I was not sure if that was pieces of Anny shining like starlight through tiny holes in Bailey's bleak cloak or if the pureness and simplicity of McKaylah's influence in my life kept me grounded and positive, but I had yet to adopt their blank stares. The veteran girls were gorgeous, incredibly gifted swindlers who meandered with an invisible plastic bag of aloofness over their heads, unless of course they were with a client. Then the bag came off and I'm not sure who came out.

I shudder at the thought of what would have become of me if not for 'Kaylah. I know how easily and permanently I would have been sucked into the cyclone of insidious insecurity. As it was, as I sat in there night after night, I could feel I was slowly becoming no different from them. I wasn't sure how I was ultimately going to continue to survive in both worlds.

"You need a massage later, Bailey?" Jamie walked past me with her massage table.

"No. Thanks."

I didn't want to spend one extra minute in this place.

Jamie set up her table in the back so after a long night, or sometimes before, if girls were sore or high, they could have fifteen-minute relaxation massages for forty dollars. Jamie was the only person that got to lay a hand on anyone in this place.

There was absolutely no touching the customers or the customers touching the girls. My second night dancing, I tried to balance on a client, and I placed my hand on his shoulder. One of the bouncers saw me and reported me to Mike. My first offense cost me fifty dollars and I was told that if there was a second offense, I'd be out. There were no third chances here. The money was too big for the rules in the club to be broken.

I batted my fake lashes and reviewed my makeup in the mirror. My wild blond locks were ironed flat, bringing my thick ends almost to the middle of my back. Ready to roll.

In my six-inch heels, I descended the stairs carefully, slowly. When I passed the bar, I longed for a seven and seven cocktail. *Just have one*, Bailey taunted me, and I ignored her.

I continued along the bar to a small hallway, almost secret. The alcove where I stopped reminded me of one of my hiding places in my dad's stadium when I would pretend to be Anne Frank in the secret Annex. Everyone in here had Anne in them, running and hiding from something, they just didn't know it. I shook off thoughts of my family. I looked up at the camera above the doorframe and buzzed the button on the wall. The knob clicked and unlocked. I walk inside.

The manager's office wasn't big. There were two desks, a couple of safes, a small refrigerator, and a wall full of video screens. The first time I was in there, Mike showed me every angle that each camera in the club could see.

"There is nothing that isn't shot or recorded that can't be used as evidence in the club, even when you're in the toilet. Remember that." This information wasn't meant to be a scare tactic. He said it like my father would. Just a heads-up. No jerking around.

Every girl had to check in with Mike before starting her shift. He was the gatekeeper to the floor and was responsible for making sure part of our breasts were covered and our thongs were big enough. Tonight he sat with his leg on a chair, his ankle gun clearly visible for everyone to see.

"What's wrong with your leg?" I looked at him.

"Sliding into home plate this weekend." He took off an ice pack from his knee. Mike was a former Chicago police officer. He had a gun under his jacket to match the one under his pant leg.

"You guys make your rec league play-offs?"

"Jag-off scored two runs on us in the ninth."

"Too bad."

"You covered?"

I pulled down my top to show him my breasts. Then I turned around and pulled up my dress, showing him my T-bar and doing a quick turn.

"Nice spin, debutante."

"Thanks."

"You're good to go."

I liked Mike, as he was not disgusting. He was doing his job and he was not impacted by the hundreds of pairs of boobs he saw on a weekly basis. He was a Roman Catholic who talked about his wife and eight kids as if he managed the club at the Four Seasons Hotel and not this place.

The red DJ booth blended in with the red velvet walls of the club. The DJ here wasn't a "hype guy." There was no hitting the siren lights and calling for girls to get up on tables "two for thirty." It was not that kind of place. But we all checked in with him for rotation. Some things in every club were the same.

"Bailey, I got you following Karma," he said.

I almost laughed at the ironic nature of his statement.

Karma was a stunning dancer who looked like Halle Berry. Her body was impeccable—not juiced up with silicone or Botox—and she could rock her short, sassy haircut just as well as one of her long, sexy wigs. Karma had showed me the ropes on my first night and was the closest thing to a female human being in this place. She was the only girl who actually spoke to me in a way that didn't sound rehearsed. She was a top moneymaker, so while in the VIP room, I soaked up her moves like a sponge. I'd studied her hand gestures and the way she could lick her full lips to arouse her unsuspecting client. Mr. Mike and the other managers fed her regulars from the Chicago Bulls and Chicago Bears. I'd watched her count out stacks of hundred-dollar bills knowing that she was taking home over two thousand a night.

I came in at four p.m. to be ready for what was usually a rush of Chicago Board of Trade guys who stopped in for a happy hour at five p.m. before going home to their wives and families. Coming in early ensured that I could make an extra five hundred off the yuppies from the trading floor, who couldn't spend, snort, and swallow excess fast enough. They practically sprinted from their historic skyscraper in the Downtown Loop area, a building topped with a thirty-foot statue of the Roman goddess Ceres, to our suburban bacchanal. You would assume that losing millions of dollars in the trader pit would have curbed their appetite for corruption, but it just made them easy targets in need of validation in the VIP room.

Another wave of clientele came in around eight p.m. These were the preparty guys; they came to Crazy Horse Too to set a lucky tone for their evening, but it ain't lucky if you have to pay for it, you know? After ten p.m., a steady flow of "gentlemen" arrived looking for their regular naked therapist.

Huh? Gentlemen? There's an oxymoron.

Bailey needed a cocktail.

Coming onto the floor, I was surprised to see two flashy-dressed younger men sitting at a table near the stage.

Two things a dancer learns quickly: check out the shoes and watches. Wealthy men don't wear dirty Nikes and Swatches. The first man, F.S., was too tan and had on Gucci loafers and a gold and diamond Rolex watch.

They motioned for me to join them. I hadn't had a chance for Bailey to fully kick into gear and wasn't prepared for the insidious nature of their personas. I pulled up a small, circular soft stool, perched on it perfectly, and displayed a sultry smile.

"How are you doing tonight?"

F.S. paused long enough to take his eyes off his text. "You're good just sitting there."

But it wasn't a compliment. He was telling me to shut my mouth. His boy, who was dressed more casually but still dripping with three-carat diamond studs in his earlobes, laughed.

"I like your shirt. Is that custom?"

Still nothing.

I sat bored. Now I really wanted a drink.

I don't sit and stay like a good poodle who is on display for the money boys from Miami. Bailey was getting heated.

"F.S.? Are those your initials?" I looked at the engraving on his cuff links. "I'm Bailey."

My eyes shifted to a group of traders coming in the door.

I'm done with Mr. Personality and his sidekick. I stood up.

"Where you think you're going, blondie? I told you, you look pretty sitting there."

"I have to work." I tried to remain charming. "Do you work?"

He set his BlackBerry down and said, "I'm a drug dealer."

He was playing me for a fool. This man didn't deal drugs. I know those men. Now I was insulted.

"And I am a librarian."

His one-man audience laughed at my joke.

But I didn't amuse F.S.

I walked back to the dressing room. He had gotten under my protective layer with his ambivalence. I may be a stripper but I'm not some Al Pacino from *Scarface* wannabe's pet.

Karma was waiting for her latex to dry as I pretended to retouch my lashes in the mirror.

She and I caught eye contact but I wasn't about to tell her anything. Not in there. Not when other girls could hear me. When I headed back out, Karma walked with me toward the office.

"You okay?" she asked.

"That guy's an idiot."

She quickly turned on the stair to me.

"The tan guy?"

"Yes."

"Bailey, that's . . ."

He was a platinum-selling artist. He wasn't a gangster or a one-hit wonder and certainly not a drug dealer.

"I don't care who he is. He's still an idiot."

The girls in there were impressed with prestigious labels and brands, but I had seen them my entire life.

Whether the money came from Michael Jackson or a lotto winner, it was all the same to me.

I purposely avoided F.S. all night. He sat in the VIP room with three girls most of the evening. He spent over ten grand. I played with one of my regulars from the trading floor and made one of the biggest nights in there. I was fueled by his arrogance. I didn't need any music moguls to hustle in there. Hustling was just hustling.

Two weeks later F.S. was back in the club when Mike approached me.

"F.S. wants you to sit with him in the VIP room. He's been in the back corner with a group of executives from the label. He had one of his guys purposely ask for you."

I started laughing cynically, and said, "For what?"

"Bailey, he is a lot of money to the club."

"Pick someone else. The guy's an idiot."

"He picked you."

Owned. You're always owned.

I was reluctant, but I agreed to one drink. You couldn't say no. Plus, my feet hurt tonight as I was breaking in a new pair of shoes.

I could use the sitting time as a break, I conceded.

As I approached the table, his face changed from arrogant to slightly inviting. He stood up and the other men at the table noticed.

"We got off on a bad foot." I could barely hear him over the music. "Have some champagne."

⌘

Over the course of the next thirty days F.S. began inviting me to private music industry parties in high-rise penthouses, the studio, and at his three-million-dollar home on Lake Shore Drive. For a night, the "F.S. company" would pay girls like me a grand or two to show up and look pretty and make sure the guys had fun. Fun meant talking to them. Listening to them. Laughing at their stupid jokes. Girls from Crazy Horse were not for sale, just window dressing. At this point I had danced at the club and been schooled on investing tips by Fred Durst. I had watched Pauly Shore whip it out of his pants and get tossed from the club. I wondered if Bill Maher's audience knew he liked strippers who would debate atheism with him. After all, we were in a nonexistent hell together. Each one of the celebrities had their own niche woman. I had watched them, along with the Harlem Globetrotters, the Chicago Bears, and anyone who was in town to play the Bulls, meander in and drop their dough.

They can deny their perversion all they want—as Mike said, it's all on tape.

I was with McKaylah at the zoo the first time F.S. sent me a non-work-related text from his private phone: "Hope you're good. In San Fran. Be back Friday." I didn't respond. Having his voice, just nine short words on a text message, creep into *my* real world with *my* daughter made me wince. I had kept Bailey and Anny completely distinct in Chicago.

F.S. would eventually become one of the many clients I would meet out of the club. They were emotionless relationships that had to be managed with laser precision. This wasn't *Pretty Woman*. The men paid me for my affection, and whether the sex and their company was enjoyable to me or not was irrelevant.

He wasn't as sleazy as some of the others, and I found his infatuation with me entertaining. Still, he was a customer. He would never know my real name. The portrait of a stripper having a real relationship with a customer has a limited perspective. There's no romance in stripping or prostitution. You're owned by your own addiction to money or drugs or a rich man or pimp who keeps you like an animal. The size of the cage doesn't matter.

Don't think that's love. Bailey fueled my anxiety tank. *This guy is only one of many. You deserve a golden ticket. Look what we're doing here. Focus on the prize. Money. Money. Money.*

Was I insane?

Bailey justified it for me: *So what if it's not what society deems appropriate. What do they know? Frauds. Most of the rule makers are frauds. I know this because I see them in the club. I see them with their drool, all cracked out, facial twitch driven by unresolved childhood issues. You're going to judge us? Me? Get in line. The back of the line.*

I dreamed that night that McKaylah and I were in a hot air balloon about to take off. She was wildly clapping with excitement. As the basket lifted off the ground, I could see all the spectators below watching us. Then the balloon caught fire and I was frozen with fear. McKaylah cried, and because I was unable to respond, because I failed to console her, Bailey jumped to attention, grabbed her, and threw her out of the basket.

I screamed.

Then I realized 'Kaylah was floating safety down, and then the balloon whizzed like a rocket into the sky, engulfed in flames.

I woke up panting with a deep despair.

chapter sixteen
THE BOMBING OF CHICAGO

There are an estimated 400,000 strippers in the United States, raking in over $3.1 billion for clubs across the country.

Statistic Brain, http://www.statisticbrain.com/strip-club-statistics/, 2012

I believed the pursuit of happiness was money. But when I attained the money I wanted, all it did was spotlight my misery, as the very thing I was chasing wasn't real.

Anny

I tried to shelter McKaylah from the dark underbelly of my life. My mother had pegged her an old soul from birth and she was right. Just four years old, my daughter was funny, intuitive, and caring. It was becoming harder and harder to hide my job from her, as it was becoming harder and harder for me to skip back and forth between the realm of darkness and absurd fantasy that was the club and the real-world sunshine that was my life with her. The more access and extravagance that I attained as a stripper, the brighter McKaylah's light would become.

Her purity and milestone moments highlighted the false highs I enjoyed from money, parties, and stage worship. I wanted her to have all the luxuries that dancing could provide, but I didn't want her to be anything like me. I struggled with my own ability to balance motherhood and life in the sex industry. I started to drink again, only this time in much larger glasses. It was a choice that wounded me deeply later in life.

On my nights off I would take McKaylah to my parents' lake house in Michigan. She missed them desperately, but I had a love-hate relationship with the state. So many of my personal problems had happened so publicly there and so much was still emotionally unresolved. During my drives home, at the one-mile marker I was longing for the comfort of family and all that was familiar, but with every little green sign that brought me closer, I'd grip the steering wheel a little tighter. I could feel my tenacious attitude coming to the surface; I was ready to fight at a moment's provocation. On the other hand, the lake house was the only place that I could sleep for four or five hours straight.

"How's the job search going?" my mother asked me as we sat in white Adirondack chairs, drinking lemonade and watching the waves lapping at 'Kaylah's ankles.

"I'm making good money cocktailing."

Liar!

I'm becoming a better and better liar.

"You can't cocktail your way through life." My father had quietly walked out of the house, and I didn't hear him approach. Did his voice cut through the serenity of the lake or my lie? Or both? He made his way to McKaylah.

I understood that the passive-aggressive anger he felt for me was from the number of times that he had pulled me from the muck hoping that I'd make something of my life. He wanted me to be a social worker or therapist, anything that fit with the college education and the blood, sweat, and tears they provided me with.

"We just want the best for you. Something will come up," my mother encouraged.

I didn't want to be argumentative with them. I had enough chaos in the club. I refrained from rebutting their disillusionment with who I was supposed to be in life.

Really? I am supposed to make twenty grand a year? We need to get out of here. Bailey had a way of taking an ax to the wood of normalcy and splintering it down the middle. *Can someone get some vodka for this lemonade?*

I felt there was a boxing ring inside me. In the left corner, there was the angel, McKaylah, and the pockets of joy that I felt with her. In the other corner of the ring was the devil of accumulated pain from childhood that everything here reminded me of. When I left Michigan, the inner demon and angel would concede the fight to be a draw.

I turned off the valve of real hope to help me maintain distance from the shadowy world that was slowly beginning to envelop me. I was killing myself with F.S. and the other men that I was dancing for, or sleeping with. I had never committed to anyone other than my daughter. Taking care of her and trying to take care of myself was enough for me.

I was incapable of feeling anything real for anyone other than for McKaylah. Life was safe in our little bubble. I was a broken vessel, but for all of my brokenness, I was a good mother.

I can't talk for specific clubs, but many clubs are owned by the mob. They are not crooks but they are predators on human desire at its worst. Where there is a demand, there is supply. You think you know the Mafia from movies like *Goodfellas* or *The Godfather*, but the men who run clubs where sex is for sale sell girls. Girls get trafficked and are branded like cattle with tattoos and are sold or overdose. They find your headless, rotting body in a Dumpster next to an abandoned building. Today's gangsta pimps don't have the old-school tradition of their grandfathers. As society has become more gratuitous, the fixations have become sicker. Women are not put up on pedestals to be valued, unless you're at an auction. It's not a game. You don't get to walk out of the theater after ninety minutes of entertainment. It's fifteen-year-old girls from upper-middle-income families trafficked by pimps and truckers, who force them to perform sex acts on command, and after they repeatedly try to run away, they are found dead by the feds. This is a sick, twisted demonic playground.

My demons are pretty bad, but their demons are way bigger than mine. The clubs make money at every pour, tip, turn, bend, and squeeze. Our club was a waterfall of cash but also a streamlined legitimate business. Dancers were paid an hourly wage, so there were taxes to be paid. The bars ran long tabs of liquor and various supplements, and managers made sure that business was business and no one risked the currency cow of the club. When men ran out of twenty-dollar bills from their wallet, the club could provide them with funny money. Funny money is like the chips in Las Vegas, only made to look like dollars with a cash value. Men could draw from their credit cards in exchange for black laminated money with gold writing so the clients could tip their dancers. The girls hated funny money, as at the end of the night you had to cash it in for real money, and the club charged ten percent for the exchange. It was also taxable income for Uncle Sam.

From the keypads on the wall that resemble an alarm keypad in a luxury home where dancers punch in their stripper code to record every lap dance, to the doorman keeping an exact head count of patrons in the VIP room and dollars paid for the entrance fees, the owners monopolize and manage the sex-for-sale business in a gentlemen's club, just like Steve Jobs from Apple parlayed the iEverything into an empire. Clubs are the iSex with a bada-bing-bada-bang inflection, and the bosses have the ability to make anyone disappear for talking trash about the family.

On a Sunday afternoon, I was sitting with a customer when three slick, well-dressed men in their early thirties came into the club. Security quickly escorted them to a VIP table to the right of the stage. The VIP tables were reserved for the high rollers. One by one, dancers made their way over to the table. We knew the drill: we were all supposed to allow the VIPs to get a good look at us so that they could select which girls would join them at their table. Tonight was different: all the girls were politely told to keep moving. The men had no interest in the girls, they just kept ordering drinks and talking among themselves.

It seemed odd. The men ordered drinks and sat in deep discussion. As I left my client, I made eye contact with the man seated in the middle. He was good-looking, with a strong jaw and a shaved head. His glasses were Armani and his white dress shirt was heavily starched. He looked like a younger, hotter James Gandolfini.

That's a nice watch, Bailey noticed.

My plan was to sit with him and get him into the VIP room for five hundred an hour after I finished my stage set. As soon as I got up on stage, I looked over to my next victim and the table was down to two. The man in the middle had left.

There's still hope with the other two. That money in their pockets? It belongs to me.

The X-rated song "What's Luv?" by rapper Fat Joe spun in the DJ booth, mixed with Tina Turner's classic "What's Love Got to Do with It" in the chorus. My moves were calculated and seductive as I turned off any goodness inside and twirled my way around the pole. One of the other gentlemen at the table came over and held out a hundred-dollar bill for me. He tucked it into the garter on my arm.

In this club girls couldn't carry a purse, so men put money in a garter on your leg or wrist. I kept my money folded origami style and rubber-banded for safety until the stack got so big that I had to go to my locker and put it inside.

"Thank you." I smiled at him.

"Did you see my friend?"

I looked at the table.

"The one who left?" I nodded. *Yes, I saw him.* I danced for this guy a little longer than usual, as I could tell he wasn't finished talking to me.

"He wants to talk to you but he didn't want it to be with your clothes off. Will you come sit with him when you're done here?"

He knew he was in a strip club, right?

I agreed, finished my stage set, and as sure as sugar, as soon as I was done, there were three men at the table again.

I went to the dressing room and freshened up my makeup and put my stage money in my locker. When I came back out, there was an empty chair placed next to the man in the middle.

I sat down, but before I could get a word of smooth, manipulative talk out, he moved his chair toward me so that his whole body was facing me.

"Do you believe trust is the basis of every relationship?"

After being in the industry for almost five years, I was rarely surprised at what people said to me or asked me to do. But this one statement caught me off guard.

Focus, Bailey. Give him the answer he wants and get him into the VIP room.

"Yes."

"Good. I'm leaving for Vegas and I'm giving you this."

He gave me a key.

"What do you want me to do with this?"

"Drive it. Have fun. I don't need to know your name or where you live. Honestly, you can do what you want with it."

He's crazy. He's a crazy mobster and there's a dead body in the trunk of his car.

"It's a stick. Can you drive a stick?"

Girls in clubs get set up all the time. Set up by cops.

Set up by the Mafia. Set up by other girls wanting their clients. Taking this key was against the rules. There were no exceptions. I remembered Mike telling me, "Everything you do we have recorded on these cameras."

"Can you wrap that up in a hundred and give it to me? It's against the rules for me to take anything from you. I'll go put it in my locker and come back."

He pulled out his money clip with hundred-dollar bill after hundred-dollar bill and peeled one off and wrapped up the key.

I got up slowly, looking around at security. I walked toward the stairs but instead ducked into the hallway and buzzed the door of Mike's office.

"That guy?" Mike pointed at a monitor.

"Yes. That guy."

"I'll take care of it."

For Mike that meant escorting the man out of the club and banning him from coming back. I dropped the key on Mike's desk and went to the dressing room to freshen up and wait for the middleman who was trying to set me up to get thrown out of there.

I'm not a sucker.

"Bailey." My name came over the loudspeaker in the dressing room. "Please come to the office."

Time to get back to work. I eased out of the makeup chair and went back to Mike's office, where he sat with a burly man in a three-piece suit.

The man began, "You have to take the car." Mike was sweating. I'd never seen him sweat.

He got up and poured himself a drink, and walked out of the office. The man said, "Sit down."

I sat down in the swivel chair opposite his desk.

The man said, "You cannot tell anyone he gave you that car. It's illegal. You can borrow it. I don't want any of the other girls knowing. You got me?"

"Are you for real?"

"He's *family*."

I was in over my head.

"Go back. Be sorry. Buy a round of drinks. I'll cover it all."

What had I gotten myself into? He was for real and I'd just ratted him out.

I took the key from the man's hand, ran it up to my locker, and went back on the floor.

"I thought you were setting me up." I sat down.

"You didn't want the car?"

"I didn't want to get in trouble."

"Doing the right thing? You're a smart girl."

"Thank you." I tried to be charming but the odd awkwardness of fear was pouring out of me.

The waitress came over and set down drinks. "Don't be ridiculous," he said as I tried to pay. "Do you still have the key?"

"I do."

"I'll get it when I'm back from Vegas. Don't leave it here." He drank his drink and then got up.

"You're leaving?"

"I have a flight."

My shift ended at four a.m., and after I tipped everyone out, it was almost five. I stood at the valet's spot and he just pointed to a black car with a gray racing stripe down the middle.

Inconspicuous it was not.

"It's a Viper," the valet said. "Only a hundred and twenty grand."

As I got behind the wheel, I realized that my heart was racing. I had no idea what his name was or if there was a kilo of cocaine in the trunk. This was too much.

His name was Anthony. He was thirty-four years old and running a legit business financed on mystery money. For a single man, he didn't live a bachelor life. He partied like a rock star in private. He wined and dined me, all the while knowing I had no intention of quitting dancing. I had to keep three worlds in the air and two of them were becoming increasingly knotted together.

McKaylah stayed with my parents for an entire month after her fourth birthday. It was during that month that, without her beacon of light, I was unable to keep myself from crashing into the rocky shore and breaking myself to bits. I became an empty shell of my former self, just like the other dancers. Without my daily routine with McKaylah, there was nothing to keep me alive.

I would drink two or three cocktails at home and then Anthony would take me to posh restaurants, but I was too bent to eat. We would go from the front of the line at this party to the front of the line at that party. I was wildly out of control with no supervision and clarity.

I used sex as a way to control him, although I realized that control is self-deception. There is no real control of anything, let alone another person. I couldn't even control myself. Without my daughter, I had no reason to come home at night. My old divide of pain-numbing addictions and discovering joy was bridged by bottles of vodka and drugs.

I was on the top of the world, and yet I wanted to jump.

In the club on Sunday night, Mike and I sat at a table and I watched a girl dance on the stage.

On a major bender, I was unfiltered. "I've seen that look before," I slurred.

Mike watched as the dancer swung around the pole. "What look?"

I was on a roll. "On a dead deer, in the back of a pickup truck, during hunting season."

"Go home, debutante."

This club didn't have messy girls. The girls here were classy. Not drunk, nostalgic ramblers. But I continued on, my words blending together.

"I have all this money." I showed him a stack of hundreds. "And a great place to live, and limos and private jets, and I can't . . . I can't . . . *feel* any of it."

He looked over my shoulder at a security guard. Then he stood up.

"Shift's up, Bailey."

"We're all *dead*!" My voice got too loud, and he placed his hand on my arm.

I no longer possessed any of the grace, goodness, and faith that my parents had preached to me with the unconditional love that God had showed them. I had demolished it all in an apocalyptic fashion.

I hadn't really eaten or slept properly for the twenty-nine days that McKaylah was in Michigan.

Exhaustion, road sobriety, and a lack of simple nutrients began to kick in with the shakes on the highway. I don't know how I made it to my parents' house in one piece. As I pulled the key out of the Viper, the challenge I faced became clear: was I going to be able to fake strength? Would my parents return my child to this haggard, messy version of their daughter?

My father walked onto his front porch.

"Whose car is that?" He walked around the outside.

"A friend's."

He resumed his walk back up the porch.

"Mommy!" 'Kaylah came running outside and into my arms. It wasn't until just then that I realized how life-affirming she was for me. *Life. I can feel life.*

"Go get your bag, sweet girl."

I hugged her again. "Ahhh, I missed you so much."

She went running back after my dad.

"Do you want to eat?" My mother looked at the bags under my eyes that she knew all too well were from fatigue and mental and physical self-mutilation.

"I've got to get back."

"To what?"

Just tell her!

"I'm not cocktail waitressing. I'm dancing again. I have a shift tomorrow."

She didn't even flinch.

"Anny, do you want me to tell you we don't love you?"

We both stood there. Maybe I did. Maybe I wanted her to tell me that.

"Do we agree with your life? No. But we love you. Nothing can change that."

How could she stand there after all that I'd done—lied, tricked, and hurt them—and keep on telling me she loved me? *Give up already, I'm not worth it.*

"I have to get back."

McKaylah came out in my dad's arms. My parents knew she wasn't in danger with me, and they understood she was now my reason for living. Maybe that's why they let her go.

"Here." My dad handed me a bag full of food. "Eat something. You're too thin."

When I returned from Michigan, I put McKaylah in the best day care and I tried to sober up. Eliza kept me fed, took care of the groceries, and was a constant for 'Kaylah. At night I'd shove more money in the shoeboxes under my bed. Thousands of dollars that I had planned to use as an escape, but let's be honest. This was my life now. There was no escaping.

I continued on with Anthony for the two months that followed but I never let him close enough to know me. How could I? I didn't know me anymore. On our last date, he took me to an old building that he was restoring.

"It's going to be a spa."

He walked me through the structure and I stumbled a little, as I'd been drinking. He explained how his big dreams would become a reality. Everything that Anthony touched he finished with success. From business to buildings.

"Listen," he said as we drove to dinner. "I wanted you to see the spa because I want to help you get out of the industry."

Am I just a project to him?

I lit a cigarette. "And do what?"

"You can work for me. Quarter of a million dollars a year."

Sit, stay, and roll over, Anny.

It didn't seem possible that he wanted me to change. "Why?"

"For the same reason you didn't take the key. Bailey, you're smart. You don't have to take your clothes off for a living."

Just for a moment I felt something. Then that something went from zero to sixty in five seconds.

"I don't *need* you to take care of me, Anthony. I don't need saving."

"Bailey. I'm trying to help you."

"I don't need your help. I don't need anyone's help. Take me home!"

For the next three weeks I ignored all his calls. After I retreated, he walked away. He wasn't the chasing type. Thank God, or with those mob ties, I'd be dead.

In the dressing room at Crazy Horse Too that night my hands were unsteady. I was too drunk to paint latex on or think straight.

A dancer was watching me.

"What are looking at?" I yelled at her.

Two girls turned and looked at me. I picked up the powder and threw it at them all.

The next thing I remember, Mike and two security guards were tearing me off one of the girls. I had gone completely nuts and started ripping up the place. When I went back the next day to work, Mike had my things in a box in his office.

"You're not meant to be here, Bailey." He fired me.

"That's it?" I tried to sound sober.

"You're out."

I knew better. I knew that this club didn't do ghetto fights or sloppy dancers. I had imploded and bit the hand that fed me, again. I could still be a party girl though. I had a party to go to for F.S. and his crew that night, in fact. It wouldn't pay the bills, but it would keep food on the table and I had the cash in the shoeboxes.

In the studio I got a drink with a dancer named Kesha. She was a tall brunette with purple contacts that made her look like a young Elizabeth Taylor. I had met her before at the Crazy Horse Too and she also danced at a big club in Detroit.

"Have you ever danced in Vegas?" She stirred her martini.

"No. You?"

"There's more money and parties like this every night."

"Seriously?"

"Yeah." She guzzled her drink.

Maybe, I thought. *Maybe*.

chapter seventeen

PASSING THROUGH DETROIT

Between the use of drugs to medicate [their feelings for and awareness of] what they do and hearing how beautiful they are all the time, they soon experience what I call BDA—Basic Dancer Attitude. This is when the dancer thinks that no matter what friends, children, husband, and families think about her, it doesn't matter. They can all be replaced because all of the patrons around her find her attractive, beautiful, and idolized. Now, the dancers are truly caught in the adult scene. With friends and family gone from their lives, they exist alone in this dark subculture of sex, drugs, alcohol, and prostitution. All of this perverse living, to the dancer, is now just . . . normal.

Steve Gallagher, *How America Lost Her Innocence: A History of the Sexual Revolution*, Dry Ridge, KY: Pure Life Ministries, 2005

My perception of sex and money was distorted and my personal and professional boundaries became blurred. I had no real chance at intimacy with the exception of a four-year-old little girl.

Anny

Letting go of Chicago wasn't the catastrophic meltdown I thought it would be. As I drove away, I knew the tide was changing, and I wasn't one to sit around and wait to get evicted for lack of funds. I had to find new revenue sources, a new club. I didn't want to leave Chicago, but word had spread with the gentlemen's club managers that I was a loose cannon. I wasn't about to lower my stripper standards and go to work at a cheap club, so I needed to change zip codes.

I had enough money to hire a company to pack and move our special pieces of furniture and the belongings that McKaylah had grown to love into a storage unit near my parents' house in Michigan. I gave the rest of the household away to a dancer in the club. My Explorer was filled with the personal things—clothes, toys, etc.—that McKaylah and I would need for what I reinforced to my mother would be a temporary stay in their home. With the holiday season descending upon us, my parents were excited to have McKaylah, and possibly me, nearby.

"You're going to be okay." My mother lay down on the bed in their guest quarters with me during the second night I was home. She knew I was still looking to dancing as the answer to my problems. The cat was out of the bag on my chosen profession and I didn't have the energy to lie to her anymore. I was raw and honest with my mother.

"It's the only thing I am really good at."

"No, it isn't."

"Mom, this isn't patty-cake."

"You have to trust me. I know that you're meant for more."

My voice sounded monotone when I explained to her in detail what I had been doing for men night after night.

I was no longer a little girl. I was a full-grown woman who had encountered more spiritual darkness in the last few years than most women will ever know. I told her about the lap dances, stage dances, VIP room, and parties. I described the men, makeup, manipulation, and money. I told her about Bailey. She listened carefully, paused, and took a breath. After my confession, she had only one question. "Are you having sex for money?"

"No. I would never stoop *that* low."

This was partially true.

I wasn't a hooker. I was an exotic dancer. It is funny how even sinners categorize sin as a way to justify their garbage.

"I need your help with 'Kaylah," I said. "Stability for her."

I was cognizant enough to grasp that my world was too reckless for my daughter. Even if I had to leave her with my parents for small pockets of time while I worked, and I would be without her—my decency beacon, my lifeline to hope—'Kaylah's stability and safety came first. Even if it meant signing my own death warrant, it was a sacrifice I was willing to make for her.

My mother refused to believe that Bailey had killed Anny. She didn't buy the story that Bailey was the Big Bad Wolf and that Little Red Riding Hood was long, long gone. But we both agreed that my life was playing like a skipping record. I kept making the same mistake, over and over. I couldn't move the needle in a different direction.

What I did know is that I was good at dancing. One of the best. As wrong as it seems, it had provided me with the means to an end. But what did the end really look like? Did it look like me at the end of a gun barrel?

What I didn't know was that my mother was hearing from God. She wouldn't have ever tried to speak a spooky spiritualism to me at this point. She had too much wisdom. She didn't preach at me, she just kept loving me.

My stay with my parents was only until I could save up enough money to get 'Kaylah and me headed to a warmer climate. More stability. Out of the cold. The cold of my choices and the cold of the Midwest. In my mind this would take less than two months. I wanted to go west: California, Arizona, or Las Vegas. I didn't know what I was looking for. I was only twenty-five and I was in transit. I was leaving, I just didn't know where I was going.

While staying with my parents, I ignored my father. I was a guest at his house and he was the blind bellman. We never spoke about my career. What father wants to have that conversation with his daughter? He knew what I was doing; my mother filled him in. We barely made eye contact when I was home. Neither his approval nor his disdain meant anything to me and he knew it. He focused all his energy on my daughter and making sure she had a proper male role model. And she did. He was amazing with her. She followed him around like a tiny brown disciple learning at the feet of her prophet. They had popcorn together for lunch; she had a pretend shaving kit so she could put shaving cream on her face just like grandpa. She was a Mini-Me all over again for him. He focused on her, and my mother focused on me. Tag team. They were an unstoppable force.

❧

I drove to Lansing to work and stayed three nights at a motel while I danced and partied with the girls from my old club and guys I met from Michigan State. I tried to reconnect with Serena and Jill but they were gone. The manager told me they had gotten out of the business. *Smart.* I used to think they were so cool and wild, but Chicago had showed me they were tame compared to the big city.

Déjà Vu was now beneath Bailey, but it was easy money. The first night back dancing, I had forgotten that the party club was about really *dancing*, that I had to actually move and take my clothes off. By my third rotation in, Bailey was back but she was not happy, at all. What she lacked in happiness she quickly covered up with self-medication.

My last night in Lansing, I came off the stage and Cinnamon, the old dancer who had schooled me my first night of work here, was in the dressing room snorting blow out of her little tiny vial. *Some things never change.* I thought she was going to hug me, but she didn't. She pinned me against the wall with her forearm.

"What the hell are you doing back here?" Her eyes were just big, black dilated pupils.

"What's your problem, Cinnamon?" I tried to ease her off.

She was choking and shaking me, and I didn't want to have to beat her down.

"You're supposed to do something with your life. You're one of the few I thought was smart enough to get out of here. God has other plans for you."

"God?" Bailey slapped her so hard and so fast it felt more like a reflex.

Then she threw a punch at me, and I kneed her in the stomach. The rest was WWF style.

"Out!" One of the bouncers yanked me off her. "Out of here, Bailey."

"She came at me first!" I was spitting venom and blood.

Maybe Cinnamon knew if I were thrown out of the club, again, I'd actually stay out. I sneered back at her as I hit the door. She was smiling but not in a mean way, in the way a satisfied mother lioness would smile at her cub after a fresh kill.

That old broad was trying to force me off the track and take me out of the race.

Before I left town, I hooked up with a few dancers and learned about a new club that had recently opened in Detroit, and I thought we should check it out. I found out where it was located and, without a second thought, off I went.

～

The next three months I danced at a club right smack-dab in the middle of Highland Park, an all-black neighborhood in Detroit. It was famous for the drug dealers, prostitutes, thieves, and murderers that ran amok there; it was so bad even the cops stayed away. It was also known as a hangout for notorious drug dealers and pimps and rappers.

I would get a hotel room, sleep, go to work, and then

drive back to the lake to make ends meet. In Highland Park I was the only white person for miles. I had grown up around six-foot-eleven black men and had a biracial daughter, so this didn't scare me in the slightest. As for the street girl inside me, Bailey was neither white nor black. The only color she cared about was the color of money.

The ghetto-fabulous address aside, indoors the place resembled an X-rated supper club in New York's Meatpacking District. The club's two stories were decorated in "welcome to the palace" style. The furniture was purple, the VIP tables were dimly lit with bloodred bulbs, and the main stage was outlined in tubular lighting that gave it an eerie glow. Elevated booths formed a semicircle around the stage. The entire second level was restricted to VIPs. Clients had to take an elevator to get up and in. There was also a back staircase, as the dressing room for the girls was tucked upstairs. The floor on the second level and above the stage was made of some type of Plexiglas so clients upstairs could see the strippers on stage below while getting private dances. In the middle of the room, from floor to ceiling, was the pole. I was making bank and had become a well-requested piece of talent in the place. It all seemed fine until one morning after work.

It was four a.m. on Saturday. I came out of the club and turned back quickly, but the door had shut. It was snowing heavily and I didn't have security with me. I could see my car, so I went for it. My shoes crunched in the snow and I kept my head down to get out of the wind. I got to my Explorer. As I tried to push the unlock button on the clicker, I heard a strange metal sound next to my head. It was a sound I'll never forget. The sound of the hammer on a pistol being pulled back.

"Don't look or you die," he said, calling me varied curse words.

I stood frozen with just the blood rushing through my brain.

"I'm not moving," I said. "Take what you want."

"Open the door." He shoved me forward into my door.

My hands were shaking from the cold.

I hit the clicker again.

"*Now!*" He pushed a second time with the barrel of the gun.

"I'm-I'm trying." I held it up, showing him that I was pressing the button over and over and nothing was working. "It's not working."

He was pulling at my clothes. Then he tried to grab my keys but they fell into the snow and it was so snowy they were invisible in the darkness. He pistol-whipped the side of my head, causing me to fall down. My purse and Caboodle dropped. He kicked snow in my face and then stepped on my waist, crushing my ribs. He grabbed my Caboodle and ran.

I lay in the snow stunned that I wasn't dead. I was dizzy and felt like I was going to throw up. My eyes stared underneath my truck and all I could see was the glint of my keys. *There they were.* I reached out and pulled them to me and crawled to my knees. My head was pounding. There was no blood in the snow from the hit to my head, but I could feel the bump above my ear. I pressed the car button again and it opened. I saw my purse on the ground, quickly picked it up, and got in the car and locked the door. I started the engine and looked out the front window, the side windows, and the back, fully expecting whoever that was to be back. I jammed the car in reverse and got on the road.

I didn't cry or freak out. I had been beaten up before. I had been raped. I had been tossed in the spin cycle and lived. This was just another square sewn into my violence quilt. I pulled out my phone to call my mother and realized that all my money was in my purse. I normally kept it rolled and hidden in my Caboodle. For some reason tonight, I put it in here.

I hope that scum has fun with my feminine spray and vanilla lotion. Bailey tried not to sound shaken.

The next night I sat around in the club drinking heavily, trying to fill up and looking around to see if I could spot whoever had tried to rape and rob me.

I'm still here. You can't scare me.

Was he getting ready to watch me dance? It could have been a client, a regular, the bouncer, or the manager.

As I waited for the high to fill me up to work, another girl came to my table to join me. She was a quieter girl, Nina. We'd spoken in passing, but it was all small talk—we'd not had a real conversation.

She lit up her cigarette and asked, "You ever worked in Vegas?"

It was the second time Vegas had been brought up to me.

"No, but I have a friend who does."

"I live here and in Vegas too," she said, taking a slow drag. "Work all the top clubs. You should go with me next time."

I didn't have an escape plan anymore. I had nothing.

I wanted to go west but I didn't want to leave my daughter and go that far away from her.

"Just go for a weekend or two and come back. I work them all. You can hang with me." It sounded doable.

⁓

With the idea of Vegas sunshine in my head mixed with various substances, I got on the treacherous and icy road from Detroit to my parents' lake house. I should have slept off my high but I just wanted to be home for McKaylah. The snow was coming down so hard, I couldn't see the road anymore. I made it off the highway and onto the back roads along the lake to their house. I wasn't going very fast when I hit a sheet of ice and my truck slid sideways. I took my foot off the brake and turned into the skid. I wasn't a novice at winter weather, but the snow was heavy and the truck just kept moving. *This is it. This is where I end up in my dad's frozen lake, dead like they've all predicted for all these years.* But they just didn't have the details for my obituary. Instead of heading into the icy water, my truck ended up crossing the lane. Then *thump*, I crashed into a snowdrift. I remember being relieved that at least it wasn't ice water filling my truck and me sinking into the abyss.

I couldn't see anything out of my driver's-side window but the white snow. It made the inside of the car pitch black. I unbuckled and slid over to the passenger's side and pushed open the door. I had to really lean into the door to get it wide enough to get out, and when a pile of snow finally gave way, it fell on my head and wedged the door open. Now there was no way I was going to get it shut again. I grabbed my boots and squeezed out the door to assess the situation. The wind whipped all around me and chilled me to the bone. I decided I had better get back inside the SUV.

There, wet and exhausted and sobered, I climbed behind the wheel, revved the engine, and gave it some gas. The tires just spun, spun, and spun, and then I really pressed my foot on the pedal and the wheels spun violently. Just like my life. Round and round but stuck in the same place. Meanwhile, the snow just kept coming.

I started pounding on the steering wheel and yelling, "*What do you want from me!*" I was crying and sobbing. I knew God was there. I knew he had stopped me in that snow. He wanted me to stop running. I was so mad at Him. I sobbed and cried until my shirtsleeves were all covered in glittery makeup-laced snot.

I didn't want God to take over. *I didn't want him!* I was throwing a tantrum in protest. I sat there screaming until I couldn't scream anymore.

Shortly before dawn, a snowplow came by and saw me. The driver got out of his truck and offered me a ride. There was no getting my car out. He could have been a rapist or killer but I'd already faced those down and lived. He drove me to my parents' house less than fifteen minutes away. He didn't speak much other than to offer me coffee from his thermos. His name was Luke, and he had on overalls, snow boots, and a faded John Deere ball cap. The age spots on his calloused hands and the creases around his brown eyes made him look like he was in his sixties or seventies. He was just a sweet, quiet country fellow being a Good Samaritan. As we pulled up to the house, daylight broke.

My father was already up and seated at the kitchen table. "You all right?"

"My car is stuck up the road about fifteen minutes. Snowplow guy couldn't dig me out so he gave me a ride."

My dad set down his cup of coffee and sighed. He was so used to me lying, it didn't surprise him anymore. "There's no plows working these roads and won't be until Monday."

To this day I believe that man was an angel. To this day.

chapter eighteen
SIN CITY'S EXORCISM OF BAILEY

Approximately 12,000 dancers are registered with the Las Vegas Metropolitan Police Department, who issues work cards for these and other non-sex industry employees. The age of the dancers varies considerably, from underage girls working illegally (80 known) to 50+ of all genders.

Sex Industry and Sex Workers in Nevada,
UNLV Libraries Report, 2012

At some point, either the dancer (your alter ego) or the real you has to go. You can't go on forever living two lives. One of them will end up killing the other.

Anny

In the Detroit airport bar, drinking shots of tequila, I met a businessman in a wrinkled black suit while waiting on my direct all-night flight to Las Vegas. Ken had come home to Traverse City, Michigan, to bury his mother. He owned a large construction company in Vegas and his latest project was building a casino just off the Strip.

Ken had seen women like Bailey before; she was no novelty. She possessed the looks and the overtly sexual overtones of your typical XXX club dancer. Still, she had him disarmed by the fourth drink with her fond memories of the Cherry Festival and Interlochen, and when I was called to board, I learned that Ken had paid for my upgrade. He wanted Bailey sitting next to him in first class.

As the plane reached ten thousand feet, he reclined his seat and leaned into me conspiratorially so the woman in 2B couldn't hear him. "Would you like to become a member of the mile-high club?"

"Somehow, Ken, I think the FAA frowns upon that type of behavior." I returned the flirt but politely declined his offer.

It takes more than an extra mileage upgrade to get me in the sack, babe. Particularly in a cramped toilet stall. That's not happening. But Bailey was ready to play.

"Why don't you come out to a club and see me," she purred. "Here's my number." She threw him a cell phone number on an airline cocktail napkin. "I promise that it will be worth it."

He put his hand on my leg and began to massage my thigh. While this upped his arousal, I immediately felt anxiety. I couldn't shake the feeling of being thirteen years old and back on the team travel bus. I yanked open the window shade in order to get some metaphorical fresh air, but there was only darkness in the night sky. The plane was dimly lit and people were approaching a deep slumber. The side of my face began to twitch. I wasn't used to being touched by what I deemed to be a mark, and there were no bouncers aboard our 757. There were no security guards to fend off the carnivorous behavior of lonely maggots.

Truth be told, I had invited this behavior when I agreed to take his upgrade and sit for five hours in first class next to him. I placed my hand on his hand, wanting to break his fingers, but I just held it gently. When the intimacy of hand-holding began to make me woozy, I leaned in and said, "Excuse me." I unbuckled my seatbelt. "I need to go to the ladies' room."

"Do you want me to escort you?" he flirted awkwardly as he got up to let me pass.

"Actually, Ken, I'm feeling a little queasy." I was unbearably self-conscious: a trigger from my childhood.

He sat back down and watched me go into the bathroom.

Where was Bailey when I needed her?

Inside the lavatory, I slid the lock on the door that noisily turned the indicator from green to red. I began to hyperventilate in the two-by-three-foot restroom; then I was choked by fear.

You're a grown woman. Bailey had tired of fighting my battles. *Take control. Take control. Take control.*

I sat down on the lid of the toilet and put my head between my skinny knees. I flipped my hair upside down and ruffled it up. *Breathe. Breathe. Breathe.*

I miraculously regained composure, sat up, rolled my shoulders back, unlocked the door, and walked out.

"Everything okay?" Ken's face lit up in genuine joy at my return.

"Yes." I climbed in facing him, placing my hands on his seat over his shoulders, with my chest in his face, replicating a lap dance in a club.

Control. Control. Control. I have control of him.

He positioned his hand on mine as I sat down. This time I returned the gesture by taking his hand in mine and placing it between his legs.

The flight attendant tiptoed neatly down the aisle with the cart. She saw everything and gave me a dirty, judgmental look as if I were devoid of any value.

Keep moving your little drink buggy for ten bucks an hour, sweetheart.

"I'll have another." Bailey smiled sweetly as she eyed her nametag. "Tina."

"The captain has turned on the fasten-seatbelt sign. He's asked us to sit down."

She didn't *want* to give me my drink. She didn't *want* to have anything to do with me.

"Then you'd better hurry." Bailey was no longer timid.

The woman in 2B was watching us. She had the same look on her face as the flight attendant. Was she looking at me, judging me? Was everyone? I turned in my seat and looked around the cabin to see if everyone was looking at me, and it appeared they were. Was I paranoid?

The moment was a wake-up call of sorts. Every woman in first class was staring at me, yet when my gaze met theirs, they looked away. That's when I realized who I had become. I was the woman that every woman hates. I was the girl that was judged for her mistakes, abuse, and promiscuity in high school, and I was the girl that married men slunk out of their corner offices at work and out of their marriage vows and covenants to meet in empty closets and dark stairwells. I was the girl who steals away their men's money and morality through Internet porn sites and five-star hotel rooms.

Or was I the product of a lifetime on display?

This had never bothered me before, but today it did. They all hated Bailey.

Maybe I hate Bailey too.

Tina handed me another drink.

"Thanks." My sweet smile framed my perfectly straight white teeth from years of braces. I was hoping she would see that somewhere inside me a good, Midwestern girl once lived, and I wasn't the worthless stripper she was silently condemning.

We landed and Ken promised to call me to take me to dinner, or rather have me for dinner. Either way, he said he'd call, and I knew he would because they always do.

Nina picked me up at the Vegas airport in her Lexus, playing Louis Armstrong's "Hello, Dolly," and we wasted no time. I was still marginally buzzed but we immediately got to work completing paperwork for each of the clubs that she worked at. The Spearmint Rhino, Cheetah's, and another Crazy Horse Too; I was going to join all of them.

As we stood in line at the Las Vegas Police Fingerprint Bureau with sheets of paperwork, waiting to get my stripper license and my work card, I remarked on the absurdity of it all.

"You realize this is a joke, right? Getting a license to take off your clothes?" Even crazier to me: I wasn't alone. I was in a line at least ten girls deep.

"Baby, it's all very professional in Sin City. They got to run you through the National Crime Information Center and do your background checks to make sure you're not wanted for murder, you don't have any outstanding warrants. That kind of thing." A look of concern washed over her face as she leaned in to me and whispered in her New Orleans accent, "You're not wanted, are you?"

"Oh, I'm wanted all right," I said cynically.

"Without that card, there's no way for you to work in Vegas."

"But I'm an independent contractor."

"You still make wages from the club."

"Yes, but there are laws and labor rights, even for strippers. The fact that we have to do this, then pay the stage fees, booking fees, and commissions to the house; DJ, house moms, managers, and bartenders out of our *tips* is completely illegal. You get that, right?"

"Well, when you get your degree, you can stand up for naked rights across the country. Be the Joan of Arc of strippers." She was guffawing at me.

"I have my degree," I sneered, as a woman behind the desk administered my work card. She handed it to me and we left.

~

Although Las Vegas is swathed in bright neon colors, colorful flashing signs, and sparkling fountains of water, my vision was clouded and blurry. To me, this Candy Land in the desert was monotone, all shades of gray ashtrays and dusty sand and cacti. Nina had a condo in a four-story tan stucco building ten miles away from the Strip. It was surrounded by a covered parking lot congested with gray, brown, and white Ford Tempo rental cars.

Unlike the brown Vegas terrain, inside Nina's apartment was an exotic and vibrant sanctuary from another time and place. I rolled my Gucci bag into her living room and imagined that in a past life Nina was a voodoo princess.

The apartment was a blend of exotic and Ikea. She had a picture of the African voodoo queen Marie Laveau in a wooden black frame that hung behind her nineteenth-century-style couch, and various charms, tall glass candles, powder dishes, and beads set stylishly on the end tables between the contemporary chairs.

On a mantel between her windows, she had placed primitive wooden statues of naked tribal people and hand-painted masks. None of it was menacing to me. If anything it was uplifting, but the place had a tangible ambiance of another time and another place.

"Are those dolls meant to be poked to wound people?" I said, puffing something that I thought was a joint.

"They're gris-gris dolls used to bless you. Not curse you, ma friend. They can bring you luck or love or power."

I picked up one of the dolls wrapped in cloth with strange yarn-like hair. "Good. I need it."

"My birth mother was a practicing voodoo healer. She was very spiritual."

I stroked the doll a couple of times for good measure.

"What happened to her?"

Nina took a long reflective drag from the brown-paper-rolled blunt.

"Murdered."

I quickly set the doll back in its place next to the others. I could tell I had gone too far. It's like asking a dancer her real name. We don't want to be too close. We never want to be too close. We all had that moment. I changed the subject.

"What is in this weed?"

"I dip it in a mix."

"Of what?"

"Jimsonweed and honey and a tad of sulfur. Some people 'sup it but I find it nicer with a drop on bud."

"You're not trying to kill me, are you?"

"Quite the opposite, my white African dancer. Quite the opposite. It's a Nahluns treat I learned ova by ma mama's mama. She learned it in the bayou, in a shack."

Her voice changed to accentuate her ancestry.

Nina's guest room housed a futon and a cracked, beige, faux wood bedroom set. The only artwork was a framed New Orleans Jazz Festival poster on one wall, and then a huge hand-painted single lavender dogwood flower on the other.

"Did you paint that?" I asked her.

"Yes." She smiled. "I've always painted."

"It's really nice." I so wanted to tell her about my love of music. The gift of playing. But I couldn't muster the connection.

I suppose she, like me, had her escape from her history. Painting was her form of escapism, like music was to me.

"Thank you." She walked out saying, "Make yourself at home."

Then she proceeded to go blast tunes that sounded

like gospel brunch music with trumpets and loud bass players. Not the typical Tupac I was used to hearing at home.

All in all, the sights and sounds would do.

I learned her apartment was an investment property. On the weekends she wasn't in town, Nina rented her apartment out to couples that didn't mind staying off the Strip if it meant avoiding overpriced hotel fees. She was a black girl from Louisiana who sauntered along and spoke slowly, creating a protective aura of a sweet and simple Southern girl, but all the while she was masking the intelligence and savvy that lay underneath. Aren't we all?

I hadn't quite figured out why Nina had invited me to Vegas, but I knew I wasn't here to be her new BFF. No matter how tight you become with a girl from the stage, our world was about agendas and moving dollars. After six years in the business, I knew when someone was putting the con on me, but I hadn't cracked her angle yet and at this point it didn't matter anyway. Bailey was tired and wanted a vacation.

I called to check on McKaylah and see how she was doing. My mother's voice was upbeat—no long, lamenting pauses as I had expected—and she cheerfully told me to call back later, as 'Kaylah had gone out to the hardware store to get salt for our icy driveway with my dad.

I put on my bathing suit and admired my tanned, toned body. I had become obsessed with my weight and body image, as one would expect, I guess, when every night of work was the equivalent of a beauty contest. Little did everyone know that under this perfect wrapper was rotten fruit.

I went to the pool area in search of real vitamin D—a welcome change from the fluorescent purple glow of the tanning beds back in Michigan and Chicago—hoping to plug into some type of life force in the courtyard. The sun. I needed to be outside. The Midwest was so depressing, with the constant gray and snow and freezing ice storms. I lay on a chair and felt like I was melting in the heat. At first it was amazing, but my body wasn't used to being bare in the warm temperatures. It wasn't long before sweat beaded on my upper lip and rolled off my forehead. I got up and walked to the pool edge and sat on the first step of the pool, cautiously dipping my feet into the refreshing water. I slowly walked down the four steps and then completely submerged, letting the oxygen from my lungs release. All sounds were muffled and the voices in my head quieted as my body sunk deeper and deeper. My eyes closed, I thought about inhaling and letting the water into my lungs. It would be so easy to let go of the familiarity of what my life was now and stay submerged in this aquatic darkness. I opened my eyes and looked up at the sunlight rippling through the aquamarine water. I searched the blue and yellow rays for answers and heard 'Kaylah giggling. The thought of her made me smile and remember to come up for air.

Outside the gentlemen's clubs that Nina and I worked were huge video billboards. Film of nude girls sordidly dancing played on a loop. The guts of the clubs all looked the same to me now: lights, camera, and action. The exception was the girls. They made the girls in Chicago and Detroit look like they were pure and sweet and full of the resurrection power of Jesus Christ. Beautifully painted and sculpted, with names like

Heaven and Serenity, you could wind them up and watch them go for sale between rows and rows of dancing and drinking and partying men and women. Yet, like me, they were all broken and hollow on the inside.

Despite a Vegas club's five-star decor and impossibly beautiful women, it has a disturbing atmosphere. Girls can pretty much do whatever they want as long as you make the client pay. No one is enforcing anything. Prostitution is virtually legal here, like jaywalking, and it's part of the culture. There are girls with girls. Boys with boys. Couples with couples. Repression is masked as expression and debauchery as freedom. It is absolute synchronized madness. It's a pre-orgy scene from the Roman Empire during the rule of Caligula. Being there, I felt I was watching an absurd room full of soulless hedonists overdosing on sex, drugs, power, and control.

I would sit for hours in a club just watching and trying to come to life. Trying to get up. Trying to make it work, but I couldn't. Some nights I'd just sit there paralyzed, getting more and more wasted.

Whether you're a devotee of the Bible, Qur'an, or Torah, you know the story of Sodom and Gomorrah. I remembered my father telling me how God consumed the cities with fire and brimstone in judgment for their sins. Now it was in my memory, but I didn't believe in God. How could there be a God in places like this? For people like this? People like me? This city was off His Lordship's radar or He'd just given up on it. Whether the Morgan Freeman version of God with his graying beard was real or not didn't matter to me. What mattered was that the dark forces in these clubs was contagious. And so far, the wickedness and lunacy of people coming from near and far to be herded into windowless buildings where time stands still had escaped God's judgment. Whoever designed this place understood that there was fertile soil here for self-indulgence to grow. Lust and gluttony were in full bloom.

There may not be a God, but there is a devil, and he reigns in Vegas.

⌘

"You ever had sex for money?" Nina asked me one night while we were smoking a blunt in her car.

Shocked, I recoiled.

"No!" I said. "I would never do that."

I didn't realize it at the time, but that was the *exact* same thing I'd said when Serena and Jill told me I should dance.

Sure, I'd had "relationships" in which I would "date" men—rich men who wanted to never admit they were hiring me—but they hadn't ever gone like this in the Midwest. It was always softer on the psyche to "date" a customer and pretend you liked him. The truth was, customers you "dated" were just a quick way to get the rent paid, and of course eventually you had to put out, but you did it in the guise of the "dating scene." In reality, I never would have dated any of those losers had they not been multimillionaires.

Maybe it was the jet lag or maybe it was just the slow waltz every night with the darkness, but the cancer of lust was killing Bailey. She was tired and needed to sleep.

One night when I was dancing, I couldn't get Bailey to wake up. Bailey was comatose on drugs and alcohol and fatigue. I watched Nina leave the club for an hour and she came back with somewhere between five hundred and a thousand dollars, while I was working for twenty bucks at a time. Common sense told me that whatever she was doing made more sense. But I still resisted, because the idea of waking up one morning and thinking, *I am now officially a prostitute* was something I wasn't ready to stomach.

Over and over, I found myself sitting night after night for hours, only making a few hundred dollars and getting so completely wasted that I'd have to leave early and take the following day off to recover from the hangover.

I would numb myself on my drug of choice, trying to retrace my steps: How had I gotten to this place? What was I doing here? Where was my life heading? When grief would overtake me, I'd take a couple of shots or lines or hits, and pieces of Bailey would come alive and plow through the men's wallets, but even Bailey had nothing on Vegas.

❧

Traveling the triangle of Vegas, Detroit, and my parents' house at the lake to spend time with McKaylah was killing me. I was rail thin—carrying just 120 pounds on my five-nine frame—tanner than a leather couch, and bruised on the inside. I was a rat in a cage spinning my wheel. I came to the conclusion that there was no getting out. For the last half decade of my life I had always justified taking off my clothes as a short-term plan. It was just until I could do . . . fill in the blank. Just have enough . . . fill in the blank. The blank had turned into forever. This was it.

⤸

Back in Vegas, Nina and I left the club early.
My first-class flight buddy Ken had invited us to a swanky party in a casino. Our plan was to stop there to eat and drink as much as possible for free and then Nina would take me home before she had to meet one of her clients later that night.

We got to the casino and valet parked, then checked in at the concierge desk, where Ken had left me a special key card to the elevator. We crossed the marble floor to the elevator, got in, and took it up thirty flights to one of the suites overlooking the Strip.

A man in the full garb of a fortune-teller greeted us.

"Look, it's one of your people." I grinned at Nina.

"No, he's not. I promise you."

We were buzzed from the drinks that we'd already finished and thought it would be wild to have him read my tarot cards and look at my palm, so we followed him to his table.

"I'm going to get a drink." Nina headed in the direction of the bar.

"Get me something."

"You're quiet and mysterious." The fortune-teller held my hand and studied the lines and folds.

"So far, so good." I smiled and sat patiently. Part of me wanted this magic man to solve my inner conflict and show me the exit sign to my private catastrophe. The other part of me just wanted to have some fun.

His black eyes widened. "You're going to aid people." Without taking his penetrating gaze off me, he said, "Women will gather at your feet and you'll be like a mother to them."

"I hate kids." *Except for my own daughter.* "And men."

"You'll teach them."

Maybe teach them the ropes and then take their money. Bailey was listening.

With a fake laugh, I stood up and said, "Thanks, swami."

Then he took my hand again. I figured he wanted a tip, but he just said to me, "Take care of your son."

"I have à daughter, not a son." I wanted to add, *moron.*

Ken found me on the balcony having a cigarette, alone with the luminosity of the Strip below me. I had looked all over for Nina without any luck. The party was jam-packed with suits and cocktail dresses. I stuck out in my tight leopard pants and six-inch platform shoes.

Maybe Ken could save me, but I didn't have any more gas in the tank of lies. Normally, Bailey could've played him like a fiddle. Bailey's plan had always been to destroy and deliver, but being in Vegas was destroying her. *Something* was destroying her. She had been so tough, the armor around me. She and I were the same, so I thought, as the truly crazy person doesn't know they are crazy. At my worst, I always knew Bailey was a part of me, but she wasn't me, she was a coping mechanism. But something was changing as that mechanism wasn't working. The power she carried was evaporating, particularly in the clubs and now with Ken. In an attempt to hide my real self and regroup, I kept my time with him limited. I needed to find Nina and get out of there.

~~≈~~

Nina didn't want to take me back to the apartment, so I agreed to sleep in her car while she made a quick stop for one of her clients, which involved her having sex with some dude from the club at his place. I was sitting in the car smoking a cigarette about to doze off when she knocked on my window. I rolled it down.

"My customer wants to include you in the action," she said.

"What?"

"He's willing to pay for it," she said.

I didn't say anything. I just wanted to run, and it took everything I had not to.

I had the same touch I had years ago. A feeling inside me—it was there. The same sensitivity that had wanted me not to come out of the bathroom on the bus, the same sensitivity that wanted me not to go look for my roommate at boarding school, the same feeling right before I stepped on the stage for amateur night—all those times there was a protective and sensitive *something*. I thought it was my conscience. Maybe it was my dad's voice. I don't know. I just know I could hear it again. And it wasn't Bailey.

"You do this with me," she said, "and you won't have to worry about working at all this weekend—you can just head home. We'll be done in an hour."

Even though I was hesitant, her logic made sense,

especially when she told me what kind of money he was offering. In fact, with that kind of money, once I got home I could stay home for an extra weekend. It seemed like a smart shortcut. *But there are no shortcuts in life.* I wouldn't have to work eight hours the following day, which was becoming more and more of a struggle. I gave in. Bailey was losing her drive and now I just did what I thought I had to do—I, Anny, took the proposition, and into the house we went.

The guy was wealthy. Why would a rich guy like this need to pay for hookers? I needed a drink. He poured vodka for both of us. I guzzled mine down quickly and banged my crystal rock glass down on the coffee table. He filled it up again, without a word, just as I had silently asked. Then he counted out a thousand dollars in cash for me. I wasn't used to taking money up front. The way I worked wasn't so forward.

After it was finished, I showered at the man's house for a long time, standing there feeling empty and disgusted wearing his terry-cloth robe. I had reached a new low and turned my first trick, but it would not be my last.

Nina came into the enormous bathroom to check if I was all right. She didn't seem fazed by the sickness of the situation at all. She acted as if we had just gone grocery shopping. Nothing out of the ordinary.

"Let's get out of here." I reached for the watch and diamond ring in the soap dish, but she stopped me.

"Not this guy. We'll be back here."

I set them back down. "The money he gave me is in my purse." I looked at my red and remorseful eyes in the mirror.

"That's all yours, Little B. He paid me mine."

An uncontainable sob escaped me. "What did you call me?"

"Little B. You know, Little Bailey."

It was a glittering and tender reminder of my father and his nickname for me, Little Dee.

I was going to vomit. I thought I was at the beginning of a nervous breakdown. Little Dee was inescapable! Rise up, Little Dee!

Driving back to Nina's apartment, I realized that she could have conceivably made more money than me. I had seen him count out *my* money but not *hers*. Had she played me? Had she parlayed her meeting me into more money for her? Maybe this was her plan all along. This is another form of conditioning I thought I was smarter than.

⌒

I took three weeks off and stayed at the lake house. I had enrolled 'Kaylah in a local Christian preschool. Day after day she would bring home colored pictures with sayings at the top like "Jesus loves you" or "If you follow Jesus, He will lead you to unexpected places."

The night before I left for Detroit and Vegas, I was feeling utterly lost. I told my mother, "I don't think I'm going to make it." I showed her where the shoeboxes were under my bed. I had meant to say, "I'm not going to make it *back*."

"You're going to be fine. You're gonna make it."

"How do you know that?"

"Because I know."

There was something about her unmovable reply. She wasn't fazed by how messed up my life was. Having nothing else, I clung to her faith in me and the innocence of my daughter. My father was there too, but I didn't see him. I couldn't look at him anymore, I had so much shame. I thought he hated me but loved 'Kaylah and that's why he put up with me.

When I finally got out of the industry, my mother told me my father had cried a lot, but he would never do it when I was there. He would say to my mother, "We've lost her. She's going to end up either in jail for killing someone or dead," and she would assure him, "She's gonna pull out of this." He would weep for the pain in me and for what he imagined was being done to me. I see now that it was every father's nightmare for his baby girl.

The truth was that something inside me was heading to the grave. I wanted to be better for 'Kaylah, but her life was peaceful here with them. It was obvious that I needed her more than she needed me. Or so I thought.

McKaylah had packed her pictures of Jesus' sayings into my suitcase on one trip. I had become an atheist, but I took them to Vegas with me, and when I got to Nina's, I hung them on the guest room mirror, because my five-year-old had insisted. I didn't want a reminder of following Jesus or anyone, and if God existed, He wasn't for women like me. He hated women like me. Women like me didn't deserve God's love. It was much easier to pretend He didn't exist.

~

On the cusp of my seventh anniversary in the sex industry, I sat on my futon counting the money I had raked in swinging upside down on a pole, center stage, wearing silver platform heels, a sequin thong, and answering to the stage name Bailey. The week had been strangely profitable, as I had tucked away a few thousand for four nights of dancing and seeing clients on the side, but the price tag had left me physically and mentally exhausted, not to mention spiritually bankrupt.

With an orange soda mixed with Ketel One vodka in hand and a little bump of coke to energize me, my friend Nina and I loaded up her Lexus with our overnight bags and headed west to Los Angeles, the land of milk and honey, for the weekend. This had become my method of survival. Escape. Escape from what ailed me.

During the five-hour drive to California, I rang up a prominent music producer client who lived in the Hollywood Hills to let him know we were heading to town. He laid the groundwork with doormen and nightclub managers for us to roll into all the posh Hollywood nightspots VIP-style. Even in LA, there's no waiting in lines for girls like us. We make the patrons happy. This is how it works from coast to coast.

It was Friday night at the Wild Orchid, and the place was packed with A-list celebrities, Hollywood studio types, and wannabe starlets. In painted-on white leather pants, a black tank that hugged my breasts, and sexy lace-up boots, I was at my peak prizefighting weight. Nina and I cruised the bar to decipher who was really a player and who was just playing. It wasn't my intention to be working, but at this stage in my life, I didn't know another way.

We had cozied up to two movie executives I'll call Mr. X and Mr. Y. The corks were popping off the two-hundred-dollar bottles of Cristal champagne like fireworks on the Fourth of July. We were snorting an occasional line of cocaine to pick us up when I felt a tug in my soul. It was that voice again, *Time for us to leave*. But our foursome kept our party going as we headed outside to the valet stand, where Mr. X's red Lamborghini pulled up.

"At least we know he has money," I whispered to Nina.

We piled in the car and headed from the Wild Orchid to an after-hours club that I vaguely remember being named something like the Hookah Lounge. My head was spinning and foggy. When Jay Z and Beyoncé's "Crazy in Love" repeated for the third time, I started to feel weak. My heart was racing faster than normal from the drugs. Something was very wrong.

I wanted to go home.

Not home to our hotel, but home home. Home to a small town in Michigan. Home to the safety of a good Christian family where I had a loving mom and basketball-coach dad. Home to my daughter. Back in time to when I wasn't such a complete disaster. I was afraid I was going to die here, and I didn't want to.

I struggled to get up as Mr. X. tugged at my arm. His bloodshot, hungry eyes filleted me. He rubbed his hand down my hair and into the arch of my back and breathed his stale cigar breath on me with a growl. "How much?"

The next thing I knew, I was in the heart of Beverly Hills at the L'Ermitage hotel in an oversized suite with marble floors, white linens, and sweeping views of the city. Now, let's be clear. This isn't a scene out of *Pretty Woman*, and Mr. X is no Richard Gere. He's overweight, bald, sweaty, and oily. He grinds his teeth. He's an especially lonely pervert.

Mr. Y has vanished. Nina turns to me as if to say, *What now?* I just shrug. I'm praying he'll pass out and I plan to slip a Xanax into his cocktail to make sure he does.

But Mr. X was all business. He pulled out a wad of cash and paid Nina five hundred dollars to leave and wait in another room. My heart sank. My stomach gurgled and flipped upside down for the umpteenth time. I was the one who was going to have to pay the piper, and I was going to have to do it alone.

The metallic clang of the lock on the door jolted me. Despite the gallon of alcohol I had poured into my frame, I was suddenly very alert. I eased down on the bed as he counted out a thousand dollars in hundred-dollar bills. It wasn't my first time, but this wasn't something I did easily either. Like an animal led to the slaughter, I was about to be carved up piece by piece. Every time I offered up myself for sale like this, I left a piece of me behind. Tiny morsels of my humanity, my soul, were being sliced off to satiate the devil, one scavenging meal at a time. Eventually there would be nothing left. And what then?

Take off your clothes. Be Bailey, I begged myself.

They make it look easy in the movies, but there is nothing easy about selling sex. You're naked and open for the taking. No matter how tough you are—and I was raised a champion with a winner's spirit—there is a vulnerability and fear and disgust and hatred of yourself and your client in every breath and every touch. Each minute passes like hours and each hour like days. This particular night was darker and seedier and more horrific for me than any of the others. I had imprisoned myself with my own sinister choices. The horror ended sometime before sunrise when he left.

When the morning light finally pierced through the corners of the heavy drapes, I saw my beautiful, luxurious hotel room for the dungeon that it was. A wretched smell of stale cigar smoke and body odor clung to the sheets and a sourness filled the air. I stumbled like a zombie to the minibar and proceeded to down four small bottles of scotch. I made my way to the bathroom. I wished a shower would wash away the stain of filth on me. I inspected my body in the full-length mirror: a little bruise here, a scratch there. Where had my beauty gone? How had I gotten here? My rubbery licorice-whip legs gave way and I dropped to my knees and finally succumbed to limpness on the cool floor. I saw blood begin to trickle from my nose onto the white chenille mat. I reached out and touched the stranger with dead eyes staring back at me out of the mirror and whimpered, "Help me."

chapter nineteen

TWO SIMPLE WORDS: *HELP ME*

*The people living in darkness have seen a great light;
on those living in the land of the shadow of death a
light has dawned.*

Matthew 4:16

*Sometimes it's a process, not an event. Just because
you find Jesus doesn't mean you're magically healed.*

Anny

I'm not sure if I was dreaming or hallucinating,
but I know what I saw. A group of older black men
wearing stately uniforms—red jackets, dark pants, and
white gloves—walked in a line slowly down a long street.
With their brass band instruments, the jazz musicians
played a somber, slow hymn. It was an old-school New
Orleans funeral procession. I was standing under a gas
lamp and I could barely see the casket on the shoulders of
the pallbearers, but I knew it was mine. My mother wiped
away tears with a white handkerchief, as my father held
her weight to keep her steady behind the group.

The procession went by, each man and woman a
professional mourner. The music was unstable and the

cathartic spectators were there both to mourn and to celebrate the life of the deceased. As the processional reached the cemetery at the end of the street, the mourners set the casket down in front of an empty tomb.

I was one of the bystanders. I stood looking at the casket. I slowly opened the lid. It was Bailey.

She reached up to grab me with her cold hands.

Get in here.

"No!" I screamed at her. "Why are you trying to kill me?"

Kill you? I've protected you. I kept you safe.

I slammed the lid shut.

Then the line of black-and-white women were twirling their black parasols with red streamers. The crowd was going wild, swinging jubilantly to the raucous song, "When the saints go marching in, when the saints go marching in . . ."

In a hotel in Los Angeles, Bailey was pronounced dead. I laid my alter ego to rest. I buried Bailey below me, and looked up. I was still deep in the hole I had dug.

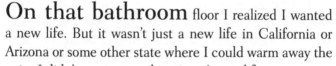

On that bathroom floor I realized I wanted a new life. But it wasn't just a new life in California or Arizona or some other state where I could warm away the pain. I didn't want a new location. A new life.

Is it wrong to just not want to be who you are anymore?

That new life came in the form of a baby. I found out I was about seven weeks pregnant after wanting to die on the bathroom floor. I wish I could tell you that I wanted to have the baby. How I desire to confess to you that I was magically healed, but I wasn't; that wouldn't be honest. The truth was, I didn't want to have another child. I had McKaylah and she was enough. I wished the baby away and went back to the only place that I knew to go: Michigan.

I would sneak out of my parents' house and try to drink the baby away. Cocaine the baby away. I was even so desperate that I went to a psychic, hoping she could tell me the test was a false positive, but none of it worked. See, I had buried Bailey, but I was not healed. I was now simply on my own with no Bailey armor.

So, with neither a job nor an idea of what to do next, I'd lie with McKaylah in my old room in the guesthouse attached to my parents' house. I'd toss and turn, fretting over my decision in the middle of the night. I couldn't sleep, I was so uncomfortable with the choice. I didn't tell anyone in my family about the pregnancy. I was kept engrossed in McKaylah and communicated to my family that I wanted to stop the madness. This was enough for them. Just stop the dancing. The drugs. The drinking. The depression. The darkness.

I made an appointment to abort another child. I tried staying busy at McKaylah's school and helping my mother around the house doing projects, biding my time until I could just go and get this taken care of, but every night, as I lay in bed trying to sleep, I couldn't.

The decision I made weighed so heavily on me that I did the unthinkable for someone who had no faith in anything.

I prayed.

Looking back, I'm not sure if I prayed out of desperation or just to get some sleep, because I didn't really think it was going to work. I can't tell you what led me to do it. But pray I did.

This is what I said: "God . . . I don't know if You're real, or if You can hear me. But if You're real, and You can hear me, I don't think You want me to do this. I'm not going to stop it. If you don't want me to do this, *You* stop it."

As soon as I said "Amen," I fell asleep.

I missed my first appointment due to a scheduling error—when I showed up, the receptionist, an Asian fortysomething woman who was prematurely gray, and all natural with a nose ring, informed me that my appointment had been the day before and that I'd have to reschedule. *No problem,* I thought. I made a new appointment and even got a little business card with the date on it to make sure I didn't miss it.

By the time the second appointment came around, McKaylah had become feverishly sick. I didn't want to leave her, so I rescheduled the abortion again. *No problem, right?* I still had plenty of time. I called and made what would be my third appointment.

On the day of the third appointment, I rushed out the door, buckled my seatbelt, and counted my cash to make sure I had the right amount. When I finished counting, I folded it up and stuck it in the side pocket of my purse, where I always kept cash. Upon arrival at the clinic, I went to the desk and was greeted by the same receptionist. She handed me the paperwork, and I dug in my purse and handed her the cash.

The nose-ringed receptionist counted it and said, "You're a hundred short."

That couldn't be; I had *just* counted it in the car. I dug back through that same side pocket, hoping that the money somehow had come unfolded and a hundred-dollar bill had gotten loose.

There was no other money in my purse.

Since I was further along and the window of opportunity to get an abortion was closing, I asked if I could get it done that day and come back tomorrow to pay the rest of the money. Policy was such that that wasn't an option. I'd run out of time in Michigan to get the abortion pill, but I still had a little time in Illinois (whose laws and prices are different), so it had to be the following week in Illinois. I wanted the pill, as it was less invasive to my body and soul.

As soon as I got home, there was an unfolded hundred lying on the shoe mat just inside the front door. I knew I wasn't crazy. I'd counted the exact amount *after I'd left the house*, and yet here the money was inside the house.

I started to fear my prayer had been answered.

The fourth appointment was the next week. At this point, I had no other choice but to travel across state lines to get it done, so I set out for the road trip two and half hours early to ensure I'd be there on time.

I was starting to get nervous again and was feeling that same pressure that had kept me awake until I'd prayed. I also cannot tell you how many times in that week I heard the song "Faith" by George Michael. *Really, God? George Michael?* God, whatever He was, had a sense of urgency and humor and was absolutely chasing me. As I drove, I was on edge and barely concentrated on the road.

About forty-five minutes outside my destination, I hit traffic. I didn't panic at first though, because I'd given myself over two hours of extra time for exactly this kind of situation. I was prepared for this. What I wasn't prepared for, however, was the fact that I ended up being stuck in traffic for *over three hours*. I still went to the clinic to see if there was anything we could do, and when they said I had to reschedule, I started crying.

I decided to stay in Illinois. I checked into a hotel, plopped down on the bed, and turned on the TV. The scene from *The Lion King* with the booming song "Circle of Life" was playing. *Nice touch, God*. But the pressure began to lift as I watched it. Exhausted, I turned off the television.

My fifth appointment was the next morning, and it was already midnight. When I put my head on the pillow, my heart was racing. That horrible feeling of pressure had come back, and again I couldn't sleep. I stared up at the ceiling and said, "God? This is Your last chance. My appointment is at eight a.m. If You don't want this to happen, You better say something. I have no idea what I'm going to do at the clinic tomorrow, but You have to make it clear this is not what You want. Please help me." I fell asleep.

It's ironic that there's a Bible verse that says, "Come to me all of you who are weary and I will give you rest." An atheist praying is almost comical, but my pattern of prayer and sleep was irrefutable.

In the morning I got in the shower, and I'm not sure what happened, but this voice inside me overwhelmed me and told me not to go. It wasn't a voice over the school PA system, but it was entirely clear. I think God was telling me not to go. At first I tried to shake it off. But it was utterly convincing. I felt enlightened and scared to death at the same time. I'd never felt so understood. I knew that God heard me. He was real.

I just didn't know who He was.

⮞

I canceled the appointment, went back home, and broke the news to my family. My mother suspected why I had gone to Chicago and was relieved to find out I hadn't gone through with it. I'm absolutely positive she had been home praying for me to do what God wanted. She's always known the right thing to do but has never been the type of person to interfere with other people's lives. Her wisdom and insight always run deep, and I could tell by the look on her face when I told her that she was happy.

My father, on the other hand, wasn't so excited; instead, he had legitimate concerns. I'd just gotten home from Vegas. My life was an overall explosion of nuclear proportions, and he knew it. This wasn't the way he wanted his daughter's life to go, but at this point you'd think he'd be used to it.

I was upset at my father's reaction but I understood it. Ironically, my daughter was the most excited about the news of my pregnancy. She was exhilarated to have a sibling. I believe her enthusiasm bridged and healed the initial pain of my actions and consequences for my father. When he began to show signs of acceptance, my resentment for his initial response faded away.

I had kept in touch with one friend from high school, a boy who was in the Navy. I ran into his mother, Agnes, at the grocery store in town around this time. As we stood in the checkout line, she asked me if I had a minute to speak with her. I was in a hurry, but there was something about the look in her eyes that made me want to take time for her. She had lost her husband the year before, and her son was gone on a naval ship and her daughter was in college. I just assumed she was lonely.

We walked outside the store and sat on a wooden bench. I watched a small child put a quarter in one of those mechanical horses and ride it as Agnes began to speak to me.

"I want to tell you that I've been praying for you."

She began to explain her faith to me, but not in a daunting or over-the-top way. She was a Christian, she said, and the Lord had spoken to her and to some of her prayer partners about me. I wasn't even sure what a "prayer partner" was at the time, so I sat on the bench and just kept nodding and smiling.

"See, Anny, I knew at some point God would put you on my path, I just didn't know where and when," she said. "And here you are."

She told me a story of how, as her husband was passing, his best friend was there and received a word from the Lord that described me. I had never really gotten to know these people, and the thought of strangers praying for me was odd to say the least, so again, I nodded and smiled.

"I am beginning to believe in God." I shared with her how I'd prayed about the abortion. "I'm just not quite sure who He is."

Why I felt the need to tell this woman about abortions or prayers or God was beyond me.

"When you're ready to talk more, here's my number," she said.

She didn't force anything on me. She just let me know that she was willing to listen. That was it. She stood up and hugged me. I didn't want to let her go. There are just people in the world like this. No pressure. No judgment. Just listening and doing what God told her to do.

When I was six months pregnant, I started going into preterm labor. Agnes and her daughter took care of me at my parents' house. They'd take me to lunch or just talk with me on the phone. I'd dialogue with them almost every day. I was a disaster and they never, ever seemed to judge me. If I wasn't talking to them, I was talking to my sister or my mom, and when they got tired of talking to me, I read books.

I read a lot of books. Now I knew God was real, but who was He? I read about Buddha. I read about Allah. I read about the universe. I read a lot of books by Deepak Chopra, who had the most "truth" I could find at the time.

I was searching for ways to get God to answer me again. I prayed to miscarry almost every day. He seemed so distant now. I knew He was real, so I demanded that He show up again. This was His plan, right? But now I was alone, with two kids by two different fathers, and I had no job, no house of my own, and no money. My life seemed to be in shambles again, only this time, I couldn't fix it by "taking care of it" at the abortion clinic and running back to work as a stripper. I couldn't even get a real job at this point, because I was bedridden from constantly going into preterm labor, and I was relentlessly wearing out my sister, my mom, and Agnes for companionship.

"Pray, baby," Agnes told me.

So I did. I prayed for money. Yep, money. "God, I need money." I almost laughed at the hypocritical nature of it all. But within two days, I found out I qualified for financial assistance, and that it was exactly the amount of my car payment plus twenty bucks. I didn't know the scripture about God being able to do "exceedingly abundantly above all we could ask or think" at that point. I just took it as another sign that God was still alive and could hear me.

The question then became, why wasn't He answering me about my *life*? I was completely unattached and had learned that the growing baby inside me was a boy; I even began to research adoption for him. My sister said she wanted him, but I couldn't have that; I didn't need a constant reminder of how I left my kid.

I had a lot of time on my hands to sit and think. *God, who are You?* was the only thing that kept getting stuck in my head.

About a month before my due date, Agnes asked me to go to church with her. I went, trying to prove to her that Jesus wasn't the only way to get to God.

And yet, I noticed a difference between her and Christians I'd met in the past. Other than my family, most religious people I'd met all told me I was going to hell. All I could remember was being in that Sunday school class in the basement and being a bad Apple Jack in the hell pile. Not the good pile going with Jesus.

But Agnes actually loved me and supported me no matter what crazy thing was coming out of my mouth. I told her about my past, the desire to abort, and I had even bashed her Savior . . . and she never went anywhere. She was there for me all the time.

God had given unconditional love to me my entire life, with my mom and dad, and yet it took virtual strangers for me to truly see that unconditional love doesn't naturally come in the DNA of our parents. My parents loved me extraordinarily, and my mother was a rock God had placed at the center of my world, but I never realized that that wasn't part of her motherly duty. I thought she was just doing her mom thing. That all mothers did what she did. I didn't realize how blessed I was until I learned how other parents had abandoned, given up, or abused their children.

It made no sense to me. I was at the lowest of the low points in my life, and yet Agnes was a constant. So to entertain her, and then to prove her wrong, I went to church. The crazy thing was, as I sat there listening to the message from the pastor, it was as if he was talking directly to me. The thought crossed my mind that Agnes had told the pastor my business, but as I looked around, I realized this church was far too big for her to have that kind of relationship, so I chalked it up to coincidence—that the universe in its infinite power must have been talking to me.

Soon after that sermon, I had another attack of preterm labor. I was only at thirty-eight weeks when they admitted me to the hospital. Mom was at home with McKaylah and Agnes was at work when the preterm labor became real. I was given an epidural and I went to sleep. I woke up early in the morning and began to push. It was just the midwife, the nurse, and me.

My son was born at five a.m. on February 6. He was beautiful. I named him Amais.

❧

The first month was hectic. I was barely able

to take care of one kid, so caring for two by myself was a stretch. My parents were in the adjoining house, but they put the responsibility of parenting on me and set proper grandparent boundaries. This was tough, but it made me responsible. My daughter, who had gotten used to sleeping in bed with me, had to be put in another bed in our suite so I could put her new baby brother next to me for middle-of-the-night feedings. Unlike McKaylah, Amais was fussy. I think he sensed my anxiety about adding to my family and not having a plan.

I had spent basically my whole pregnancy bedridden, reading, trying to figure out who this *God* was, and now I was up every forty-five minutes to two hours with the new baby. I started to burn out very, very quickly.

When I had my daughter, I physically bounced back within a week. This time it took a bit longer, causing major body image issues in my life. I was dirty and smelled like breast milk, my hair was matted, and I had sag—everywhere. I didn't know this was normal. I didn't know all mothers experience this, as I came from a stripper subculture in a bubble of perfection.

A month after I had my son, I was on the phone with my sister Lisa. She had kept me sane throughout my pregnancy and continued to do so. We were deep into one of our normal conversations about Mom or Dad or just *What the hell am I going to do?* She was trying to talk me out of some crazy mental process that had become my norm. Keep calm and carry on. While we were talking, I suddenly got a sort of audible thought in my head: I wasn't hearing voices, it wasn't Bailey-like, but it was comparable to when a song gets stuck in your head. It was repeating itself over and over and over, growing in volume, until it became louder than the conversation or any other train of thought that I was having.

Out of pure irritation, I interrupted my sister and said, "Who is Matthew, and what does four sixteen mean?"

"What?" she said.

"I have this thought stuck in my head, like on repeat. I just keep thinking *Matthew four sixteen* over and over."

"It sounds like a Bible verse," she said.

The thought that anything to do with a biblical reference was in my consciousness was enough to make me want to hang up the phone. I thought of the Bible as "man's way to control a woman," even though, ironically, I had never read the book. Still, out of respect to my sister, I let her get out her Bible (I didn't own one), look up the passage, and read it to me over the phone.

"Those that have sat in darkness have seen a great light. For those living in the shadow of death, a light has dawned."

Speechless, I dropped the phone.

❧

Agnes called to explain some of the things she'd been praying for me about, as well as some of the spiritual dynamics of what was going on in my life. After talking with her over the previous six months, I was growing to trust her wisdom and support. After our phone call, and with my son calming down from a colicky spell, it hit me. I gasped and said out loud, "*I get it!*"

There was no one around besides my almost six-year-old daughter and newborn son. I sat there for a minute trying to figure out exactly what had just happened to me, but as it unfolded in my mind, I realized that Jesus Christ was the way for me to get to the Father; that heaven was real; that hell was real; that I was forgiven. . . . It was like an instant download from a heavenly iTunes.

It felt as if Jesus Christ Himself was sitting there with me, because He was.

The first thing He said to me was, "Don't let people tell you who I am, let me show you who I am."

In that instant, I had a new view on life, a new set of eyes that saw *everything* differently. But more than that, I realized that the voice I'd hear from time to time when I was working in the industry and about to get myself into a situation I couldn't get out of was the same voice I was hearing now—it was Jesus Christ the whole time! The voice before I got on stage. The voice in the club. The voice that always tried to alert me. I knew it was Him.

Everything the religious people had told me about Jesus wasn't who He was after all. God wasn't mad at me. God loved me. He was with me. He'd been with me the whole time. That meant He knew everything I'd done, and He was *still there*!

It blew my mind.

So many times we think Christianity or God has something to do with who people say He is, but we don't realize they may be misrepresenting who He *really* is.

This idea revolutionized my life.

The first thing I knew I needed to do was get a Bible. If that single verse from Matthew had been planted into my brain and heart while I was talking to my sister on the phone, and it had the capacity to jump-start this level of understanding, then I needed to know what *else* the book said.

I called my sister the next day to try and explain what'd happened; she believed in God and was a Christian, but we'd never talked much about it until now. She mailed me a Bible and a Beth Moore Bible study book—a six-week study on the fruits of the spirit.

I did it in less than a week.

I read the entire New Testament in a few weeks. I was starved for knowledge.

I couldn't get enough.

All the while, I was learning, being taught by the Holy Spirit. I no longer felt lonely. This is so important for people to understand. I no longer felt lost. I no longer felt like I had to figure it out on my own. I wasn't on my own anymore.

I started attending church—I was there every time the door was open. I hadn't been to church since childhood, other than with Agnes, so on Sunday mornings, when they had two services, I didn't know I could stay for both. I thought they'd kick me out until someone asked me if I was staying for the second service. My response was, "You can *do that?*" I felt like I'd hit the lottery. Every service felt like a conversation with God. Whatever the pastor would speak on, it was exactly what was going on with me through the week. It was so new.

When the worship music would start, I always felt like I was going to spontaneously cry. I didn't understand it, so I'd excuse myself from the pew and run to the bathroom until I got myself under control. It'd been so long since I'd felt *anything* that even crying felt foreign. I had no idea my tears came because God was touching my heart and reviving my soul.

After church, I would go home and reread all the notes I'd written down during the service, going over them again and again until the Wednesday night service happened, and I did it all over again.

No one at church seemed to notice—or care—that I was a dirty mess. I'd come in and sit in the back and never let my kids go to the nursery. It made me nervous to think about my kids in the hands of strangers. Sometimes, someone would ask to hold my son, and I'd always tell them no. I wondered why they wanted to, scared they were trying to steal my son, when in reality they probably saw what a mess I was and wanted to pray over my kids.

Finally, after five months of attending church and meeting the children's pastor, I started to see that these people might not be a threat to me, so I allowed my son to go into the nursery and my daughter to go into the kids' classes.

I ate it up. And in everything they taught, I recognized His voice. He talked to me everywhere I went. I was actually happiest when I was alone, because then I could spend time with my new best friend. I would sit down to read the Bible and He'd pour out revelation.

I was being transformed at the speed of light. I was able to feel again. By that time I'd accepted that crying was going to be a part of church, and once I let it go, it happened every service. I was being rocked by His Power. I still didn't talk to very many other people; I didn't trust them. But there were a few I befriended; the lady at the nursery who favored my son became a friend of mine. We exchanged numbers and talked on the phone every day. I told her the things that were happening to me, and she, like Agnes and my mom, was able to explain what was going on. These three women were my spiritual tour guides.

◁≥

About eight months into my church experience, I started to feel like God wanted me to go back to Los Angeles. I wanted to pursue a life in LA in the daytime out of the industry.

I wanted to be reborn where I had buried Bailey.

To make ends meet, I'd gotten a job at a local radio station doing marketing and advertising, and had a little bit of money stacked up, so when tax time came around and I got a big refund, I booked a flight and a hotel room to see if God would open any doors and explain why I had this desire to go to California.

When I arrived at the hotel—which, unlike in the old days, was nowhere near Beverly Hills—I learned that there was an issue with my reservation and I was upgraded to a suite. I took that as a good sign God wanted me there for sure. Each day, I'd wake up, pray, and go explore the city, hoping to find a divine appointment that would confirm my move. Each day went by and nothing happened. I was so ridiculously frustrated by the time the trip was over, I went out and had a couple of cocktails before my flight home in the morning.

Even with the big love I had found, I was still flawed.

More than anything else, I think this is what shocked me—*how* quickly I reached to self-medicate. I was mentally beating myself up.

What was I thinking? That I had heard His voice and magically He had turned the world into Oz and I was going to be skipping along the Yellow Brick Road for the rest of my life drama free?

This was an incredible misconception I had until Agnes and my mom reminded me that Christians make mistakes. *In fact, all the time.* That I was still going to have problems and issues, but it was how I was going to deal with those situations that made the difference.

Did I want to do it alone, self-medicating, or with Him, God-medicating? The second gives you much less of a headache in the morning.

I still went to church, but I avoided my time with Him alone. Maybe I felt embarrassed for my behavior. Shame was still an issue for me. Finally I broke down and I prayed.

"God, I don't know what You want me to do. Clearly, You don't want me to go to LA. If You have something for me to do, have someone at church tell me. Do something. Please."

And that's exactly what happened.

Easter Sunday was a few weeks later. A friend of a friend came over during the meet-and-greet time—my least favorite part of the service—with an uncomfortable look on his face. It was clear that he had something he needed to say but wasn't sure how he was going to say it.

After we greeted each other, he said, "I know what you're supposed to do. I had a vision."

I chuckled, unsurprised, and explained to him not to be tentative or freaked-out; I'd already prayed for answers. The look on his face was priceless; it was as if he was getting ready to say something that was going to cause my head to spin, and he didn't know how to break the news. "You're called to preach!"

Before I could think about it, out of my mouth came, "I know."

This is how God was showing up in my life. I never knew the answers to my questions, but I knew with deep confidence He would answer. So when He did, it wasn't startling or creepy or odd because as far as I understood, this was just how He worked.

chapter twenty
A TREASURE HUNT

But by the grace of God I am what I am, and his grace to me was not without effect.

1 Corinthians 15:10

Let's all just stop playing church and start teaching His grace and love.

Anny

I spent the entire next three years chasing God. It was wild. I'd wake up every morning and pray, "Lead the way, God, and I'll go!" And one day, He did, and the directions were very specific. He'd tell me to stay home one day and then the next day He'd tell me to go to the YMCA. On a morning in June after praying, I felt God interrupt me and tell me, *There's a gas station on the corner of Forty-Fourth and Eastern. I want you to get up now and go there. You will find a man in a blue BMW pumping gas. His mother is in the hospital and he is on his way to see her. I want you to tell him I'm going to heal her, and offer him prayer. Tell him I sent you.*

I was reluctant to do it. I wondered whether I was starting to lose my wits. But the instructions were so specific, so clear. This wasn't about being obedient, as they say in church. It was about checking my sanity. If I heard all this stuff, and what I heard came to be true, I couldn't be crazy. It had to be real, right?

I doubted first that the man would really be there. Then I worried he would think that I was some Bible-thumping kook who needed a ride to the psychiatric hospital. The way I saw it, the only way to find out if God really was directing me to go was to actually go to the gas station, so off I went.

When I arrived at the gas station, the man that God had described was pumping gas into his dirty blue BMW. *Whoa!* I almost fell out of my car.

I walked up to him and told him what God had told me. His eyes flooded and he quickly wiped the tears away. He was stunned and just kept murmuring and thanking me. Both of us were speechless in the shock and awe of it all.

From that point on, when I would hear from God, I did what He told me to do when He told me to do it. And sure enough, each time, the location, the people, the situation, and my participation in it all were completely accurate.

It got surreally strange. I was such a new Christian and I had no idea what was happening to me, but there was no doubt that astonishing occurrences and changes were happening. I began to research these types of occurrences and found a school in Northern California called Bethel. Students of this school of the supernatural participate in something similar. They called them "treasure hunts."

And that was what I was experiencing. God kept sending me on little treasure hunts.

Looking back now, I'm not surprised God was directing me. He has been giving unsuspecting individuals precise directives for thousands of years. He didn't just tell Noah to build an ark. He said: "Build yourself a ship from teakwood. Make rooms in it. Coat it with pitch inside and out. Make it four hundred fifty feet long, seventy-five feet wide, and forty-five feet high. Build a roof for it and put in a window eighteen inches from the top; put in a door on the side of the ship; and make three decks, lower, middle, and upper." He did this with Gideon and Abraham and Moses and David. Over and over there are *specifics*.

So of course He was going to use specifics when He talked to us. I'm not special, I was just listening.

During that time, I was having daily encounters with His grace. Love and acceptance and mercy met me everywhere I went. It was powerful and exciting and radically altering. Everything that was open within me was changed. I honestly could not get enough of Him.

At home I was relentlessly reading the Bible and studying the deep mysteries of God. I was digging deeper and deeper for the truths. It took me eight weeks, but I read the Old and New Testaments cover to cover. Then I read them again. Every time I felt that I didn't comprehend something, I'd raise my arm to God like a schoolgirl in class and ask a question. And He'd show me. Many times He'd lead me to study ancient pictographic Hebrew. He wanted me to get to the root of it. The door was opening to His Kingdom. The Spirit of Truth was leading me. Everything was shifting in my heart at such a rapid rate that I never questioned why. I just went with it.

~

I was finally at peace at home with my children and parents. Peace. I had overcome a huge obstacle by finding acceptance. Calm. I learned to enjoy the moment and let love wash over me. I just stopped running from—I don't even know what—and began trusting God. I experienced harmony on a level I'd never known before.

There was always temptation to revert. A handful of my old friends would call and want to go out to bars or dancing, but I declined their offers. I just wanted to stay in and stay serene. My social life at once minimized and expanded to include only other people who were also teaching, learning, and praising God. We would worship and delve into history and allegories of the Bible and Jesus' life for days on end. It sounds bizarre to the unbeliever, but we would pray and worship the Lord until the wee hours of the morning. It was as if the Spirit was pouring into me and I was just beginning to understand what that meant and the prevailing ramifications.

My family never articulated it, but I think they were worried I had lost it, that the drugs had finally pickled my brain. And why wouldn't they be? I'm sure anyone who had watched the drama of my life unfold, or even some who may be reading this now, must be thinking that I went from one end of the spectrum to the other.

But that is how God works, when you let Him work. He takes the least among us and transforms them.

I didn't describe the most horrific acts in my life—as I have done in previous chapters in detail—and my own willing participation in them to try and entice you. I wanted to show you—to prove to you through my experience—that Jesus loves us even when we are at our worst.

He can take the most screwed-up sinners—and I really don't love that word—and change them, from the inside out. For me to sugarcoat my brokenness and how atrociously I behaved to appease certain individuals' sensibilities would be doing Jesus a disservice.

It's easy to love the lovable, but it's not so easy to love in the other direction. I spent a great deal of life acting out in ways that were utterly unlovable. But there is no doubt that Jesus loved me through it all.

My family couldn't deny that a serious change had taken place. I went from a hard, promiscuous, drunk, out-of-control party girl to a relentless, passionate follower of Jesus Christ. My mood had changed. There was an easiness that was making its way to the surface. My words were kinder. My thoughts were less judgmental. To be honest, I just stopped being so horrible all the time. Even my appearance was different. I had always wanted to come across as *hot*. Let's face it: I was a stripper. Or at the very least, I wanted to be fashionable. I laid down all of that, as I knew my appearance had been my shield, and just wanted to experience how He had made me. I let go of my bleached-blond mane and dyed my hair back to its natural brown and donned a uniform of comfy T-shirts with loose jeans.

This was a season in my life, and it was and still is a process. I am by no means holier than thou. I still struggle with my personal demons, and anyone who knows me will tell you that I love great shoes and fashion. But at that time it was important for me to just be simple.

To not be distracted by anything. Gone were the fake lashes, glittering body parts, fast cars, and high (stoned) life. I needed to shed it all and let God transform me into whatever He was designing.

I had no idea where He was taking me—I just knew I couldn't get enough. I was undergoing a metamorphosis in a divine cocoon, and He was in there with me.

I was in complete revival, which is a churchy word for restoration and revitalization.

I was attending Agnes's church, which was predominantly an African American congregation. When the choir sang "Freedom" by Eddie James, the lyrics "No more shackles, no more chains, no more bondage, I am free. Now help me dance the dance of freedom" spoke to me. As the congregation sang the words *freedom* and *hallelujah* over and over, they were describing exactly how I felt: free. My soul and feet leapt in unison.

The music would stir my soul and open a passageway to my heart that had been closed since I had played the piano in my basement and listened to my neighbor howl at the moon. I was flooded with a passion for music and life that I thought I had lost long ago. I had never experienced anything like it. The Holy Spirit would rain in ways that would shift the entire atmosphere for me. It's hard to explain without sounding mystical or full of smoke and mirrors, but the easiest way to articulate it is to imagine the complete opposite of where I had been, in the seedy underbelly of darkness and hate and oppression that exists in windowless strip clubs with their perversion and bondage. That to me was hell, and what was coming out of me was divine love.

I was serving in the children's ministry, which was hilarious, as I didn't enjoy being around children other than my own. But I didn't mind doing it. The kids made me laugh and smile. I found joy, as I was doing what God wanted me to do, so their whining and tantrums didn't annoy me the way they had in the past. I was so hungry to submit to what was being asked of me, I did anything the church asked me to do. Anytime there was something the pastoral staff needed me to do, I flew. From stuffing pamphlets, putting bracelets on the kids for security, and setting up and breaking down the kids' rooms to working with the pastor's wife to make sure she had her Bible and belongings in her seat, I just wanted to serve. My spirit was in such a place of gratitude that I would have happily cleaned the toilets for Jesus in an airport if that had been what was asked of me.

～≫

I had been saved for a few years when I finally got baptized. For me, the reasons for water baptism are clear in the Bible, but at that time they seemed more important to the church than to me. To me God had already saved me. I could hear Him. I could feel Him. I knew He was real. But I wanted to follow the proper order of things, so I signed up to be baptized after church at the local YMCA. I just assumed that baptism was a mandatory component to my salvation.

I think that is where I missed my mark—I forgot to pray about it. *It happens.* I spent a great deal of time saying yes to *good* work without making the distinction between God work and God-directed work.

McKaylah was almost in the second grade. My parents watched my son as I packed our towels and bathing suits and off to the YMCA McKaylah and I went. It was a sweet ritual but more meaningful to my seven-year-old than to me. Two different men baptized us at the same time. When we came up from the water I didn't feel anything. We went to the dressing room to change and I pondered, *Where was the* aha *moment?* Nothing. It left me slightly disappointed.

In my mind I expected fireworks or a little waterworks show. I dried off and dried off my little daughter's body and helped her get dressed.

As I tugged her shirt on, she said, "Jesus said I didn't have to lie anymore." Maybe that was my fireworks show. Brushing her hair, I realized I was still trying to earn Jesus' approval. I was serving in church (*which is awesome, keep doing it*), but I was trying to manipulate an encounter with Him by doing this baptism when maybe it wasn't my time to do it. I still believed that I needed to *do things* to deserve God's love. But my daughter, who had approached the baptism and, well, God's love as a total gift, was giddy about how Jesus had spoken to her.

There was an underlying tug on my soul, *even now*, that believed that if I served enough, submitted enough, prayed enough, followed the rules enough, if I was good enough, He wouldn't change His mind about me.

I had repented. And when I use that word *repent*, I don't use it willy-nilly. The Greek word for repentance, *metanoia*, means "to change one's mind." Now, for me, the only true way to have my mind and heart changed was by God—by the Holy Spirit. There's no other way to explain it. I was changed and it didn't come from anything on this planet.

My thought process from years of feeling unworthy and dirty and a lifelong fear that God could crush me at any time had not completely gone away. I mean, if God was going to be mad at someone, it should be me. Somewhere inside I figured I had used up all my grace coupons when I was running amok. I had felt my own version of hell and I didn't want to go back, and so I definitely needed to keep doing everything *right*.

Well, that's impossible.

After a long conversation with God and just being still, I finally grasped that I didn't need to do anything anymore. I didn't need to work to get Him to love me or approve of me. It was enlightening. So many people get caught in this web of *playing* church or religion, pretending to be good enough, dressing the part.

That belief system is the flip side of the same coin of exactly what I was doing in the sex industry—performing for approval.

I had believed that what I *did* was who I *was*. That by being a stripper or a *sinner*, I had disqualified myself from God's love. And now if I just did enough pleasing things for Him, I would be taken out of the "sinner" category and become prequalified for the "heaven" category. I was still that little girl in Sunday school separating the Apple Jacks, only now I was putting all my nice deeds of good service into the good pile, hoping if there were enough, I could tip the scale of God's judgment in my favor.

What I learned was that the cross is the great equalizer.

I had it backward for so many years. That's largely what kept me from ever really believing anything about God. To believe would have meant I was completely busted and going to hell for sure.

But the Holy Spirit was with me long before my trip into the YMCA pool. It was between Him and me. It's between *you* and Him. We're like the criminal next to Jesus at the cross. In short, the Bible says the bad guy repented to Jesus. He knew who Jesus was, and his thoughts were changed. Did he need to have a baptism or to stop stripping? No. He didn't even need to beg for forgiveness. He just *knew* Jesus. And Jesus *knew* and loved him, and through that love the man believed and said, "Jesus, remember me when you come into your kingdom" (Luke 23:42). For the criminal it didn't depend on anything in his life that he had done to be with Jesus, as frankly it was all baloney, and there wasn't anything good. I can relate. He could only depend on God's love. And God's love is what he got. God's love is what I got. Free of charge.

This was when the lights truly went on for me.

I am happy that I got baptized, and for many people there are overwhelming reasons why one should do it. I just wasn't doing it for one of those reasons. When I realized how deep and how wide and how long and how grace-filled His love is, I knew it wasn't about being dipped in pools or bending in pews or blabbing in confessionals.

It is by His love and mercy we are saved. I had things in reverse order.

chapter twenty-one
NOW WHAT?

Trust in the Lord with all of your heart. Lean not unto your own understanding. In all of your ways, acknowledge Him and He will direct your path.

Proverbs 3:5–6

Sometimes His plan and your plan are really, really different. But trust me when I tell you, His plan is always the better plan.

Anny

On my thirtieth birthday I wanted to know what was next for me. I decided to do a five-day fast. I had learned the importance of fasting from the Bible. From John the Baptist to Jesus and heroes and heroines in the Old and New Testaments, people prayed and fasted for a breakthrough. I wanted answers. I prayed, "Jesus, You started Your ministry at thirty. What am I supposed to be doing?" I prayed, "What did You save me for? You saved me for something, *something*. What is that something?"

When you pray these types of heart prayers, be ready for answers. It wasn't that I wasn't prepared; it was simply that I did not expect what He would say.

When my fast ended, I was watching McKaylah, who was now ten years old, teach Amais, who was five, how to play chess. I had taken the television out of our equation for a period of time while studying. I didn't want to be sidetracked. But on this night as I sat there playing games with the kids, I felt the Spirit of God say, "Turn on the TV."

Two things about this are funny. I had to actually lug that old television out of the closet and I nearly killed myself doing it. And then I had to hook up ancient antenna rabbit ears to it. *Yes, we had antenna ears,* because we didn't have cable.

I was shocked to find a channel that would never normally get reception coming in as clear as the blue sky.

I watched as a pretty woman in her thirties gave an interview about how she'd been a stripper for a few years, and now she was spending time going into strip clubs and other places where sex is sold, and she was ministering the love of Jesus Christ to women in these places.

In the last decade in the clubs, never once had I experienced an evangelist type trying to love on strippers. Maybe tip them, but never deliver them. As I watched, I felt God say, "I have something similar for you to do."

In my body and mind, I questioned, *Really? Me? How in the heck am I going to do that?* But at this point the supernatural stuff that was happening to me made far more sense than the *who, what, where, when,* and *why* questions everyone, including myself, kept asking. I knew if this were what God wanted, He would make a way.

That week I went to the library to research whether there were ministries that had places for women in the XXX business to go, like housing for women who are escaping abuse. I felt we needed to give them a place, a home where they could stay free of charge and we would love, feed, and help them move to the next stage of their lives. We needed to provide a home of hope. I scoured the Internet for more ministries that existed for women in the sex industry that needed help.

You see, I had been blessed over the years to have my parents to support me and show me love and keep reminding me that I was going to survive. I had them when I needed to escape. But 99 percent of the girls that I knew in the clubs did not have a place to go, even if they wanted to leave.

I learned about a handful of ministries across the country where Christian women were going into the XXX world and reaching women in the industry. I couldn't believe it. I was so thrilled that I e-mailed two of the women. The first was Annie Lobert. She was a former prostitute; she had been trafficked and beaten. She had struggled and fought and then given her life to Christ. She had started a ministry called Hookers for Jesus in Las Vegas.

In the back of my mind, I was incredibly thankful that God had picked her and not me to minister in Las Vegas. To this day, the thought of Vegas makes me shiver. She had a home for women in the sex business called the Destiny House in conjunction with Hookers for Jesus. I examined every step of her journey, taking notes as I watched her do interviews on shows like *Dateline*, *Nightline*, and *The Tyra Banks Show*. Annie was a maverick, radical Christian making a statement: Jesus loves women in the sex industry.

The second woman I found was Theresa Scher. At the time she headed a ministry in San Diego called JC's

Girls. She has since stepped down from the organization. Theresa e-mailed me back immediately and we began a dialogue that lasted for months.

We realized how much we had in common; we had both started at the same club chain, Déjà Vu, only she was in California, and we both ended our careers at the Crazy Horse Too in Vegas. We both had children the same age, and we were both in the industry for the same amount of time.

There was something special about connecting with Theresa, as she had witnessed the same darkness and shame and struggles in her life that I had been through. It is so important that women in the industry have someone to share their rawness. It made me no longer feel like an alien in my life. When we chatted, we were like two aboriginal people from the bush figuring out how they had survived in the middle of Times Square.

My triggers from the industry about men and my ongoing inner numbness on many topics made sense to her. See, even though I had found hope in Jesus and I was being transformed, it's a process. Theresa taught me, as a woman, to begin to love myself again, that there was more to adoration than being a sex object, and that I could love myself, even though I struggled with shame.

I had a deep respect for her. She helped me learn the next steps I had to take if God was really calling me to house women in the industry. Again, I believed God had put someone in my life to help me. She began to teach me how to love others—that *love* is the answer to everything. She was a wonderful mentor and is still a dear friend to me.

⇜

I felt God telling me to go back to the first club where I had danced. I didn't know why I was supposed to go back there. I just felt the tug from Him to go. Maybe there was a girl in the club that I was supposed to help. Share the wisdom Theresa had shared with me. I had no idea; I just knew I had to try.

The night before I had planned to go, I had horrible nightmares. I woke petrified. Remarkably and right on time, Theresa called and told me that whatever I was meant to do today, "Go."

So I went.

The club had been moved and rebuilt and was twice the size it was before.

I sat in the parking lot and just prayed. I prayed and prayed for about an hour. I didn't know what to expect when I went inside. How would I feel? Would it be too much? Then without knowing what I was supposed to do, only knowing I was meant to go inside, I felt a Power inside, and I went.

As I walked into the lobby and looked around, I realized I was holding my breath.

The only other time I remember holding my breath this long was when I was thirteen in the back of the elevator, when I was trapped with the basketball player who was assaulting me.

I sat at a small round table near the stage and ordered a Sprite. A girl whom I knew and whom I used to dance with came up and offered me a dance. She didn't even recognize me. I don't know if she was too high or if I looked somehow different.

Is this the girl you want me to encourage, God?

But I got nothing. I just sat looking around at the wickedness hiding in the shadows of the place. I perceived the aching and the loneliness. I hadn't ever allowed the real emotions of it to infiltrate me. Never sober. I couldn't let it bore inside me.

I prayed in the spirit, and I prayed in my voice. When it became clear to me, I knew it was time to leave. *Just go.*

I walked out to my car and got inside and sat there for a long time just lamenting and grieving.

I knew God had brought me back to this place not to help some new girl but to show me what He had saved me from. When the reality of where I had been and what I had done really hit me, I began to release deep whimpers and cries that turned into uncontrollable sobs of gratitude.

He had brought me back to show me what He had done for me.

It was another indication for me that if He could love and save me, He could save many.

I was beginning to understand that this had to be God's plan for me. He was forging new business and ministry relationships for me, and opening doors with each person I met. He was teaching me to learn, understand, train, and equip myself to properly minister to women, but also to be who I was and not sell out within the context of the church.

He was placing stone after stone along the foundation of my new life. It was all at His fingertips. With guidance from Theresa and others, I began the long road of research to launch my own ministry for women in the sex industry.

With my degree in family studies, my upbringing in a world of influence, my screwed-up life in the sex industry, and my desire to offer hope, I knew God was making sense of it all. Everything I had gone through in my past and at the church seemed to be part of this great destiny to start a home for women looking to exit the sex industry. With Him, I had a clear focus. I finally knew what I was supposed to do with my life.

I cannot tell you how grateful I am for the pioneers in this type of ministry, the women—Theresa and others— who mentored me. They wrapped their arms around me to prepare me for what was coming next. They offered me inspiration, possibility, relevant messages, and serious game plans. Thank you.

During this time, I had tried several ways to meet with the pastor's wife, as I wanted to articulate to the leaders of my church that God was telling me to go love on strippers, as strange as it sounded. I wanted their guidance and support but nothing was coming to fruition. I knew that she was going to be thrilled for me that I had finally come to know what my role would be in the Body of Christ. I had served under her and so many at the church, in a variety of capacities, but she knew my heart was yearning to have more vision and that I hadn't yet heard from God. I couldn't wait to share it all with her.

When we finally had our meeting scheduled, I waited two and a half hours, but she never showed up. I tried to reschedule three times, but she would never call back to confirm a time.

I began to sense coldness in church from the leadership, but I didn't understand why. I had shared my vision for ministering to women in the sex industry with a few of the parishioners and the youth ministry leader: I had told them that I believed I had found my calling. But there was no way they could be upset about that, *right?*

I tried not to let it bother me. I maintained my heart for God and progressed toward launching a nonprofit. As much as I wanted my church leaders to assist me, I knew they were busy and had their own missions, and this was something God had told me to do. *Press on.* So press on I did.

With a few friends from Lake Forest Academy who were involved in legal professions and nonprofits, I began to properly build the framework for a nonprofit ministry. They, along with a woman named Carol Reed, whom I had met through Sid Roth's show, *It's Supernatural!*, came together to form a board of directors for me. Carol's testimony is incredible. Mind-blowing. God again showed up with another woman from the sex industry for me to hear and learn from.

I spent two months filling out all the paperwork to submit to the IRS—a twenty-eight-page document that I nicknamed the Beast—and become incorporated in the state of Illinois.

I wanted a name for the organization that wasn't Christian-cheesy. My favorite revelation story of the Bible was what happened in the Garden of Eden with Adam and Eve. I believe it tells us what God originally had in mind for us before the serpent showed up, before there was evil.

Eve was Woman's *fallen* name. She wasn't Eve until Woman (and Man) had fallen into sin. *Angels* means "messengers." Essentially, Eve's Angels is what we are—what I wanted my nonprofit to represent. We are the messengers to tell women that you no longer have to live fallen lives anymore. No matter where you've been or what you've done—or are still doing. You don't have to live under the curse of what the devil is tricking you to believe. He wants to destroy the hope that real love exists for you. *Lie. Lie. Lie.*

Eve's Angels was born.

⤙⤚

Just as one door opened, the Lord shut another. One afternoon I was working in the church's children's ministry, painting mime faces for a children's program.

I became overwhelmed with what some would consider a "gut feeling."

I had to sit down.

I must've looked white, because another volunteer asked me if I was okay.

"This is the last time I'm going to be in this building." It just blurted out of my mouth.

She scrunched up her face and said, "What does that mean?"

"I have no idea!"

We continued to get the youth ready and then were going to watch them perform, when the pastor's wife walked up to me and said, "I need to talk to you."

Finally!

I was so enthusiastic. I couldn't wait to share with her all the pieces that had fallen into place. I wanted to tell her how God had taken me back to the first club and connected me with other women in this type of ministry, Theresa, Annie, the board. So much had happened.

When we got to her office, a room adjacent to the sanctuary, I was bursting at the seams, illustrating to her all that had transpired—all of the little and huge miracles that had happened.

At some point in my up and down and pacing and laughing and talking about this and that, I realized she wasn't rejoicing with me. She was just standing stone-faced.

I sat down slowly. "Is something wrong?"

It seemed as if she was trying to choose her words carefully, as there was a long minute of silence before she said anything. Then she began.

"I can't believe you would go into *those* places. You and this so-called ministry need to find where you're supposed to go, because it isn't here." Her tone was condescending.

Wham. Direct hit to the belly. I wasn't expecting that.

I was shocked and didn't know what to say. My heart sank. "Why?"

"Anny, why would God tell you to start something and not also tell the pastors here? We're the leaders of the church. You should have run this by us."

"I tried."

This was so confusing.

I was just naive enough to not understand the difference between religious and Spirit-filled people.

All of a sudden I realized that I was still an ex-stripper to her. Or maybe in the hierarchy pecking order,

I had broken some invisible code, skipped some boxes that are supposed to be checked, but I hadn't done it intentionally.

I had loved it there and I was grateful for the good people like Agnes who had walked me through these last seasons. But my time there was over.

The pastor's wife made it clear: "There is no place for this type of ministry in this house."

But, but . . . it's God's house. I wanted to say it so badly. To remind her that Jesus said "Feed my sheep" and "Just bring them to me." I wanted desperately to rebut, but I didn't want to be disrespectful. What's the point?

Had I not gotten that gut feeling, almost preparing me for what was coming when I was painting faces that afternoon, the premonition that it would be the last time in that church, this turn of events would've been far more than I could've handled.

I drove home mourning that this season of my life was changing like the autumn leaves. I prayed to God that this was the right direction and that He would bring a new place and crop of people for me to serve in my life.

A month later, I was on a plane to San Diego. I went to visit and train with Theresa and her team, to go on outreach to clubs with them. I sensed that her ministry was an incredible grassroots outreach and felt sure that if Eve's Angels could touch women with God's love, we would be able to provide housing when they were ready to walk off the stage. We would be the follow-through home.

During this time, the IRS sent a letter stating that my nonprofit's 501(c)(3) status was approved. Everything was going well.

Theresa is a captivating brunette with an ethnic background that is Hawaiian, Portuguese, Japanese, and Chinese. She has a face that is so unusual, you can't help staring at her.

When we were sitting in a club, I asked her, "Don't you ever tell the girls to quit?"

She said, "No. That's none of our business. It's not our job to convict or convince them. It's the Holy Spirit's job. Remember when *you* worked? Could anyone tell you to quit?"

It all made sense while I was there. That statement changed the way I looked at how to do ministry in this industry. It was all about the *love*. The goal was not to get them to quit—it was to show them the love of God. If they could get that revelation, then quitting would be the by-product.

⟡

My son was in the hospital with bronchitis and asthma, which was seriously affecting his lungs. While I was in his room, a nurse who tended to him began talking to me about God. Now, she knew I was a believer, as she had witnessed me pray over him many times.

When he would rest, I would tell her about all the mystical things that were happening in me and in my life to both set me free and give me vision to help women in the industry. She told me about a revival meeting that was taking place at a church in Grand Rapids. They were having some of the same streams of ministry teams that I was talking to her about and getting out into the community.

When my sweet baby was well, I decided to go to the revival and check out the church that hosted it, and sure enough, it was my type of scene. During the weekend, they were sending people outside the four walls of the church to do ministry. Even during the conference. It was all part of it. It was awesome.

During one of these exercises to minister outside the church, I felt God tell me to go to another strip club and then report back to the group. At this point I was doing more listening and learning and had not shared too much about my past with them.

But I went to a club and did what God told me, and when I got back to the church, I was asked where I went. I got on the microphone and began to tell them that I had gone into the XXX club and taken the girls Bibles and invited them to the church later that day. You could have heard a pin drop.

Everyone just sat there shocked. Someone actually looked back at the door as if it were going to fly open and a parade of naked strippers was going to march down the aisle.

The girls didn't come. I think they didn't believe they were really welcome in the church, just as I never had.

No one in the church responded, and the story seemed to suck the oxygen out of the room. It wasn't the response I was hoping for, but at least I wasn't booted out!

Where was the crossover God?

Then I received this irresistible sensation that God had someone there I was supposed to connect with. I felt God nudging me, as if He was standing behind me pushing the back of my shoulder gently forward. He had a connection for me there. I talked to several women but nothing seemed out of the ordinary.

When I was leaving, the senior pastor came up to me and said, "Aren't you the girl who went into the strip club?"

I explained to him that I was building a ministry that desired to house girls from the industry, and that I believed God wanted to send me back out to California to set it up and partner with the outreach ministry Theresa was spearheading. I was *sure* with every fiber in my being that's where God was sending me.

"I know my wife and I would love to hear more about that. Would you meet us for lunch tomorrow?" he asked.

"Sure." I was hoping they were the connection that God was revealing and they had some type of direction or backing that would help me reach these women.

The following day, I showed up at a Mexican restaurant decorated with hanging red chili lights, sombreros stenciled on the wall, and a mariachi band. I was ready for chips and salsa and to hear what they wanted to talk about. *Download me with some good Godly news.*

When we sat down, his wife began.

"God is telling me that you're not meant to go to California."

I know I am a Christian, but her so-called prophetic word made me choke on my chip.

"He wants you to start Eve's Angels right here, in Michigan."

No! I wanted to yell at her.

"That you are to take the training you've been given to begin outreach in Grand Rapids. The house will come later."

My inner Madea was right on the verge of exploding. This lady had to have a bad connection with God or something.

I thanked them for the lunch and we all began to leave.

I walked to my car and then she hugged me unexpectedly and said, "It's going to be amazing."

It made me feel awkward, moved, and mad all at the same time.

I did nothing but sit there replaying all the plans I had under way to begin my life with my kids in California. I had a good plan. In my mind I was done with ice storms and gray skies. And outreach wasn't my ministry. Housing was to be my ministry.

About ten minutes away from the restaurant, I was rolling along in a haze when out of nowhere a man ran a red light and smashed into my car.

Now I know what you're thinking. God doesn't cause bad things to happen in our lives, but I believe the bad things that do happen can be used for good. The good part of getting T-boned, of breaking my bones and having no vehicle for a bit, was that I was going to need to stay in Michigan and follow the plan . . . His plan.

chapter twenty-two
PLANTING EVE'S GARDEN

I am the vine; you are the branches. If you remain in me and I in you, you will bear much fruit; apart from me you can do nothing.

John 15:5

We can do many good things to serve God on our own. But allowing God to do His works through us takes our surrender and brings true glory to the Father.

Anny

I continued to extract practical wisdom from the Bible. It was my resource for restoration. New awareness would come daily during my mediations and discoveries of the Word and the significance and methodology of the characters in the Old and New Testaments. The contextual meaning behind Jesus' parables leaped off the pages for me as if each moral tale was to be used as a new lesson for me to put into practice in my life or to save for the ministry work that was ahead of me.

The process required a daily surrender—and that process was never ending. Surrendering was an enormous emotional, mental, and spiritual hurdle for me to overcome. I had been raised in an extremely competitive bubble that required multiple levels of coping mechanisms for winning. What I learned from God's word was that I had to completely surrender if I was to ever find my purpose and peace.

Surrender in our house meant forfeiting, and *forfeit* was a dirty word. But for God, surrender didn't mean giving up but rather *giving in* to His will. Having a willingness to let Him lead. My will or His will? This one contradictory inner interrogation will always dictate the outcome of victory for me.

When I would lose over and over in the real world, losing would catapult me back to my darkness. Learning to forgive myself and forgive others—countless times— was the major turning point for me in becoming able to lead Eve's Angels. That and discovering that only His will would stop the devil from continuously undermining any progress that I was making.

I was invited to speak in Grand Rapids at a church led by the pastor and his wife who had declared to me that I needed to plant the Eve's Angels' flag in Michigan.

The pastor only had one suggestion.

"Don't go into too much of the stripper stuff." He tried to say it delicately in the pew as they were passing the offering buckets.

"I get it." Keep the niceties on, and don't get too graphic.

Narrating accurately what goes on behind the scenes of the sex industry makes people uncomfortable, particularly in the church. And it should; that's the point. It should be so disturbing that it calls them to action. Church should be the one place where people can come and honestly tell what has happened to them, and receive healing, mercy, grace, and love. I heard a poet named Jefferson Bethke speak a line in a video that he put together, and it jumped out at me: "The church has become a museum for good people, but it should be a hospital for the broken." Not all churches are this way. I have been exposed to many wonderful, spirit-filled leaders and churches that are completely dedicated to serving and helping. They are truly mirrors of Jesus' vision. And what I have learned is that there is a time and season to tell appropriate stories from the pulpit.

I was grateful that the pastoral couple was brave and supportive enough to pass me the microphone for five minutes to explain Eve's Angels and give the particulars regarding our upcoming Bible studies and how we were going to reach out to women in the sex industry, offering them hope and belonging.

The church donated their building for Eve's Angels to meet and conduct Bible studies on Tuesday nights with the ultimate goal of equipping our street teams and sending them out to clubs. I was witnessing God moving. He always delivers on His promises.

Monday afternoon I received a call from the pastor's assistant.

"Can you come in to the church today?"

My initial reaction was that the pastors had changed their mind about letting us use the church for our studies. "Sure."

Much to my surprise, her next sentence was, "There is a woman, she's got some demons. She's a prostitute and wants to talk to somebody."

Amazing. I agreed to meet with the woman and two

other women from the ministry team from the church. The secretary showed me to a small room where all three women were gathered.

"They've already been in there for twenty-five minutes." The secretary's mouth cringed slightly as if she was trying to warn me of what was in the room.

I opened the door quietly and spotted a black folding chair near the three women, who were sitting in a small circle facing each other. As I made my way over, the group turned and looked at me.

"Sadie, this is Anny," Miriam, who worked as a greeter on Sundays, introduced me to the prostitute.

"Good to see you," Louise, who served with me in the teen ministry, said.

"You don't look like no pastor." Sadie snarled at me through her semirotting teeth.

Right away I knew that Sadie was a serious addict. I had known plenty of junkies in the industry. From her one-inch black roots contrasting with her platinum-blond hair, pulled back in a ponytail, to her hollow brown eyes and skin with divots and acne on her cheeks, I could see she was wasted.

She started scratching up the arm of her Gap T-shirt.

"I'm not." I sat down in a chair next to her.

I held her stare as long as I could but there was something crawling behind her eyes.

She kept tugging at the mini jean skirt hugging her bony frame. She must have fallen, as she had scabs on her knees and she was wearing Ugg boots.

"I'm dying," she blurted out.

She was high on something—meth, PCP, LSD, crack—or else she was completely mentally ill.

"Can you fix me?" She sounded desperate, looking at Miriam.

A growling noise that wasn't feminine or in the English language came out of her mouth, and at first I thought it was an elongated burp, but then a revelation came to me that it wasn't her voice.

Whatever that sound was rebutted her desire for help. A demon.

When the secretary at church had called me, I thought she was saying "demons" as a metaphor. But she meant it.

I closed my eyes slightly, calling on the Spirit of God.

I had read about these types of demonic spiritual encounters, and I could tell my new friend, Sadie, had had enough of her demon. *I could relate.* She wanted it gone but usually demonic influences don't go away easily. Ask any heroin addict. The drug speaks to them, calls to them, and haunts them.

The whole idea of demonic possession has gotten widely dramatized and overblown by everyone from religious fanatics to Hollywood, and it is usually accompanied by a creepy deliverance ritual meant to wean unsuspecting victims from the dollars in their wallets in exchange for freedom from depression, addiction, anger, and sickness.

In Greek, Latin, or even Spanish the term *possessed* loosely translates as "under the influence." A demon can be in control of a person, but the word *possessed* doesn't mean that the demon owns the person; the person is just tethered to the evil. The good news is that God can cut any soul free from demonic influences. How many times have we heard, *The devil made me do it?* Well, maybe he did. Today we live in a world filled with extreme diseases, mental health issues, crime, addiction, perversion—the list goes on and on. And at some point, we have all wrestled with what I would call a demon inside us.

Ninety-nine percent of the time *casting out* a demon isn't ghoulish. But what was inside this woman was untamed and undaunted. I have since, over the past decade, seen much darkness inside people, but seeing this type of demonic tapeworm fighting to stay inside this woman was for me indeed a unique case and straight out of the movie *The Exorcist*.

There's a reason that little girl in *The Exorcist* scared the hell out of America. The supernatural evil realm, when manifested in a human being, can be more frightening than one can imagine.

My two syrupy Christian friends began to speak over her about sin and salvation. Thirty minutes passed. I began to fear more for the church ladies than for the prostitute.

This was no joke, and no one was prepared for what was coming, me included.

I didn't know how they wanted me to help them, and when I feel confused, I pray.

When I looked up from my prayer, there was a sensation hovering around. I put my head back down so as to not look at her, or it, and continued praying.

Matthew 8:28 in the Bible came to me. It was the verse about when Jesus cast out the demons from two men. The men were so violent no one could reach them. I remembered the demons yelling at Jesus.

Then the prostitute stood up and her chair fell backward. Both of the churchwomen jumped to their feet and stood back out of her way. I kept seated, not moving, praying.

Her mouth opened and she had the voice of hell, with cursing and vulgarity laced with human fear.

I am fine with the f-word and c-word and b-word, but they shocked and scared the church ladies in this holy house.

I kept praying and remembering that Jesus had the power over the demons in the men from the Bible. He ordered the demons to leave the men.

Sadie's thrashing and trash talking were meant to terrorize the ladies, and they were working. But for me, her words were nothing new. I had heard them used over and over in clubs for years.

There was a power struggle of good versus evil going on inside Sadie, and now the evil in her had verbally slapped the church ladies with a couple of curse words.

I recognized that if push came to shove, and this got out of control physically, I could tackle Sadie if she tried to hurt one of the women. I wasn't going to let a ninety-pound demon-influenced hooker take them out.

The church ladies kept looking over at me as if I had some superpower with women in the sex industry. I wanted to remind them that I wasn't Jesus or Captain Save-a-Hooker. I was an ex-stripper trying to change lives in a new ministry.

Yes, I had been given supernatural revelation, but this demon manifestation was novel to me.

One of the church ladies began quoting from a book, "Deliverance . . ."

I looked at the cover and saw it was a basic how-to-cast-out-demons book.

Really?

Beetlejuice. Beetlejuice. Beetlejuice, I thought she might yell for help.

Maybe we all should've read the book before that demon started manifesting in Sadie, because I knew that if whatever was in her came out, it was not going to be pretty.

Didn't anybody remember *Alien*?

Then Mark 9:29 came to me, and I recalled that certain types of demons can't be driven out by anything but prayer. I ignored the women doing the so-called deliverance and I began to pray in the Spirit, trusting that God would give me the words. I prayed the Holy Spirit would show up.

There was no magic water or sage to burn or Indian dance, just hard-core prayer.

No Christian covert operation of weirdness. Just the Holy Spirit.

In between praying in the Spirit I would make this *Ummmph!* sound. Like my own verbal exclamation point.

The woman started twisting her neck in ways I am not even sure are possible unless she had extra disks between her C5 and C6. She was profusely sweating, and her sweat smelled like a trash dump. Wetness seeped through her skirt and she was dripping fluid down the insides of her legs.

She was right. She was dying, and what was trying to kill her was more powerful than her addictions or prostitution.

I stood up from my chair, with a mighty power that was not my own, and finally got her attention.

"Submit to God. Resist the devil, and he will flee from you!"

Wow! Thank you, Jesus! Thank you, Holy Spirit!

Looking into her eyes, which were darting back and forth, I tried again. "I said, submit to Jesus. Submit to Jesus. Resist the devil and it will flee you."

I shook her shoulders. *"Flee her in the name of Jesus!"*

She began to cry and break down. "Help fix me," she begged.

Then she dropped to her knees and I went right down with her. She was heaving in cries of pain.

Out of compassion, I just wrapped my whole body around her and hugged her.

"God loves you, baby. God loves you. We love you. We love you. God loves you. Thank you, Jesus. Thank you, Jesus. Thank you for loving this woman." I just kept saying it over and over.

This one moment seemed to be the most effective thing we did in hours.

Calmness fell on the room.

I know it sounds nuts, and if I hadn't seen it, I wouldn't have believed it. But I was there, and it wouldn't be the last time I would see this sort of thing.

I went to bed that night feeling as if a car had rolled over me. It was the same kind of aching in my body that I had experienced when I came home from dancing at the clubs. Everything on me was sore and hurt.

So God, this is how it's going to go? These are the ones You have for me?

I fell asleep before seven p.m. and didn't wake up until seven the next morning.

❧

Word began to spread that the Holy Spirit was moving within Eve's Angels.

Women (and some men) wanted to be a part of the ministry and began to reach out to me. Each woman had her own story and each had her own gifts, and the love of Jesus was connecting them all. It was exciting to be on the battleground used by God but also exhausting, as the more I dug in, the sadder and darker the realities of humanity were becoming.

Joyce, a woman from the church, approached me asking to be a part of the Eve's Angels Grand Rapids team, but she wanted to tell me her story first.

We agreed to meet at a coffee shop. I had prayed, since I needed the Spirit to show up before I went in, and I heard Him say, "Go, and be strong *in Me*."

The place was almost empty. We sat in a booth by the window across from each other. She was a kindergarten teacher dressed for school.

The waitress came by and took our order.

Joyce began slowly, "I feel like I want to help. But I am not sure if I can. I just have so much . . ." She looked down like she was in trouble.

"I grew up in a small suburb near here. My father had died, my mother worked all the time, and my grandfather was a pastor at a church."

The waitress poured coffee and we both sat silently until she finished and walked away.

"My uncle used to take me to the basement of my grandfather's church as a small child. I was maybe five or six."

She stopped and looked at me for reassurance.

"My son's age." I related to the innocence.

"My uncle and my grandfather would . . ." Her eyes went down immediately toward her black coffee.

Be strong in Me.

"They would . . ." She looked out of the window for a minute at the people passing on the street, and then directly back at me with no emotion at all. "They would have sex with me, and they would videotape it."

I swallowed hard, brokenhearted for her.

Child pornography.

The evil that was being revealed to me was a constant barrage, and my survival techniques were starting to kick in. I started to numb out.

Numbing out is not good in ministry when you need to feel empathy. But I was numbing. And she needed *something*.

When she finished telling me the details of her rape and trauma by her family in a church, I reached across the table and put my hands on her hands.

"You're okay."

It was all I could muster.

"I've never told anyone. And sometimes, being at the church even now makes me so . . ." Her eyes looked at the ceiling, searching for words. "Uncomfortable."

I said nothing.

She forced a smile. "You're shocked?"

I cocked my head at her. "No. I am in awe of you."

"Why?"

"You're still somehow finding God."

"God is the only thing that I remembered for so long. I blocked out all the rest. When those things were happening to me, there was this picture of Jesus that hung on the wall and I would just stare at Him, and it was as if I was out of my body. I can't explain it. He was alive in that picture for me. He didn't make what happened happen, but somehow He just removed me for a minute."

I knew exactly what she meant. "You survived."

Relief drained from her face. "Yes, I did."

The waitresses came to refill the coffee, giving me an exit opportunity.

"I'll be right back. I need to go to the bathroom."

I had to fight a secret war within myself to not let other people's stories trigger my own memories of humiliation and hurt. When I got into the bathroom, I went into a stall and locked the door and prayed.

"Lord, this is all too much."

Hearing her talk about how her family could do this, and her first impression of Christianity and sex and men and Jesus, ripped me in half. I closed my eyes and silently prayed. I didn't pray to comfort her but to comfort myself. To somehow keep me present and attached.

Be strong in Me.

I walked back to the booth and looked at her, and I could see light in her. She survived because of a picture of Jesus. *A picture of Jesus.*

"I just don't know if I'm good enough to help these women, you know? Holy or whatever," she said.

I tried to loosen the atmosphere. "You know I was a stripper, right? That I took off my clothes for money?"

This time she smiled for real. "Yes, I know that."

"And you're not judging me for what I did?"

"No! I would never do that."

"I promise you, Joyce, you're going to be amazing at loving on these women. Jesus made you that way."

I would have to be able to lean on Him and be strong and connected to Him in all of this if I was going to endure not just my own past but also the future. If this was really what God wanted me to do in ministry, there would have to be a continuous surrender and a pouring out of His Spirit into my team and me. There was no way to do it without Him.

The burnout rate in nonprofits that minster in this type of environment is fast and furious. You have to be born to do it. Touched by God with a purpose. Much like FBI agents who hunt down child traffickers and predators, you have to recognize that you're in it to save lives, for a divine destiny and purpose, or it can become too excruciating to attempt to rationalize and comprehend the evil that goes on every day in this world.

chapter twenty-three

BUILDING OUR TABERNACLE

Jesus said, "but when the Holy Spirit has come upon you, you will receive power and will tell people about me everywhere."

Acts 1:8

We are modern tabernacles where the Holy Spirit can hang out as our closest comrade, helping us sometimes sidestep life's land mines and walking with us through the heartbreak and the joy.

Anny

About fifteen people showed up for our first Eve's Angels Bible study on a Tuesday night. I was perched on a metal-backed barstool with a tan leather cushion watching the crowd saunter into the small room and indiscriminately take their seats.

Once seated, they looked at me as if they were hypnotized. *Wow, this is really happening. Eyeballs everywhere all on me, and I have my clothes on.*

"I'm Anny." I stood up from the barstool. "Can you please stand up?"

They looked at each other, confused. "Okay, everybody up. Take a deep breath." I raised my hands above my head, reaching for the heavens.

Each person halfheartedly stood up and then followed my movement.

"Now a really big one," I took a deep breath—*whoosh*—"and let it out."

I took another big breath and then said, "Here we go."

They all said it with me, and then I asked them to sit down. The exercise drained a tiny bit of nervousness out of the tightly stretched balloon of expectation.

"I want to start by thanking you for coming. Really, thank you. Eve's Angels really needs dedicated, Spirit-filled teams. And I want you to feel relaxed. I'm going to start slow . . ."

They opened their Bibles, expecting me to ask them to look up scripture. I just shook my head and said nothing. A few seconds of awkward silence passed. My foot bounced up and down on the bottom bar of the barstool.

One by one they reemerged from the ritual of Bible *study* and looked at me again for dictation.

"We need to cover a few things before I begin. The first and the most important thing is that we are *all* going to need to trust God in this ministry. Really, really trust Him. We're not going to be playing church or debating theological rhetoric. We're here to follow where Jesus wants us to go. We're here to help the ones that others have forgotten about."

More wide-eyed silence.

"Can someone say okay or amen or something, so I know you're getting it?"

"We hear you," Joyce said.

Thank you, Jesus, for Joyce.

"I founded Eve's Angels to help women who are trapped in the sex industry find restoration by ministering the word of Jesus to them in a nonjudgmental, hope- and mercy-filled way. Our goal is to become both a symbol to stop sex trafficking and a ministry that reaches into the local communities and places where sex is being sold, to offer grace and a way out to the women."

I paced back and forth in front of them.

"I'm going to equip you as God and other incredible women who have been doing these types of ministries have equipped me. But know it all comes from Him. We're going to initiate small grassroots teams with messages of love, realism, and courage for these women to take a step toward Jesus. We're not trying to drag them out of the club or preach hell and sin at them; we're trying to show them Jesus' love. To ignite inspiration and educate them on a new way."

I sat back down on my barstool. Some of the people were taking notes.

"It will be through His love and the Holy Spirit's conviction that they will either reach out to us for help or they won't. But like it is for every single one of us when we choose Christ, it has to be their personal choice to have a relationship with Him. We are the messengers. Through an encounter with Jesus, with you showing His love, and *if and when* they are ready, we *will* find ways to transition them out of the industry with the resources they need. Look, one of the ways for a woman to get over the past is to see a real vision for her future. We will help them discover that vision—their gifts, talents, purposes—and then we will help them achieve those. We will help them set passion- and God-based goals and reach them. Some will need immediate housing, counseling, and rehabilitation: we'll find it. And if they never want out, we will *still* love them. They're people, just like us. And all of them will need prayer and grace. All of them. We never stop loving and praying."

I looked around the room at each volunteer, trying to connect with each person's heart.

They nodded at me like willing soldiers.

"People believe this trafficking issue and women trapped in the sex industry is only happening overseas. That"—I covered my mouth in faux shock—"oh, no not here in America, not in our little town. But it is happening in this town and every town around America, and you're about to be a witness to it in our community. Together we are going to change cultural viewpoints and save lives. I know it's a lot to take in, but we serve a mighty God. Amen?"

"Amen," they said.

"The Holy Spirit is going to lead us. *Not me leading us—Him always leading us.* He has gotten me this far, and believe me, that is a long, long way, and we are going to have to trust in Him more than ever, just so everyone is clear."

A man in the back spoke up. "Are we going to go to strip clubs?"

I could see and feel his spirit wasn't right. "You, sir, are not going to go to a strip club. At least not with us."

He got up and left.

After doing countless speaking engagements and Bible studies, I've come to learn that there is always the inquisitive, kinky, strange guy who shows up.

I leaned forward and closed my eyes. "I pray that my words will be anointed and that the Holy Spirit will lead me." I opened them back up.

I'd been praying this all day.

I asked myself a rhetorical question out loud: "Why me? Why did I, Anny, want to do this?"

This is when it gets tricky.

"Because I was one of them. On the stage and on the drugs and out of control. Sure, I had plenty of cash and booze and even fancy cars. Oh, you can have money in the sex industry, but the devil had stolen my hope. I had no good reason to want to get out, and I was slowly killing myself and everyone around me. I had so much shame inside me, and denial and pride and anger. It was a powerful and delicious cocktail the devil had served me. We all have something that can hold us in whatever bondage we are in."

A few people nodded in agreement.

"I want to tell you my truth, my testimony. *Testimony?* That word comes with such"—I made my voice deep— "dun, dun, dun."

They laughed.

"But in reality, what is a person's testimony? Well, it's meant to be their story of redemption, but the meaning of a testimony for most nonreligious people is when you have to go to court and get into a witness box, place your hand on a Bible, and under oath tell the truth. It's supposed to come with supporting facts and proof. Be your own open declaration of what has happened. In Exodus, God told Moses to put down the law on the tablets. For us today, our Christian testimonies are our truths of how the Holy Spirit has changed us from the inside out."

I told them my testimony, but back then my testimony never started with my childhood; my testimony always began at the birth of the sex industry in my life. I would allude to the fact that I had come from a good home but never, ever said who my father was or anything about my upbringing. Despite all that I had been through during those younger years, and what was miraculously happening to me now, I still felt tremendous humiliation for the suffering I had put my family through. I didn't want to continue dragging them into my story of muck, even if *now* the story included redemption. In my heart I felt I had hurt my family over and over, and I didn't want my public testimony to draw any attention to them or remind them of who I *was*.

I also still carried fear: fear of the travel bus, the hotel elevator, ball court hallways, and rape. The beginning of my story was a torrential secret I had not disclosed. I had not openly spoken about the experiences that had catapulted me into the industry. I kept those details between God and me.

Unveiling where I had been, particularly the prostitution of my body, heart, and soul, was dreadful, but recounting how God had showed up for me on a hotel bathroom floor was easy to verbalize.

I wanted to leave my family out of it.

Truthfully, I had yet to *fully* comprehend, accept, and forgive the toll those years of chaos had taken on me and on my family. I was in the process of doing it. It was a day-to-day unearthing, grasping, and pardoning. An everyday cup of grace and mercy, compliments of the Holy Spirit.

What I did indisputably understand was that all of it

had come with a hefty price tag, but thankfully that price had been paid at the cross. The path to my salvation was my continual focus on and relationship with God. This I could easily admit.

Be strong and filled with Me. This became my mantra. I wasn't looking for perfection in myself or anyone else, just progress. That progress was part of Eve's Angels' inception and all part of God's sovereign plan.

When I finished telling them my testimony, I concluded by saying, "Eve's Angels isn't selling any type of miracle cure for whatever ails these women, or me or you. We don't get cured from our past, we get healed. And that healing comes from Jesus. Any questions?"

"Is it going to be dangerous?" the woman next to Joyce asked with a pained look on her face.

"The easy answer is no. But we live in a bizarre world, and the sex industry is a subculture of darkness under a layer of crazy. But it's no more dangerous than crossing the street when God is protecting us."

I addressed the group. "We shouldn't expect our lives not to be stormy, just because we're Christians or trying to help others. It doesn't mean we're not going to fall into a sinkhole. But you will need to have courage. You will have to have faith. Faith that this is what God wants you to be doing. How He wants you to be serving. Have you prayed about it? Have each of you asked God if you belong here?"

Some nodded yes. Some didn't do anything.

"Can you look at Matthew 14:25?" I turned the pages in my Bible and began to read.

"Shortly before dawn Jesus went out to them, walking on the lake. When the disciples saw him walking on the lake, they were terrified. 'It's a ghost,' they said, and cried out in fear. But Jesus immediately said to them: 'Take courage! It is I. Don't be afraid.' 'Lord, if it's you,' Peter replied, 'tell me to come to you on the water.' 'Come,' he said. Then Peter got down out of the boat, walked on the water and came toward Jesus. But when he saw the wind, he was afraid and, beginning to sink, cried out, 'Lord, save me!' Immediately Jesus reached out his hand and caught him."

I closed my Bible. "The last thing that I'll tell you is that you have to have faith. You have to be called by Jesus to be here, doing this type of ministry work, and you must have that courage to keep your eyes always on Him."

⁓

I chose two women—Joyce and the assistant pastor of the church—to go to the club with me that night. I put to work what I had learned from Theresa in San Diego and what God had imparted to me.

I gathered my bearings, smoothed down my hair, and paid for the three of us to get into the strip club. We sat down at a small table near the stage. They had questions; I gave them answers that were not always politically correct but were true. When I didn't know the answer, I was honest. We sat, talked, discussed, and I waited.

I had no true idea of what was coming next; I just knew God had led us here. And God showed up.

Two half-naked strippers walked up to our table robotically.

"Do you want a dance?" the first girl asked, shifting from one six-inch platform shoe to the other.

"No, but thank you," I replied.

"Well, if you don't want a dance, what are you doing here?" the second girl asked with a Minnesota accent and a sarcastic tone.

"We just want to tell you that we care about you. See if you need anything. Prayer? Hope. . . ?"

I tried not to sound like one of those orange-robed, bald Hare Krishnas at the airport.

The second girl rolled her eyes at me and walked away, but the first one stood there.

I continued, "Look, I used to be a stripper, and sometimes I just needed a reminder that God loved me."

I went on to briefly tell her a little about Eve's Angels and how we all just wanted to come and to say, *We're here and we care—no judgment.*

She pulled up a chair and started bawling. She was so deeply heartbroken from working in there. My goal wasn't conviction; it was just love, but God's love moved on her so quickly, it overwhelmed her. It overwhelmed us all.

"I grew up in a Christian home, but my life has gone haywire," she candidly began. "I got pregnant, and then I needed money, and I met some girls and ended up here." Her confession left her face flushed.

I reached for a glass of ice water across the table and gave it to her.

"I want to go to college. I have, well, I had, dreams." She insisted on looking at the two other women with me. "Honestly, I'm just going to do this until I can get on my feet."

I remember those ideas. It's called coping.

After we talked to her and let her know we'd be praying for her and that God was on her side, not against her, I asked her who the manager was.

She told me the woman's name was Laverne and where I could find her.

Off I went to the attached adult novelty store to go ask Laverne if she would allow us to bring some gift bags into the club for the girls.

"What's in the bags?" Laverne was hardened and jaded and wore it on her face. She looked weathered from this brutal business.

"Nail polish and, um, brushes, candy, and Bibles."

"Bibles?" She repeated mockingly.

"I just want the girls to have something nice from us. That's it. No judging or recruiting or trying to brainwash anyone." I tried to sound soft-spoken, hoping she'd keep an open mind. I again explained about Eve's Angels.

I thought she'd be fine with it; after all, she was a woman. Surely she'd understand.

"Get out. And take your Bibles and religion with you," she said resentfully.

"No problem," I replied humbly. "I understand where you're coming from. I was in the industry, and a lot of Christians treated me like a second-class citizen and did a terrible job of representing God's true love. No problem."

Laverne's demeanor changed to grievous.

"You were a stripper?" she asked skeptically.

"Vegas, Chicago, Lansing, . . . Detroit."

"You can stay." She turned and curtly walked away.

"You know I'm done with dancing, right? I'm not going to dance?" I added.

She erupted over her shoulder, "I said you could stay with your bags." Then proceeded on with cool anguish.

Later that night Laverne came up to our table to make sure we didn't need anything. "You girls want a soda?"

I wanted to tease her and tell her that I knew she had a kind soul under all that anger, but she wasn't ready for it. Her pain lived inside her and kept her safe. Life in here was choking my tired new friend. The Holy Spirit told me to wait on her and just pray.

We left our gift bags with the girl who'd cried. She said she'd be in touch.

"Do you think she'll call?" Joyce asked as we walked toward the parking lot.

"Maybe?" I pondered.

"I hope she does," the assistant pastor added.

"What I do know is, right now she realizes that God is thinking about her. That God loves her. That was the mission."

The night ended, and the two women I had brought into the club with me had their lives changed forever. They had witnessed firsthand how badly they were needed there. They learned how the simple love and kindness that Jesus preached could impact one woman's life—one life in need of hope that would probably never have been touched had we not gone to the club. And they began to grasp that customary missionary work skips these addresses and keeps moving. They recognized that Eve's Angels was the ministry willing to go inside.

This was the beginning of the huge impact Eve's Angels would have on the women in the sex industry in Michigan, but it was also the seed God was planting to grow the ministry team He was gathering for us.

～

Before our next meeting, I felt God telling me to preach. Preach His word.

I prayed the entire day, "God what do you want me to speak on?" He gave me a revelation about the tabernacle, how it can be an analogy for our lives. That everything and everyone uniquely has a purpose, a place, and a connection to Him. It would be my first *real* message, and it would eventually become a part of the first Eve's Angels curriculum guide.

Our group of attendees had doubled. After opening with a prayer for guidance, wisdom, and to be led by the Holy Spirit, I looked up and saw the preacher, his wife, and their twentysomething daughter sitting in the back.

I began, "In the Old Testament, they would build a place for God to live." I made eye contact with Joyce in the front. It warmed me that she was back. "And everything in the Old Testament is a prediction of what is to come. In Exodus, God gave Moses instructions to set up the tabernacle, and the building of the tabernacle is an awesome example for us today."

I shifted the microphone from my left hand to my right, as my fingers were beginning to hurt from gripping it so hard.

"Moses built a physical tabernacle in a very detailed way after hearing from God. In the New Testament, we . . ." I paused to make sure they all understood.

"*We* are His tabernacles. Today, God lives inside of you and has a very unique way He has designed your life, your journey, and your story. Your tabernacle is no different than the one Moses created."

I looked up. "Are you following?"

The preacher's daughter, Liz, was intently looking at me. She said, "Yes, yes!"

"We are the tabernacle and the Holy Spirit dwells in us."

I was talking so fast that I knew it wasn't me but the Spirit of God in me.

"When God gave Moses their laws, He wrote them on stone tablets to be placed in the tabernacle. Now that *you* are the tabernacle, He writes the laws and His word on your own heart and mind. Jesus gives us the key to Him and our purposes with the Holy Spirit."

I got up off the stool and walked down to my group, touching each one on the shoulder. "In our lives, even when bad stuff happens, God has a way of taking the worst of what we've done or has been done to us, and if we'll let Him, using it for His purposes and for the purposes He has specifically for you."

This was why my life in the sex industry made sense to me now. God was taking all that I had done, that He had allowed me to choose, and now He was using it for good.

I walked back up to my stool and took ahold of my Bible. "He gives us this blueprint, and as a bonus you have the Holy Spirit constantly with you like your own personal contractor who fixes all the broken pieces and connects them again—for free."

I set my Bible back down, sat down, and leaned forward, placing my elbows on my knees.

Almost at a whisper: "When you align with the pattern God has for your personal tabernacle, you'll feel peace and joy and a sense of *Yes! This is my purpose.* Jesus came to this earth for one reason, to love you. It all starts there. Just let Him love you. His plan for you is more than you can imagine, and His blessings are endless."

He was working that night, and by the end people were praising and praying and love was there.

Thank you, Jesus.

❧

After the meeting, the pastor approached

me. "Nice job, Anny. I like what you're doing here."

"It's all the Holy Spirit. He's really moving the ministry, and quickly."

"We knew. He spoke to us. I am just glad you're here."

I wanted to keep the momentum going, and I had felt God telling me that we were going to be in the media. I could feel something big brewing, but I didn't know what it was. It prompted me to ask the pastor, "Do you think that we should do a press release or something to announce the ministry?"

"Yes. That would be great. We can show you how."

"Okay, that would be terrific. I need to get going. I've got to get to a club for outreach."

Before I turned to leave, he said, "Have you heard about what's going on in Ohio?"

"No. What?"

"There's a church that has been picketing a strip club for years, and now the strippers are picketing the church on Sundays in their bikinis."

I would have laughed if it weren't so sad. "That's too

bad. I'll make sure and pray for the situation."

"Okay. Keep doing what you're doing," he encouraged me as I left.

On my way to outreach, I went back to the club where we'd gone before and took Laverne a fruit basket.

She didn't really know what to say. I knew the industry had taught her that nothing comes for free, but I hoped she was getting the message that we weren't like other religious people she'd clearly encountered who had probably judged her and made her feel like less than she was.

As I walked off, I wondered what would've happened if someone had visited her years ago and just loved on her. That simple act of kindness could've changed the rest of her life. The thought inspired me to keep finding more women like her and showing them the true love of the Father.

I got in my car and began to pray for her, and then I prayed for those girls in Ohio and the pastors. I prayed Jesus would help them put down their picket signs.

chapter twenty-four
JESUS DOESN'T CARRY A PICKET SIGN

If I speak in the tongues of men or of angels, but do not have love, I am only a resounding gong or a clanging cymbal. If I have the gift of prophecy and can fathom all mysteries and all knowledge, and if I have a faith that can move mountains, but do not have love, I am nothing. If I give all I possess to the poor and give over my body to hardship that I may boast, but do not have love, I gain nothing.

1 Corinthians 13:1–3

In the end it is all going to be about how much we loved Him and how much we showed His love to others.

Anny

My new sister-in-law, Marta, was a petite, beautiful Brazilian with tan skin, thick, curly jet-black hair, and a fiery heart. I understood why my brother, Bob Jr., had married her. She exuded a spicy zest from her full lips when she spoke, even if I couldn't understand a word she uttered in her broken English. The newlyweds had come home to Michigan for a quick vacation from

China, where he was the head coach of the Shanghai Sharks. He had become an international and Chinese phenomenon, and Marta was a radiant companion for him.

My brother returned to China early, so I offered to chauffeur Marta to the Chicago airport, as her animated, fiery personality was entertaining to witness for the three-hour drive. With her hilariously heavy Portuguese accent, she tried to describe my brother's friend, Yao Ming, the Chinese team's owner, and then she warmly wondered whether my brother would land the position as the Chinese national basketball coach. It was entertaining, virtually eavesdropping on her thought process.

During the lulls in our one-way dialogue, I would feel something in my spirit that was making me uncomfortable, an inward angst itching at my soul, and I couldn't quite scratch it. I flipped the radio station three or four times, searching for decent tunes to relax me. I let out a deep frustrated sigh and turned the radio off.

"You are irritated. No?" Marta questioned.

There was no way to explain the supernatural tug at my spirit, given our language barriers.

"Not irritated." I tried to keep it simple. "Maybe I am just excited to be going to Chicago."

"Like me and Brazil. I love Brazil, and my family there, and the beaches . . . and . . ." She daydreamed out the window.

I looked at my GPS on the dash and realized we were only twelve miles away. Although Chicago had been a place that contained ex-stripper baggage for me, I felt attached to it.

Intense spiritual morning dew lay thicker and thicker on me with every mile that we got closer to the airport. I had arranged to leave Marta at the airport and head directly back to Michigan. It had been a mentally and physically time-consuming week of ministry, and I was longing for moments of innocence and simplicity with McKaylah and Amais once I got home.

Parked in the departure zone at O'Hare Airport, I heaved Marta's overstuffed designer luggage out of the trunk of my dad's sedan, kissed her on both cheeks, and watched her curvy body walk into the international terminal.

Another wave of enthusiastic anticipation tangibly hit me, causing me to take a step forward to maintain my balance.

I knew it was God.

I looked up at the clouds floating in the blue sky. "What? What are you trying to tell me?"

I climbed back in the car and sat behind the wheel, not moving.

I asked again, "What are you saying? I can't understand."

An airport security guard tapped on my window, startling me and causing me to bang my head on the door window. "Ow!"

I thought he was a messenger.

"Keep moving," he said with annoyed vigor.

I turned the key in the ignition and drove out of the airport. I recognized that there was a specific mission I was supposed to do in Chicago, I just didn't have a clue what it was. My heart was heavy from the heightened awareness. As I drove, I searched everywhere for signs from above, from marketing slogans on passing billboards to the license plates on cars in front of me. I was looking for a dispatch from the Divine to pop out and give me direction.

Nothing came.

I pulled into a gas station to get a Mountain Dew and fill up the gas tank with unleaded fuel. I knew this perplexing apprehension wasn't going to stop until I really prayed and He answered.

Does He want me to stay in Chicago? Does He want me to go home? Is there someone He plans for me to minister to in the city? What? What is it?

I set my large caffeinated drink on the hood of the car and placed the gas nozzle in the tank, feeling resigned that His time and my time are different, and apparently patience was a fruit of the spirit that I still needed to work on.

I halfheartedly said, "Can we make it easy? Just have someone call me. Because I am not quite getting what you're trying to tell me."

I finished filling up the gas tank, screwed the cap back on, grabbed my drink, and got in the car and headed back onto the road toward Michigan. I craned my neck toward the windshield and looked up again.

"You know God, I feel like a teakettle down here ready to blow. I know you have something for me. But I'll wait. It's okay. Really."

My phone began to ring and I almost knocked over my giant soda fumbling to grab it out of the nearby cup holder.

"Have you heard what's going on in Ohio?" I recognized the number: it was a woman who worked for Theresa's ministry in San Diego.

Immediately, every hair on my arms stood up. Chills ran down my body.

God was telling me to go to Warsaw, Ohio.

~~~~~

Theresa had been tending to her dying mother, but she, along with my pastor in Michigan and the media, were closely following the church-versus-strippers clash that had erupted in Warsaw. I desperately wanted Theresa to come with me on the trip, but she had family business to tend to following her mother's passing, so instead another woman would join me. Theresa imparted many words of wisdom, prepping me, as she understood this type of conflict and how it can turn volatile quickly. The mission was to be on God, and then me, and thankfully her representative, as there would be gift bags to stuff and media to manage, and two are always safer than one.

From Chicago to Michigan, the nuances of the trip began to unfold: travel, hotel, and goodies for the dancers. As my brother or father would call it, the game plan.

Home in Michigan, I packed my bags, kissed my babies good-bye, and set off for the five-hour drive to Columbus, Ohio. I met Theresa's girl at a hotel and we set up base camp at a Holiday Inn. Inside our room, we began to put the gift bags together on our double beds as I prayed and wrote prophetically for each of the girls on individual cards. Every card would be a different message from Him, not me. We prayed that each note would be specific to each dancer's particular situation.

Less than forty-eight hours after I dropped my sister-in-law off at the airport in Chicago, God had us ready for Warsaw. Our strategy was to rest and spend Friday night in the hotel and leave Saturday morning. The journey had been long and we both needed sleep, but when I got into the small shower and yanked the plastic curtain shut, I knew we needed to go *now*.

The Fox Hole strip club in Warsaw was an hour and a half away from Columbus. It took us three hours. We were adrift on county back roads with no street signs, driving in circles. Damn devil had us lost in nowheresville among the overgrown trees and farmland and raccoons.

Warsaw is a classic Americana community that can't have over eight hundred residents. It has one main street and one football team. It was hard to miss the strip club in the middle of town, with the local police cars, onlookers, and picketers outside. It was a ramshackle XXX spot with a small fluorescent billboard in front that had a drawing of a stripper in a bikini on the pole on one side, and the words THE FOX HOLE in large black letters. On the other side was their own special message, CHECK OUT OUR 3 X 4 $30 SPECIAL.

Wearing my heels, jeans, and a black and sparkle tank top, I walked through the picket line and passed the police cruisers and made my way toward the club. I was hesitant, worried about how the ladies would perceive me, but I pressed on until a female gatekeeper stopped us just inside the door. She was a full-figured veteran wearing a blank, stretched-out tank dress that barely covered her bottom cheeks and breasts. Her name was Jean.

My instincts took over.

"Do you have a house mom?" I was nervous.

"I'm the house mom." She squinted suspiciously at me.

I knew winning her over would be a step in the right direction, but I wasn't completely in control of how to do that.

"We come in peace." I tried to sound Native American.

Then my sidekick held up the box of gift bags and said, "We are Christians."

The woman cringed.

I jumped in. "I just want to apologize for what you're seeing out there." I gestured at the picketers. "I used to be a stripper. Honestly, we just want to show you a different side of what you're seeing and what you've been hearing. Because it isn't quite accurate."

"Well, you got that right." Jean's lips puckered.

"Jesus doesn't call people a whore or dirt or a home wrecker. And, and . . ." I closed my eyes, waiting for the Spirit to move. "He wants you to know that you're not forgotten."

She reached out and pulled me in for a bear hug. "Come on in."

I spent the next two hours in the Fox Hole dressing room with Jean and some of the dancers, telling them not only about Eve's Angels but about my background in their business.

"Why did you come?" a pretty blonde in a cowboy hat asked me.

"Because God told me to come."

"But why?" she kept digging.

"He wanted you to know that He doesn't carry picket signs."

"You're telling me that you came to tell us that Jesus doesn't carry a picket sign?"

"Yep . . ." I got a lump in my throat and my eyes began to swell because I felt God's grace and the hope it offered. "And that He loves you." Tears poured down my cheeks.

I really don't like crying, particularly in public.

The woman who questioned me began to cry. It seemed as if we were all crying.

I went on to tell them what had happened on my drive to Chicago, and the phone call from Theresa's ministry, and that there had been an extraordinary directive for me to come to them. That the situation needed to be rectified here and now.

They were overjoyed and cynical at the same time.

"Anny, you have no idea what you're dealin' with out there," a dancer with a white garter belt on her thin arm apprehensively said.

"No, but God does. Trust me when I tell you, He's already got this worked out."

And it was a good thing, because by the time they finished telling me about the endless years of threats, negativity, and hate that had been put on them by the church, the more I understood it would have to be God standing in the gap between these two completely opposite viewpoints.

As we left that afternoon, I promised to return the next day with pizza and more prayer and hopefully more clues on the next steps.

I walked out of the small club energized with the Holy Spirit. It wasn't until I read what was on the picket signs that my own anger started to brew. *Human anger.* Yes, despite all the prayer, I still wanted to whack someone over the head with their own picket sign.

As I drove back to the hotel, my anger turned to sadness.

In the Holiday Inn, I researched backstories on the events that had taken place in their small town both in the name of Jesus and in the name of freedom of expression. The dancers had their viewpoints, their right to work, their right to do what was legal, and the church had a very legalistic interpretation of God's word.

The picketers, who were led by the local pastor at the church, were filled with hellfire and brimstone, and the dancers were filled with rage and pain. It seemed to me that both had made a mockery out of what Jesus came to this earth for and had died for on the cross. Both had missed the mark and taken such strong positions that there was no light to see the truth of His love for both of them.

I had more empathy for the dancers than I did for the religious picketers. I tried not to judge either side, but I couldn't help speculating that the Christians were more responsible for the turmoil. How was it that as followers of Christ they weren't imparting what Jesus taught?

How had they missed Matthew 22:36? "'Teacher, which is the greatest commandment in the Law?' Jesus replied: 'Love the Lord your God with all your heart and with all your soul and with all your mind.' This is the first and greatest commandment. And the second is like it: 'Love your neighbor as yourself.' All the Law and the Prophets hang on these two commandments."

The pastor and the picketers had all the right in the

world to teach their viewpoint, but I couldn't comprehend how loving the women was not seen as the one answer. They didn't have to agree with the stripper's chosen profession. But, what if for every picket sign that was purchased, created, and held in a Christian person's hand, a Christian person instead went and bought a bag of groceries and left it on the doorstep of the club? Or flowers, or just kind words of hope?

They certainly weren't getting anything accomplished trying to shut down the club in their town. But they were getting the women's hearts shut down to the possibility of finding love and transformation through Jesus.

The next morning as I got ready to go back to the club, I talked to my family and our ministry teams and asked them to pray for us. I sent messages to my pastors and to others and asked them to keep this trip at the top of the prayer list.

The Fox Hole was an hour-and-a-half drive from our hotel, and yet again we got lost and it took three hours.

There was a Little Caesars pizza close to the club, so we decided to stop and get five pizzas for the dancers.

I stood looking up at the pizza menu.

The kid behind the counter stared blankly at me. He pulled off his black pizza logo baseball cap and pushed his dirty blond hair back off his forehead and smiled. "Are you ready to order?"

Then I heard God say, "Get one for the picketing Christians."

Really, Jesus? A pepperoni or sausage?

They were the last people I wanted to feed, let alone have to engage. But obedience is something that I had finally learned after twenty-something years of rebellion.

We walked inside the dressing room of the Fox Hole carrying pizzas. The dancers all clapped. They were joyful to have us back, or at least free pizza.

Over the next several hours, the Holy Spirit began to move, as the girls would rotate in and out as they had to meet with customers and get on stage. They began to tell me about their lives and their dreams. Their children, their hobbies, their bills. As they were talking to me, I would simply begin to pray with them. God was giving them an encounter with His love right there in the strip club. He turned their dingy dressing room into holy ground.

Four women gave their lives to Christ that night because of His message of hope and nonjudgment and free pizza.

As day turned to night, the myth that God was mad at them was lifted as they could tangibly feel the Holy Spirit washing all over that place.

"Would it be okay if I prayed over you all before we leave?" I asked the girls listening.

"Yes, Anny! Pray." They were shockingly open to His words.

"God's message," I began. "His true message has nothing to do with whether or not you are strippers. Your Father in heaven is going to love you no matter if you decide to walk out of here now or stay in here forever. He is the same yesterday, today, and forever, and His love is unconditional."

I get much negative flak from religious people for this one message. They tend to think I should be encouraging these ladies to get out of the industry. But it isn't my job to condemn them, it is my job to show His love to them. I have no authority to judge them or tell them they are going to hell if they don't immediately stop whatever it is that they are doing. My job is to impart His most important message. Love God. Love each other. And He will handle the rest.

"God loves each one of you, and there is nothing that you can do to be *qualified* for that love, nor is there anything you can do to be *disqualified* from that love. He isn't mad at you. He wants you to feel His grace. He made you uniquely His and knows how many hairs are on every one of your heads."

"Will you pray with me?" I took a stripper's hand and she took another. "Repeat after me?"

I began, "We pray this message takes root, Father. We pray to know your love more. We pray that you will forgive the picketers—"

Some of the girls stopped. But I kept going and then they repeated it.

"We pray that You will forgive the picketers for misrepresenting You. Father, we pray for You to forgive us where only You know where we need it. We pray for hope and we pray for love to continue to cover us." I squeezed the woman's hand next to me extra tight.

"Amen."

And the ladies said, "Amen."

Thank you, Jesus. I was almost blown over by how God's mercy isn't weird or kooky or strange, it's just love and we all need it.

Outside the club I saw the picketers. The pastor eyeballed me as I walked toward them. I think he was expecting me to hurl dirt at him, but instead I held out my hands and gave him their slightly cooled pizza.

Calmness was in my soul as I began to tell them all who I was and why I was there. I didn't want to offend any of them, but I wanted to tell them what I felt was missing from the situation: *Jesus.*

I began to tell them my story. Being saved by love and grace and mercy. Where were the love and grace and mercy here?

The sound of one wooden picket sign being laid on the ground resonated in my ears.

"It wasn't the wrath of men, but the love of God that transformed my life," I pleaded with them. "These women need to feel Jesus' love through you. You are supposed to be His people here."

Another picket sign was laid down.

"Everything going on outside, here, is turning them away from Him. Making them defensive toward Him. Making them scared of Him."

"Sin is sin," one person tried to explain. "And we're tired of sin around our kids and in our community."

My face softened. "None of us is without sin. None."

One by one, I looked directly at each face. "We've all made mistakes. We still make them. I'm not saying Jesus agrees with stripping. I'm not saying that they are right and you're wrong. What I am saying is what Jesus said: 'The sinless one among you, go first: Throw the stone.' The love of God transformed me. I am walking proof that if you show them His love, it will change the atmosphere in your town. Isn't that what you want?"

They listened and then we all prayed in a circle. We prayed for peace and restoration.

"Will you come speak at our church tomorrow?" the pastor asked me.

⤸

That night in my hotel bed I could barely sleep. I kept replaying it all in my mind: dancers giving their lives to Christ in a strip club. *Incredibly awesome*. Each one of them understanding that God was for them—not their stripping of course, but their souls—and that He loved them. Having the right words to be able to share my testimony with the people picketing on the sidewalk in a way that could—just maybe—change their hearts. It was all so supernatural and amazing.

I woke up early the next day, and we set out for Warsaw again, to the local church called New Beginnings.

We pulled up outside the small, single-level, tan wood country church and witnessed two or three camera crews that were ready to again cover the controversy. I got out of the car as the girls from the Fox Hole showed up in their bikinis to picket the church.

I hugged a woman. "Can you please put that thing down and come inside?"

"We just don't feel welcome," she said.

"But you are. Someone has to start somewhere. Come in and hear me speak."

I couldn't convince them. The years of bitterness ran deep.

"It's okay. I'll be back." I wrapped my arms around her again.

I stood in the pulpit and a hushed silence fell on the congregation. I began to reveal my testimony to them in an honest, Spirit-filled way and explain the wisdom God had given me that transformation in the flesh is possible.

I called out Matthew 4:16. I could hear pages turning to the scripture that had saved me. "The people living in darkness have seen a great light; on those living in the land of the shadow of death a light has dawned."

I closed my Bible and conveyed the reason that I had chosen that particular scripture. The meaning of it for me, and the meaning of it for all. I concluded with a prayer of peace.

As we started to leave, I walked with the pastor and a few of the parishioners and reminded them of God's word in 1 Corinthians 13:1–3: "If I speak in the tongues of men and of angels, but have not love, I am only a resounding gong or a clanging cymbal. If I have the gift of prophecy and can fathom all mysteries and all knowledge, and I have a faith that can move mountains, but have not love, I am nothing. If I give all I possess to the poor and surrender my body to the flames, but have not love, I gain nothing."

We were some of the last out of the church after the service concluded. When I got to the door and looked at the crowd outside, it was astounding. The strippers had put down their picket signs and the church people were talking to them and embracing them. I knew God had shown up and had ordered our steps, but it was still humbling to see these two groups peaceably caring for each other. The media crews had come to tape the ongoing explosive feud for the five o'clock news, but had instead arrived to capture a miracle in the making.

chapter twenty-five
WE PLAY TO THE BUZZER

Post–traumatic stress disorder (PTSD) is a mental health condition that's triggered by a terrifying event. Symptoms may include flashbacks, nightmares, and severe anxiety, as well as uncontrollable thoughts about the event.

—Mayo Clinic

A trigger embodies my entire being with the emotion of a childhood torment. I know that I am in the present, but it doesn't stop the emotions from overtaking me. It makes me feel insane. I want the hell out of wherever I am at. Out of my own skin and away from whatever that trigger is at that precise moment. It feels like you're emotionally trippin' on the LSD of the torture.

—Anny

A stampede of media requests came to me after the events in Warsaw hit the national news. Ideas, from Bible studies to making a Broadway musical, were floated, each with a unique version of how the ex-stripper brokered a peace treaty in Ohio. I was sensational movie-of-the-week material. The Eve's Angels Facebook page began to blow up and we had a barrage of inquiries on how people could get involved in the ministry. I received an array of messages that ranged from death threats to marriage proposals.

My commitment to making sure all our outreaches must offer love and prayer instead of judgment and condemnation only grew stronger.

Finally I understood. I had so many of the answers to the meaning of my journey.

I could look in the rearview mirror of my life and see how He had indeed ordered my steps. Perhaps not the ones that involved swinging naked and upside down, but how He had used my choices for His purposes. I vividly recounted each stone in the river of my life: each one He had purposely placed.

He began my life in the home of a high-profile, believing, and resilient family. Had I not been born to Bob and Kathy Donewald, I would not have been able to decipher and handle the intense, vastly different spotlights that shone on me. Had I not been presented with and taught grace and the love of God through the *actions*, not just the words, of my parents, I would most likely have died of a drug overdose or ended up in prison. Had I not wrestled with the devil in the subculture of the sex industry, there would be no eyewitness recount, and had Jesus not saved me, and the Spirit not filled me, there would be no Eve's Angels.

God had placed the stones in the river of my life and there was splendor in the revelation of how He placed them.

꿈

I spent the year after the Ohio experience praying with and preaching to women in the sex industry, asking God to heal their deepest wounds. But I came to realize and admit that I had still not let Him do it *all* for me. If I was ever going to truly be honest and love myself, and fully love others, men included, I had to submit it all to God completely. The secrets that I kept under lock and key needed to truly be set free.

So many pieces of my puzzle were coming together, with the exception of men. I seriously distrust them. I can accept God's love for me, as He's God, but accepting that a working-class Joe won't judge—and can somehow accept that a former sex-industry worker will make a good wife and mother—is a difficult proposition. And a part of me believed that most men—rabbis, priests, pastors, pro athletes, and businessmen, the guys that look normal, the ones that drive home to gated communities and pretty blond wives—well, aren't really all that good under the surface. Those are the men that I had spent years dancing for as they ate chicken salad sandwiches and drank Coors Light during lunch meetings with their buddies.

As much as I'd like to say that I have reached some divine space that has no problems or issues, that's just not possible. *Process. Process. Process.* I keep saying it! And I still haven't completely surrendered this little piece to God.

My last attempt at a relationship ended after I successfully sank it. His name was Sam. I emotionally blindsided him with a knuckle-to-knuckle metallic cross ring. A decent, hardworking guy, he had come into my life offering only kindness. He accepted my past and had expressed interest in helping me with my ministry.

Why did I keep self-sabotaging the possibiity of life in surburbia with a two-car garage? Why didn't I want to have dinner on the table at six o' clock, wearing a June Cleaver apron? For the record, if I did, my apron would be *fly*. Instead I chose to eat alone most nights, or with my children. Like the men before him, I flushed Sam down the drain and discarded him like scraps from our plates at dinner and turned on the garbage disposal of my life. *Again*.

Here I was preaching and praying over girls backstage in XXX clubs to let God heal their wounds, yet I still hadn't healed my own gashes that lay dormant three inches below the skin. My inability to commit and to submit had been off the therapy radar for years. It was just part of who I was, an obvious chink in the armor.

At thirty-three years old, I knew I needed backup support. I went to talk to my mentor, friend, and pastor to try and determine when and where it had all gone off course.

He is a large, imposing, dark-skinned man possessing the wisdom of a certain 483-year-old spiritual counselor; I like to call him Yoda. Our open-door talks in his small, nondescript office with his secretary outside are Spirit-filled and never involve religious rhetoric. He knows I am not a typical hallelujah parishioner. I think my two-foot-long blond hair weave, skinny jeans, tattoos, knee-high boots, and stripper ministry have given me away.

Sitting behind his desk, wearing a pressed suit, bright-red tie, and crisp white shirt, he would have been the picture of "official" if it weren't for the fact that his shirt collar was cutting into his thick, stout neck. Perhaps he'd bought that shirt two years ago and, like the rest of us humans, was expanding with age. We began to discuss my inability as a woman and a ministry leader to have a true, Jesus-infused romantic relationship with a man.

"Why in the heck can't I sustain a healthy relationship when it comes to the opposite sex?" I asked Yoda. "I thought my scars were healed. I thought my past was undone. I thought I was made new by the cross."

Dating someone came with an unconsciously weighted backpack of brokenness and distrust.

"What is it about men that you associate with vulnerability?" Yoda asked. It was a heavy question delivered with professional nonchalance.

I instantly felt uncomfortable, a sign that good work was coming. "I think men don't understand my power and they try to control me." I cross my arms. "I intimidate them."

"That's nice, Anny. But you don't intimidate me."

"You're not trying to sexualize me." I lean forward. "The place I've been attacked the most, the place where I have seen the enemy, Satan, has been within my interaction with men."

"But at some point in your past you had to have had a normal relationship with one man."

"Not really."

"How's your relationship with your father?" Yoda didn't know anything about my upbringing. No one really did. He just knew my redemption story.

"My dad is great."

"Then who?"

"What I've come to learn is that we play the hand we are

dealt—but there is a dealer. Everything is God-allowed but not always God-given. Sometimes the devil is your dealer. The cards come out of the deck and we must play them. How we play them is up to us."

I had manipulated my spin so completely that my answer actually sounded logical.

"When was the last time you felt safe?"

The muscles in my neck tensed and quietness overtook me. I could feel heat inflaming my back, as if warm blood was oozing slowly down my spine, first over my Asian-inspired tattoo that represented "Imagine the powerful woman," into the lollipop-esque symbol representing the female of the species and pooling around the date that I had etched into the skin at the base of my tailbone: 6.29.98. My daughter's birthday.

"When I was thirteen."

Yoda straightened in his chair. "Who, Anny, had access to you at thirteen?"

The pole to the pulpit was an easy story for me now. But how had I gone from Pollyanna to the pole is a story I was not willing to give up. I didn't want to ever talk about my parents, basketball, players, or NCAA reputations. My story was enough on its own. I didn't need to throw anyone else into the blender.

Later in life, no matter how filthy my sex-for-money escapades had been, I had been an adult. I was responsible for my actions, and God had restored me. But what about when I hadn't been? What about when I was powerless? How could I find the courage to speak to anyone about the moments the devil stole my innocence from me?

I placed my hands over my face, hoping my long

fingers and French manicure would cover my dampening lashes. "I can't do this," I whimpered.

Yoda looked at me with compassionate eyes. "Come back when you're ready," he said gently.

I stood up and left.

Two nights after I limped out of Yoda's office, I was in the lake house that is connected to my parents' residence. The nightly news was televising a loop reel of salacious images surrounding the NCAA scandal of Jerry Sandusky's sexual exploitation of young boys and how the university had stuck their heads in the sand to protect the legacy of the school and Coach Paterno and his team. Watching the pictures of the Penn State scandal prompted the hounds of hell in the mental catacomb that was a classic trigger for me.

This time instead of running from the lion chasing me, I stayed and watched as Coach Joe Paterno stood outside his house in an old gray sweatshirt, his large, thick black glasses dwarfing his cancer-ridden hollowed cheeks. I was mesmerized by that sweatshirt.

I had seen it before: on Matt in the bus.

Coach Paterno's wife stood by his side in her red blouse and messy Avon lady hair as media, fans, and townspeople crowded into their yard.

I muted the television, tossed my head back and forth in disgust, lit a cigarette, and turned on music to calm my fragile nerves.

With Alicia Keys on my CD player, I lay down on the

floor. I watched the smoke rise from my Newport and concentrated on the curlicues of the plume. I let its lightness wash over me as I inhaled a long drag.

I began to be the Indian snake charmer who was able to play her flute and seduce the cobra from her basket. The memories of my childhood belly danced around and unwrapped and enveloped me. I was awake, but in a dreamlike state, finally a willing participant in my own rescue.

I grasped that I should have told my parents about what had happened on the bus, in the elevator, and around every dark corner. I should have disclosed more, but we weren't that kind of family. Even now I didn't talk to them about money, sex, or their private matters. There were boundaries set in place that we all still adhered to.

My mother was the only one who knew about Matt, and I had only told her in a moment of clarity after I became unglued in the sex industry.

"You know your father would have killed him," she had responded.

Perhaps that's why I never told him.

I am sure she told my aging father, as they never kept any secrets. But he and I had never spoken of it. I had forced my parents into so much unfamiliar territory and pain from my life in the sex industry that I just could not heap more onto them. They knew more than I believe either of them could understand. Even during this time, a part of me felt it was better to keep it all buried, as if it didn't exist at all. I tricked myself into believing that if I kept it locked up in a box marked IRRELEVANT TO THE OUTCOME, maybe it didn't happen.

Now, twenty years later, the secret was scurrying and

clawing its way to the surface like a sewer rat finally needing fresh air. I could no longer suppress the feelings and images that kept blowing my notorious manhole cover off. I had to talk to my father.

God's grace was as present for him as it was for me.

I had to rewrite the subtext from my primary Sunday school classes, the Apple Jack analogies of good and bad, and insert hope and grace instead.

I turned off the television and got on my knees, my forehead against the hardwood floor. I said a silent prayer for all of Sandusky's victims, the ones who had come forward and the ones who still had their secret death bombs inside. In the middle of my prayer, I started to tremble and in a very non-Christlike way I blurted out, "I was only thirteen years old!"

As I sobbed, a revelation hit me: *Broken people do broken things.*

"God? Where does it stop?"

Forgiveness.

I had to forgive. I had to forgive them all, from Matt to my XXX clients. I had to forgive them and release them from me to God.

Simply and honestly, I said, "Father, I forgive those who have sinned against me as you have forgiven me."

But the magnitude of what He had forgiven me for is immeasurable and overwhelming.

My little son, Amais, came into the room and stood looking at me on the floor.

"Are you okay?" He spoke like a little man.

"Yes, baby. I'm okay." I held out my arms.

On my knees, we were the same height. He hugged me tightly.

God had given me a son, a son who would grow to be a good man. God had given me a good man as a father. And He had sent Jesus, a man for me. Each one showed great love and kindness toward me. With a clear heart and vision, I could have healing love in the men around me, and forgiveness for the others.

It is my conscious decision, not a feeling, to forgive. It is supernatural and not something I can do on my own. I simply let those men who have hurt me off the hook.

I forgive you, and you owe me nothing.

If my ministry is to be about love, it has to be for *all people*. And if I am going to have a shot at an intimate loving relationship with a man, I can no longer hold on to yesterday's baggage.

I was liberated with forgiveness and surrounded by peace.

⟿

Later that evening, I walked toward my parents, who were sitting in Adirondack chairs on the small dock outside. The sun was fading late on this warm evening. They looked like a sweet retirement postcard from the Michigan vacation bureau.

"I want to talk to you about some things that have happened." I eased down between them on the wooden planks over the water.

My white-haired father poked the fire pit. "Um-hm."

My mother ran her hand down over the top of my head, her fingers in my hair, as if I were still a small child.

I suppose that they both believed this discussion was

going to revolve around my recent breakup with Sam, but it was time to finish the last piece of the puzzle.

I began our talk as a small confession to my father about my desire to protect him, the team, and the school from the events that had gone on under the cover of cheering crowds and community adoration. I explained why I had kept silent for so long. My recognition and remembrance transformed into an admission and ultimately the breakthrough of forgiveness. I admitted that I needed both his support and his approval if I was to ever honestly divulge, and ultimately remove, the roadblock that was keeping me from trusting or sustaining a healthy relationship with a man.

It may sound odd that I was seeking my father's permission to publicly reveal the facts of what happened to *me*, but you see, I love my father and I respect him. I would never want to hurt him any more than I already have.

After all, this was more than just my story from the pole to the pulpit, although that portion alone is enough to allow me to easily continue my ministry work and legitimately advocate for women in the XXX industry. Now I was talking about spiritual growth and truth. It was about coming clean with my *entire* life. And because of who my father is and was, I knew that at some point what had happened when I was a child would be revealed publicly.

When I finished, I dropped my head into my crossed arms that were resting on my knees.

My father spoke softly. "You don't need to protect any of us, but let God protect us all."

It was pure and perfect.

He didn't care that there might be extreme scrutiny and controversy that could rock us if I was honest about what had happened to me. He read the headlines about NCAA scandals and cover-ups and improprieties at the top of the sports section every day. All he cared about was me, and how to continue the healing road I was on. He now knew that I was only telling 75 percent of my truth, trying to protect everyone, and the other 25 percent of my story had me shackled and had changed my vantage point toward men, sex, life, and love. This, my father would never accept.

"We play to the buzzer, Little Dee. To the buzzer."

We all prayed together that day, and as I listened to my father's words, I realized that I have in me the same desire he has to press forward when life has us down by twenty points. And I have my mother's positive attitude.

Although for many years the soil of my soul did not look fertile, every assured seed of the Word they had spoken over me, for me, and with me had landed and grown.

My father began praying what he had prayed our whole lives whenever things began to shift.

"Lord God, we come to you and humbly ask that you guide our steps for what is honorable and pleasing to you. Let our lives be not about"—he rested, choosing his words—"the attention grabbers or superficial details and confusion, but let it be a mission of goodness and honor to You. Lord, let every door be open that You would want open and let every door be closed that You want closed. Help Little Dee to make clear decisions to be a help to others. Lead us all to make a difference on and off the court, whatever that court may be. Lord, we humbly ask

You to hear us, protect us, and guide our plans. In Jesus'
name, amen."

I am so grateful for the good men God has placed in
my life.

chapter twenty-six

A NEW STAGE

Do you think I speak this strongly in order to manipulate crowds? Or curry favor with God? Or get popular applause? If my goal was popularity, I wouldn't bother being Christ's slave. Know this—I am most emphatic here, friends—this great Message I delivered to you is not mere human optimism. I didn't receive it through the traditions, and I wasn't taught it in some school. I got it straight from God, received the Message directly from Jesus Christ.

Galatians 1:10 (*The Message: The Bible in Contemporary Language*)

It doesn't matter if I am speaking in the White House or at the Porn Convention, I am grateful to share with all how God's grace, hope, and love have changed my life. But predominantly I am grateful for the true recognition that I only take the stage for an audience of One, Jesus Christ.

Anny

"Yes, I am the Lorax who speaks for the trees, which you seem to be chopping as fast as you please."

Dr. Seuss, *The Lorax*, New York: Random House Children's Books, 1971

The ballroom of the hotel is beautifully lit with a white glow from the opulent chandelier that hangs over the room. At tables draped in lavender linens and crème organza topped with tall vases of flowers, attendees in suits and cocktail attire sit, attentively listening to Master of Ceremonies Ron, a Michigan news anchor. The topic: sex trafficking.

The sex-for-sale trade has become a serious and growing problem in the state. In July of 2013, after the FBI conducted Operation Cross Country, its seventh nationwide law-enforcement sweep of select cities to liberate victims of child sex trafficking, Michigan was second highest in arrests and recoveries. According to the FBI, more pimps were found in the Detroit area than any other city involved in the crackdown, and ten children were recovered. It crushes me to imagine that any of those children could be my own son or daughter, or yours.

I stand backstage waiting for my cue from Ron and holding two books in my hand: the Bible and the Dr. Seuss classic *The Lorax*. The first, my constant reminder of grace, tells me to begin with God's love for *all* people. The second is my reminder from the Lorax to have courage to speak up no matter the agendas of the audience— corporate, political, or even religious—to speak love and truth and speak them loudly for the ones who cannot. It's humbling to share my message, and I hope and pray it gives an intimate portrait of at least one woman from the sex industry and the true nature of the sex-for-sale subculture in America. I am ever careful not to sensationalize, glamorize, or water down my own experience, as I believe most of humanity tunes out the disingenuous tap dancing.

Tonight I use the Lorax's message to speak for my trees—the women in the XXX business who either cannot or choose not to leave the snare of the trade. I will try to illustrate that women who end up on street corners, center stage on a floor-to-ceiling pole, or in high-end hotel rooms selling sex are not all the same. Many are mental, sexual, and physical abuse survivors desperately battling depression. Many have been trafficked all over this country from every walk of life. They range from teenage girls to suburban mothers, and a large part of society has given them up as garbage, trash, and cast them out as *sinners*. Each one has her own inner and outer antagonist, the Once-ler to her Lorax, and the battle is not over for them. Tonight I stand with them and fight with love and hope, not hate and damnation.

I close my eyes, grateful to have walked, prayed, worshipped, and spoken Jesus' name in places that others might consider to be crazy. I have watched G-string-wearing XXX dancers sing gospel music on strip stages, and I have seen dancers get prophetically Spirit-filled and speak in tongues in their dressing rooms.

I've watched lives be transformed, and my heart has broken watching lives tragically end.

Ron, the speaker, says my cue, "Eve's Angels," and it brings my attention back to the task at hand.

I begin to pray. "Lord, I know there is still so much work to do—in me, and across this country. I know I am far from holy or perfect and as always I need your help. I ask that you fill me with Your Spirit. Go out ahead of me and make a path. Let these be Your words and not mine. Let lives be impacted with Your vision, not mine. Help me to have wisdom and maybe some humor. I ask that you help me to always remember that the most important audience I have is an audience of One. And that One is You. Amen."

As I took the first step onto the next stage of my life, I took the mic and said, "I am Anny Donewald, and this is my story."

about eve's angels

Founded in 2009 by Anny Donewald, Eve's Angels is rapidly becoming the restoration answer for women trapped in the sex industry. The Christian not-for-profit organization ministers the word of Jesus Christ to women in the sex industry and is both a symbol against sex trafficking and a community that reaches into places of employment where sex is being sold. The 501(c)(3) has a staff that includes volunteers who respond to daily e-mails, phone calls, and messages with understanding, grace, realism, and courage to help others take a step toward Jesus Christ and recovery. They have a street team, grassroots approach to educate and inspire women in the sex industry to transform their lives. Eve's Angels gives a portion of their proceeds directly to women coming out of the industry who are in need of immediate housing, counseling, prayer, rehabilitation, and resources to equip them for a new future.

Founder Anny Donewald diligently reaches corporate, law enforcement, political, and Christian leaders to educate them on the worldwide sex-industry epidemic and give them a new vision and impactful tools to change cultural viewpoints and save lives. She speaks at and participates in national conferences, events, and festivals.

Eve's Angels has also become a political force. Anny Donewald serves on an advisory board to Michigan's Senator Judy Emmons, who has created nineteen bills on sex trafficking. Eve's Angels has also launched the men's team called the ARMED Campaign, which stands for Association of Real Men Ending the Demand, in an attempt to combat sex trafficking from the male perspective. Active in several cities across the country, ARMED is in the preliminary stages of forming ARMED teams to parallel the Eve's Angels outreaches. And, in August of 2014, along with her coauthor and activist cousin, Carrie Cecil, a principal partner in Unfiltered Faith, they will launch the *Could She Be . . .* campaign on billboards across America to humanize women in the sex-for-sale culture.

Anny Donewald and her team have booths at the annual Pornography Convention in Chicago, where they get a chance to witness to over twenty thousand people for a weekend, including pornography stars and consumers. She has written two Eve's Angels Bible study curriculums, which are available online as resource guides to both secular and nonsecular consumers who are looking for additional information, hope, love, and guidance.

To learn more about Eve's Angels, go to: www.evesangels.org.

To learn more about the ARMED campaign, go to: www.armedcampaign.org

acknowledgments

To my dad: Thank you for showing me how to win both on and off the court, loving me through the unlovable times, and never giving up. You've loved me past anything I deserved.

To my daughter, McKaylah: Your strength and kind heart remind me of what is important every day. You truly are my heart with legs. Thank you for making me laugh and helping me keep my feet on the ground when I need to be a regular human. You are my wingwoman for life. I must be God's favorite that I get to call myself your mom.

To my son, Amais: For dancing, singing, and playing chess and golf. You make my soul smile and you fill me with an innocence that I thought had been lost. It's an honor to be your mom and to watch the man you are becoming after God's own heart.

To Carrie: You are my kindred spirit. Our connection has transcended the time we lost in our childhood. Thank you for taking a chance on so many things with me. You've helped me tell this story in a way that at times I couldn't articulate. You've shared your gift to represent me and millions of women with similar stories in a way that no one else could. You are a blessing in my life. I'm honored and humbled to call you my cousin and my friend.

To my Eve's Angels: Words cannot express my gratitude for you and all the tireless, selfless, and loving work you do for this organization. You are my heroes.

To the women in the sex industry: I get it. I love you. If you ever need me, I'm here.

To my creative team: Thank you for believing, shepherding, shielding, and encouraging me to tell my stories.

To my stylists: A special thank-you to Jennifer Johnson Hermes for pre-editing and to Robert Simpson for the photo shoot hair styling and to Christina Marie Artrip for makeup.